The South Sea Whaler

The South Sea Whaler

AN ANNOTATED BIBLIOGRAPHY
of published historical, literary and art material
relating to whaling in the Pacific Ocean
in the nineteenth century

Compiled by
HONORE FORSTER
Australian National University, Canberra

1985 ♆ The Kendall Whaling Museum, Sharon, Massachusetts
Edward J. Lefkowicz, Inc., Fairhaven, Massachusetts

The Kendall Whaling Museum, Sharon, Massachusetts 02067 USA
Edward J. Lefkowicz, Inc., Fairhaven, Massachusetts 02719 USA

First edition 1985.

Designed by Boyd T. Hill
Typeset and printed by Maple-Vail Book Manufacturing Group,
  Binghamton, N.Y., USA
Endpaper maps prepared by M.U. Pancino, Cartography Laboratory,
  Department of Human Geography, Australian National University

Library of Congress Catalog Card Number: 85-50792

Library of Congress Cataloging in Publication Data

Forster, Honore.
  The South Sea whaler.

  Includes index.
  1. Whaling — South Pacific Ocean — History —
Bibliography. 2. Whaling in art — History —
Bibliography. I. Title.
Z5973.W5F67 1985 [SH382.6] 016.639'28'091648 85-50792
ISBN 0-937854-22-0

Frontispiece: *South Sea Whaling* [detail] by William Edward Norton
(American, 1843-1916), painted in London circa 1900 and based indirectly on
Captain Frank T. Bullen's *The Cruise of the Cachalot*. [*The Kendall Whaling
Museum; photo by Mark Sexton.*]

Contents

Foreword

By the time Balboa "discovered" the Pacific from the heights of Darien in 1513, that ocean had already been conquered and colonized by indigenous island seafarers whose dominion and elaborate civilization, despite occasional white-faced adventurers from distant, colder seas, were to be no more than sporadically and impermanently disturbed for many generations. Superb mariners and able navigators whose comprehensive celestial knowledge was at least the practical equivalent of anything known in Europe at the time, the Polynesians especially ventured out to inhabit and trade among myriad islands and atolls that would remain unknown in Europe and Asia for another four centuries. Portuguese, Dutch, and British East India traders would develop a flourishing commerce beyond the "East Cape"—the Cape of Good Hope—to India, the Spice Islands and even Japan; papal meridians would divide the world, wars of conquest and struggles for domination of India and the Far East would be waged among Europeans on several continents and the high seas, celebrated navigators would pass through without much lasting effect, and Christendom would pass through the Reformation and the Baroque to the Age of Reason, before the Cape Horn passage became a commercial reality and the Pacific thereafter came gradually to be truly "discovered"—by newcomers who would corrupt, erode, pillage and ultimately destroy the outrigger empire they had found. By this time there was already a new Republic on the map of the New World, with several others to the south soon to follow in its image; the Iberian empires of old were on the brink of extinction, to be replaced in Europe by Napoleonic France, and on the seas and across the terraqueous globe by Britain, soon to reassert her naval might.

Once the British and American China traders pioneered the Cape Horn route in the 1780s, the whalers followed closely in their wake; and while the merchant princes concentrated their energies upon the sumptuous trade in China and Indonesia (and the Americans at wayside calling-ports along the China-trade circuit), the whalers poked along and across the Ocean itself in search of the great leviathan—out to its farthest extensions and into its most distant corners, often to regions seldom visited by anyone else. The whalemen were rarely the first to appear on any scene, to "discover" the unfrequented outreaches of the vast Pacific, though their observations occasionally added "new" landfalls to the as yet woefully incomplete charts of the South Seas. But they were often the ones who, once having been there, returned again and again to hunt whales on the broad seas, and reprovision in such ports and anchorages as they could find.

Thus had it ever been with the whalers. When the Spanish Basques sailed across the North Atlantic in the sixteenth century to hunt whales, they were neither the first to sight the coast nor even the first to fish the frigid waters of the Labrador. But they returned, season upon season, with their grimy tryworks (oven apparatus for boiling-down blubber into oil) installed at stations ashore, until they were familiar to the local inhabitants (though not entirely welcome). So it was with their successors in the seventeenth and eighteenth centuries, Dutch, British, German, and Scandinavian whale-hunters who followed in the wake of the explorers Frobisher and Barendsz to the far North, from uninhabitable Spitsbergen and Jan Mayen Island to the Greenland coast and Davis Strait, where they became fixtures and brisk traders among the Inuit in every season—whether or not a celebrated explorer had happened to pass by during the preceding decade or two.

Whatever the drama of first meeting between two disparate and potentially incompatible cultures—anecdotes of Magellan, Drake, and Cook are legion—in many locales, among the ice floes, in baking equatorial heat and balmy tropical breezes, it was the whalemen, even before the missionaries and the navy, whose presence was most permanent and whose influence was the most dramatic. They brought calico and broadcloth for making shirts, exotic European hats, tobacco and ivory for trade, steel-bladed knives, the latest in serviceable tools, and all the minor wonders of "advanced" Western technology—and they brought them not once, but year in and year out, until patterns of barter and trade became established (by habit or design) and expectations on both sides included, even sometimes respected, the protocols of a new commerce. They brought their vices and diseases; they created business, of a sort, where none had existed; and they outnumbered the missionaries, the navies, the consular officials and the government bureaucrats as principal clients for local services and consumers of local wares. They were more than occasionally at odds with the other Caucasian constituencies. In Hawaii in the 1820s, blubber-hunters and Bible-thumpers were consciously pitted against one another for influence and primacy among their hosts; eventually, Hawaii became an arena of British and American competition for colonial fealty, in which the presence of Yankee whaling interests may have tipped the balance. Farther south, it was France versus Britain vying for control, a pattern in which even Melville found himself caught up during his brief sojourn in the Islands. Where some of these imperialistic endeavors were succesful, as in Hawaii, Australia, and New Zealand, local whalers were modeled after the Anglo-American prototype.

The history of the whalers in the South Seas is thus, in a sense, the epic saga of the discovery, colonization, contamination, and subjugation of the Pacific itself, and the intriguing human drama of conflict both within and among cultures. For the simultaneous presence of the whalemen, with their slack morality and rough-hewn demeanor, the whaling wives, who created a colonial high-society-in-miniature on shore, the pious and not altogether selfless missionaries, whose purpose was metamorphosis and Westerniza-tion, and the navies, whose militaristic discipline and imperialistic objec-tives seem wholly at odds with the enchanted islands many wanted to be-lieve these places to be, not only created a volatile admixture of incompatible interests among the Caucasian opportunists, but precipitated factions and divided loyalties among the aboriginals as well, pitting them against one an-other with respect to principles of proprietorship, commerce, religion, mo-rality, and nationalism entirely new to the region and wholly alien to the indigenous culture.

Honore Forster has created a guidebook to a fascinating epoch, a taxon-omic catalogue of the diaires, autobiographies, meditations, opinions, trave-logues, natural histories, and moral polemic of contemporaneous souls—for the most part, themselves participants in the action—who, realizing or not realizing themselves to be on the threshold of something historic, commit-ted their thoughts and observations to paper. The product of her labor is a resource of remarkable magnitude. It should stand well for many years as an eminently useful vehicle by which to enter and explore this vast, polyglot region, and to examine the motives and actions of the principals, many of them whalemen, habitués of a most peculiar profession.

Stuart M. Frank
Director
The Kendall Whaling Museum
Sharon, 15 January 1985

Preface

The history of whaling is a vast topic, relating to a wide geographical area over several centuries. That this bibliography is concerned particularly with the history of whaling in the "South Seas" between 1800 and 1900 is the result of three interwoven professional activities. First, my long-term membership of the Department of Pacific and Southeast Asian History of the Australian National University; second, my interest in nineteenth century whaling around the islands of the Pacific Ocean, which developed from my work in this Department; third, my experience as bibliographer for *The Journal of Pacific History*. The lack of a satisfactory historically-based bibliography of whaling in this region, an industry of great significance to westerners and islanders alike, became more apparent as my research and bibliographic interest expanded.

My association with the Department of Pacific and Southeast Asian History also influenced my view of what constitutes history. The two Professors of Pacific History—the late Jim Davidson and, currently, Gavan Daws—have both taken a broad view of the subject matter of concern to historians of the Pacific area. In the context of this bibliography, I have chosen to include not only items which are straightforward historical records, but also other material which I believe helps to expand our knowledge about Pacific whaling. To this end, there are sections on art and story-telling, the nineteenth century examples of which reveal something of the impact that the South Sea whale fishery had on contemporary imagination, especially in the United States. Melville's *Moby-Dick* is only one example, albeit the greatest one, of the creativity inspired by this essentially non-romantic, commercial enterprise. Publications about scrimshaw, a notable artistic by-product of long Pacific voyages after the sperm whale, also have a place in the bibliography.

There can, of course, be no finality in a compilation of this sort. But I hope that what is presented here will prove to be of lasting value to those interested in the history of whaling in the Pacific Ocean.

Honore Forster

Acknowledgments

The compilation of an annotated bibliography on a subject as international in scope as whaling — even if one is dealing with one aspect of it only — must draw on sources beyond those existing in any one country. I have been fortunate in obtaining the assistance and cooperation of a number of people and institutions in Australia and elsewhere. In the United States, the origin of most Pacific whaleships, I should particularly like to thank Edward J. Lefkowicz, for sharing his great knowledge of American whaling narratives with me, and allowing me access to his unpublished work on this subject. My sister, Barbara Donagan, undertook invaluable research for me at the Huntington Library, San Marino, and at various Chicago libraries. Sabrina K. Alcorn in Chicago, Barbara Walsh at the Library of Congress, Amirah Inglis at the Harvard University libraries and Norma McArthur at the University of Hawaii Library all made important contributions to the bibliography. I am also grateful for the help of Virginia M. Adams, Librarian of the New Bedford Whaling Museum. Robert L. Webb, Research Associate of the Kendall Whaling Museum was most generous with his time in answering my many queries about some of the Museum's rare whaling publications. Kenneth R. Martin was another extremely helpful and knowledgable informant.

From Ireland I received much-needed assistance from Douglass C. Fonda, whose knowledge of books relating to the history of whaling was of very great value. In Australia, I am indebted to Caroline Wesley, of the Crowther Library, State Library of Tasmania, and to the members of the Inter-Library Loans Unit in the Menzies Building of the Australian National University Library. I am also grateful to this Library for giving me access to the magnificent Mortlake Collection of children's books. Finally I wish to express my great appreciation of the support and encouragement for this project given me by Professor Gavan Daws of the Department of Pacific and Southeast Asian History, Australian National University. Special thanks must go to Komsiri Anomasiri and Sue Rider of this Department for their work in preparing the MS. for publication.

Abbreviations

A.B.C.F.M.	American Board of Commissioners for Foreign Missions
A.M.	*Artium Magister* - Master of Arts
annot.	annotated
bibliog.	bibliography
ca.	about
comp.	compiler
DA, DAI	Dissertation Abstracts, Dissertation Abstracts International
D.C.L.	Doctor of Civil Law
ed., eds	editor, editors; edition, editions
facsim.	facsimile
fn	footnote
F.R.G.S.	Fellow of the Royal Geographical Society
illus.	illustrated
LL.D	*Legum Doctor* - Doctor of Laws
L.M.S.	London Missionary Society
mc	microcard
M.D.	*Medicinae Doctor* - Doctor of Medicine
M.L.	Mitchell Library (State Library of N.S.W.)
n.a.	not available
n.d.	no date
NK	Nan Kivell (Nan Kivell Collection, National Library of Australia)
N.L.	National Library (National Library of Australia, Canberra)
ns	new series
N.S.W.	New South Wales
N.Z.	New Zealand
PMB	Pacific Manuscripts Bureau (Research School of Pacific Studies, Australian National University, Canberra)
pseud.	pseudonym
R.T.S.	Religious Tract Society

Note: "The Pacific Ocean" in the context of the bibliography extends to, and includes, the Auckland Islands in the south, the islands of Hawaii in the north, the Galápagos and Juan Fernández Islands in the east, and New Guinea, the Palau, Marianas and Bonin Islands in the west. Inevitably references will be found, for example, to the Bering Sea, the Sea of Okhotsk, the Kuril Islands and to Japan, but only so far as these areas were included in whaling voyages to the Pacific Ocean, as defined above. "Whaling" refers to deep-sea, or pelagic, whaling, rather than to shore-based activities.

I.

Contemporary personal accounts of whaling voyages, and modern works based on nineteenth century material

As some of the books in this section are of great rarity, a library or museum location and/or bibliographic reference (see Appendix 3) has been provided where considered necessary. A PMB (Pacific Manuscripts Bureau) number following an entry indicates that the whaling voyage described is wholly or partly recorded in a log or journal microfilmed by the PMB's New England Microfilming Project. This project is described in Appendix 4.

Most of the notations to entries in this section provide details of ships' names and Pacific Islands visited or commented on; other noteworthy events relating to whaling are also mentioned. The modern equivalents of the names of islands used by the writers whose accounts are listed below can be found in Appendix 2.

The dates of birth and death of the men and women who recorded the events described are given if known. This has also been done for nineteenth century authors in Sections 2-5.

1   ALLYN, Gurdon L., Captain, b. 1799, *The old sailor's story, or a short account of the life, adventures and voyages of Capt. Gurdon L. Allyn. Including three trips around the world. Written by himself, in the seventy-ninth and eightieth years of his age.* Norwich, Conn., Gordon Wilcox, 1879. 111 pp.

Includes whaling voyage in the *Charles Henry* of New London, 1845-46, to North Pacific via Indian Ocean, calling at Hobart, then to N.Z., Society Islands, Navigators' Islands and Friendly Islands. Another voyage on the *N.S. Perkins* of New London, 1852-53, to N.Z., Society Islands, Hawaii and Ladrones. In 1855 Allyn was on the *Brookline* (*Brooklyn*) of New London from Honolulu to Rarotonga. In 1857-59 he was aboard the *Tempest* of New London to Spitzbergen, N.Z., Lord Chatham's Island, Pitt's Island, Duke of York Island, Kingsmill Islands, to Japan grounds, Ralick Islands, Wellington Island and Honolulu.

2   BARNARD, Edward C., Captain, 1799-1844, *"Naked and a prisoner":* *Captain Edward C. Barnard's narrative of shipwreck in Palau 1832-1833,* ed. with notes and intro. by Kenneth R. Martin. Sharon, Mass., Kendall Whaling Museum; Saipan, Trust Territory Historic Preservation Office, [1980]. viii, 60 pp.

Wreck of the whaleship *Mentor* of New Bedford in 1832 - cf. Horace Holden's *Narrative*, below.

3   BAYS, Peter, "Sailing-master", 1784?-1864, *A narrative of the wreck of the Minerva whaler of Port Jackson, New South Wales, on Nicholson's Shoal, 24° S. 179° W.; to which is added, the substance of an address to the Right Honourable the Elder Brethren of the Trinity Board, respecting the examination of new-made masters in nautical calculations, &c.* Cambridge, B. Bridges, 1831. viii, 181 pp.

Bays also gives particulars of *Minerva*'s stay in Tongan group in 1829, and of vessels arriving there from various places, including Sydney (see Ferguson, *Bibliography of Australia*, vol. II). In 1830 Bays took passage to N.Z. on the *Toward Castle*, and visited Korararika, Bay of Islands, which he describes. Narrative has little on actual whaling operations.

4   BEALE, Thomas, Surgeon, 1807-1849, *A few observations on the natural history of the sperm whale, with an account of the rise and progress of the fishery, and of the modes of pursuing, killing, and "cutting in" that animal, with a list of its favourite places of resort.* London, Effingham Wilson, 1835. 58 pp. + 2 pp. of list of subscribers. Illus. Reprinted [London, Holland Press, 1976]. 58 pp. (Limited ed. of 250 copies.)

"Never having, whilst engaged in the fishery, contemplated publishing my remarks, the substance of the following pages is chiefly extracted from a log book, in which, for the sole purpose of amusing myself, I noted daily, the most interesting objects presented to my notice in the course of the voyage." - from the author's preface. This book is more directed toward natural history than Beale's 1839 publication, which follows.

5   _____, "Late surgeon to the 'Kent' and 'Sarah and Elizabeth', South Seamen", *The natural history of the sperm whale: its anatomy and physiology - food - spermaceti - ambergris - rise and progress of the fishery - chase and capture - "cutting in" and "trying out" - description of the ships, boats, men, and instruments used in the attack; with an account of its favourite places of resort. To which is added, a sketch of a South-Sea whaling voyage; embracing a description of the extent, as well as the adventures and accidents that occurred during the voyage in which the author was personally engaged,* 2nd ed. (See above, *A few observations on the natural history of the sperm whale . . .*) London, Jan van Voorst, 1839. vi, 393 pp. Pls. (2), illus. Reprinted London, Holland Press, [1973]. xvi, 393 pp.

Beale's whaling voyage on the English whaler *Kent*, Captain Langton, which commenced in October 1830 embraced Hawaii, Japan grounds, Bonin Islands, Caroline Islands, New Ireland, Bougainville and Ladrones. Beale returned to England in February 1833 on the *Sarah and Elizabeth*, Captain W. Swain, via Hawaii and Society Islands.

6   BEANE, J[oshua] F[illebrown], *From forecastle to cabin: the story of a cruise in many seas, taken from a journal kept each day, wherein was recorded the happenings of a voyage around the world in pursuit of whales*, illus. by the author (inc. cover design). New York, Editor Publishing Co., 1905. viii, 341 pp. Frontis. port., illus., pls., fold. map, chart.

Voyage in the *Java* of New Bedford between 1864-67, visiting Marshall Islands, Hawaii, Phoenix and Canton Islands, Gilbert Islands (including Byron's Island), Saipan, Tinian, Guam, Bonin Islands, Hawaii (again) and Huahine. (PMB 871)

7   BENNETT, Frederick Debell, F.R.G.S., "Fellow of the Royal College of Surgeons, London"†, 1806-1859, *Narrative of a whaling voyage round the globe, from the year 1833 to 1836. Comprising sketches of Polynesia, California, the Indian Archipelago, etc. with an account of southern whales, the sperm whale fishery, and the natural history of the climates visited*, 2 vols. London, Richard Bentley, 1840. xv, 402; vii, 396 pp. Illus., appendix, fold. map. Reprinted Amsterdam, N. Israel and New York, Da Capo Press, [1970], in Bibliotheca Australiana series, nos. 46-7.

Bennett sailed in the whaleship *Tuscan*, Captain T.R. Stavers, from London, in Oct. 1833, returning in Nov. 1836. *Tuscan* had as passengers three L.M.S. missionaries and their wives, bound for the Marquesas and Society Islands. Voyage also embraced Pitcairn Island and Hawaii. An appendix, "Illustrations of natural history of the Tuscan's voyage" with first section on whales and the whale fishery is included in vol. 2.

8   BILL, Erastus D., 1826-1905, *Citizen: an American boy's early manhood aboard a Sag Harbor whale-ship chasing delirium and death around the world, 1843-1849; being the story of Erastus Bill who lived to tell it*, with notes on Erastus Bill by Robert Wesley Bills. World Discovery Books, 2. Anchorage, Alaska, O.W. Frost, 1978. 136 pp. Illus., maps, index.

First voyage in *Citizen* (1843-6) to Chatham Islands grounds, through Society and Friendly Islands to Hawaii, N.W. Coast of America, Bering Sea, Hawaii, Rarotonga. Second voyage (1846-9), to Juan Fernández, North Pacific grounds, California, N.W. Coast, Hawaii, Aitutake. (PMB 681, 1st voyage)

9   BOOTES, Henry H[edger], *Deep-sea bubbles or the cruise of the Anna Lombard*. London, Ernest Benn Ltd., [1928]. 261 + 22 pp.; New York, D. Appleton and Company, 1929. xi, 353 pp.

---

† Fellowships of the Royal College of Surgeons were not introduced until 1843. Bennett did, however, become a Member of the College on 20 March, 1829.

Based on the author's experiences on a sperm-whaling cruise to the Pacific in the 1880s. (The *Anna Lombard* is a fictitious name.) References to Easter Island, the Marquesas and Hawaii.

10   [BRADLEY, Henry], attrib. author (also attrib. to Thomas Henry BEN-NETT (Shoemaker 11798, 15319) and Washington CHASE (Sabin 12215), *A voyage from the United States to South America, performed during the years 1821, 1822, & 1823, embracing a description of the city of Rio Janeiro, in Brazil; of every port of importance in Chili; of several in lower Peru; and of an eighteen months cruise in a Nantucket whaleship. The whole interspersed with a variety of original anecdotes.* Newburyport, [Mass.], Printed at the Herald Press, 1823. 80 pp. (1st and 2nd eds both pub. in 1823, the 1st in an edition of 500.) Also a 5th ed., *Chili and Peru in 1824*, apparently from same sheets as 2nd ed., with new title page, Boston, 1824. [2], 5-80 pp.
Whaling section of narrative takes place aboard the *Improvement* of Nantucket, Obadiah Coffin, master, which author joined at Valparaiso. According to Starbuck, *Improvement* left Nantucket 20 June 1820 and returned from a Pacific Ocean cruise on 2 April 1823. E.J. Lefkowicz, in his *Catalogue Three*, p. 1, item 6, notes that the last 7 pp. of narrative is set in different type from rest of text, with separate title, "Of whaling", and appeared in 1835 in slightly altered form in pamphlet used to promote Cornelius B. Hulsart's print *Capturing a sperm whale.* (Lefkowicz, *Catalogue Three*, 6; Sabin, 100814, 12215, 12749; Shoemaker, 11798, 15319)

11   BROWNE, J[ohn] Ross, 1821-1875, *Etchings of a whaling cruise, with notes of a sojourn on the island of Zanzibar. To which is appended a brief history of the whale fishery, its past and present condition.* New York, Harper & Brothers, Publishers, 1846. [ii], xiii, 580 pp. Illus., appendix. Reprinted as *Etchings of a whaling cruise*, Cambridge, Mass., The Belknap Press of Harvard University Press, 1968 (John Harvard Library edition, ed. by John Seelye). [5], 27, [2], and xiii, 580 pp.

Browne's voyage was in the Atlantic and Indian Oceans, but his work gives a general picture of life on a whaling ship in the 1840s, and the Appendix (pp. 511-80) contains much information relevant to whaling in the Pacific Ocean.

12   CALKIN, Milo, 1810-1872, *The last voyage of the Independence: the story of a shipwreck and South Sea sketches, 1833 to 1836.* [San Francisco, Privately Printed by Weiss Printing Co., 1953.] iv, 70 pp. Port.

Account written 40 years after events described. Calkin sailed in the whaler *Independence*, Captain Isaac Brayton, from Nantucket in November 1833. Visited Nukuhiva, Hawaii, Japan grounds, and wrecked on Starbuck Island in 1835. Reached Rarotonga later and took passage on whaler *Charles Carroll*, Captain Weeks, also of Nantucket, to Tahiti. Visited Raiatea, Rarotonga, Pitcairn, Samoa. Note: Calkin published an account of the wreck and 19-day whaleboat voyage following it in letter to the *Polynesian*, 1:20 and 21 (24 and 31 Oct. 1840), 77-8, 81-2. (PMB 855; O'Reilly 902)

13   CAMP, Mortimer M., *Life and adventures of a New England boy.* New Haven, Conn., F.W. Cone, Printer, [1893]. 129 pp. Pls, port.

Experiences included service on the *Flora*, Captain Mayhew, of New London, to Hawaii and Fiji, in 1842. (Starbuck: *Flora* sailed 19 Jan. 1841 for "New Zealand" whaling ground; returned 7 Apr. 1843.) (Kaplan 886)

14   [CARY, William S.], *Wrecked on the Feejees. Experience of a Nantucket man, a century ago, who was sole survivor of whaleship "Oeno" and lived for nine years among cannibals of South Sea Islands,* [ed. by Harry B. Turner]. Nantucket, Mass., Inquirer and Mirror Press, 1922. 72 pp.; new ed., 1928. 73 [1] pp. Reprinted Fairfield, Wash., Ye Galleon Press, 1972. 73 [1] pp. (Limited ed. of 300 copies.)

Account of wreck of Nantucket whaler *Oeno* on Turtle Island (Vatoa, Fiji), 5 April 1825, compiled from Cary's log-book. Cary was the sole survivor. MS. was not published until 1887 when it appeared in the Nantucket *Journal* in instalments, Cary's log-book having been discovered a few years earlier. Little on actual whaling activities.

15   CASWELL, James, *A sketch of the adventures of James Caswell, during fifteen years on the ocean and in foreign countries. Also, a full account of the last revolution in Chili, in which the author lost one of his arms at the bloody battle of Concepcion, fought February 8th, 1859.* New Bedford, [Mass.], Written by Himself, 1860. [ii], 68 pp.

Printed for the author in a very small edition. Caswell served on whalers from Nantucket and New Bedford, some of which went into the Pacific, such as the *Franklin*, *Congaree* and *Roscius*, between 1845 and 1859. PMB has microfilmed logs for vessels of these names covering this period. (Fonda, Catalogue 9, 258)

16   [CHAPPEL (Chapple), Thomas], *An account of the loss of the Essex, from having been struck by a whale in the South Seas, with particulars of the sufferings of her crew on a desert island, and in their boats at sea. From the narrative of one of the survivors.* London, J.E. Evans, [1820?]. 8 pp. Also published London, Religious Tract Society (Tract no. 579), [1830?]. 12 pp. Illus. American ed., Philadelphia, American Sunday School Union, 1825. 11 pp. Woodcut on title page. This forms pp. [49]-59 of a larger work and is headed "no. 52".

Note: Title varies slightly between eds.

17   CHASE, Owen, First Mate, 1796-1869, *Narrative of the most extraordinary and distressing shipwreck of the whale-ship Essex, of Nantucket; which was attacked and finally destroyed by a large spermaceti-whale, in the Pa-*

cific Ocean; with an account of the unparalleled sufferings of the captain and crew during a space of ninety-three days at sea, in open boats, in the years 1819 & 1820. New York, William B. Gilley, 1821. [ii], 128 pp.

The *Essex,* Capt. George Pollard, Jr., left port 12 Aug. 1819 and was sunk by a whale 20 Nov. 1820 about 2000 miles west of Galápagos Islands. Twenty survivors were able to escape in three open boats, of whom eight were eventually rescued. Six crew-members who died of natural causes were eaten by their shipmates, and one was shot and eaten. (Shoemaker 4964; Sabin 12189)

18   _____, *Narratives of the wreck of the whale-ship Essex of Nantucket which was destroyed by a whale in the Pacific Ocean in the year 1819.* Told by Owen Chase, first mate, Thomas Chappel, second mate, and George Pollard, captain of the said vessel. Together with an introduction & twelve engravings on wood by Robert Gibbings. Limited ed. of 275 copies. London, Golden Cockerel Press, 1935. 87 [+1] pp. Illus.

Chase narrative from the N.Y. 1821 ed., cited above; Chappel's from Religious Tract Society pamphlet, London, 1830, above; Pollard's from Daniel Tyerman and George Bennet, *Journal of voyages and travels . . . between the years 1821 and 1829.* (London, Frederick Westley and A.H. Davis, 1831), vol. 2, pp. 24-9 (see no. 489). Note: Chappel's narrative also appears in Tyerman and Bennet, vol. 2, pp. 28-30, n.

19   _____, *Narrative of the most extraordinary and distressing shipwreck of the whaleship Essex, with supplementary accounts of survivors and Herman Melville's notes,* with intro. by B.R. McElderry, Jr.; "American Experience" series (AE 21). New York, Corinth Books, [1963]. xxi + vi, 141 pp. Map, facsims.

20   _____, *The wreck of the whaleship Essex: a narrative account by Owen Chase, first mate,* ed. and with prologue and epilogue by Iola Haverstick and Betty Shipard; illus. with reprod. of prints and map by Kathleen Voute. New York, Harcourt, Brace & World, Inc., 1965. 124 pp.; London, Constable Young Books Ltd., 1968. 128 pp. Illus., map.

21   CHEEVER, Henry T., Reverend, 1814-1897, *The whale and his captors: or, the whaleman's adventures, and the whale's biography, as gathered on the homeward cruise of the "Commodore Preble".* New York, Harper & Brothers, 1849, 1850. xiii, 314 [+6] pp. Pls. Reprinted 1855 and 1864. 1864 ed. includes notes and appendix which has portions of the whaling log of Joseph B. Gow. 356 pp. Frontis., pls. Another ed., Glasgow, London, William Collins, [1850?]. 232 pp. Frontis. Other eds, London, Thomas Nelson & Sons, 1851, 1852, 1858. 240 pp. Also pub. Boston, D. Lothrop and Company, 1886. xiii, 368 pp. Pls.

The *Commodore Preble* of Lynn, Mass., made several whaling voyages in the 1840s, all, according to Starbuck, principally into the Indian Ocean. Cheever's account probably relates to the voyage of 1 July 1845 to 23 June 1848, which included a visit to Rimatara (Tubuai Islands) and whaling off New Zealand. Joseph B. Gow, portions of whose whaling log are printed in the 1864 appendix, was a townsman and school friend of Cheever's.

22   _____, *The whaleman's adventures in the Southern Ocean; as gathered by the Rev. Henry T. Cheever, on the homeward cruise of the "Commodore Preble"*, ed. by the Rev. W. Scoresby. London, Sampson Low and David Bogue, 1850. xiii, 304 [+24] pp. Pls. 2nd ed., Sampson Low, Son & Co., 1855. Other eds, London, W. Kent & Co., 1859; Darton & Co., 1860, 1861; Darton & Hodge, 1862. All xiii, 304 pp. with pls.

Published also with title: *The whale and his captors . . .* , q.v. above.

23   CLARKE, Cyrene M., *Glances at life upon the sea, or Journal of a voyage to the Antarctic Ocean, in the brig Parana, of Sag Harbor, L.I., in the years '53, '54; description of sea-elephant hunting among the icy islands of South Shetland, capture of whales, scenery in the polar regions, &c.* Middletown, [Conn.], Charles H. Pelton, 1854. 84 pp.

This narrative also includes "Voyage of the Bengal, of New London" (p. 67-end), which commenced in 1850 (Starbuck: 25 Sept. 1850, under Captain Phillips). This cruise, via Cape of Good Hope to Pacific Ocean included visits to Hobart, Kingsmill Islands and Hong Kong. Here Clarke gained discharge and joined *Frances* of New Bedford, to Arctic Ocean and Honolulu. Paid off at this port and shipped for home on the *Hibernia* of New Bedford, reaching port in 1853. (New Bedford Whaling Museum)

24   COFFIN, G.A., *There she blows, or the story of the Progress*. Chicago, Arctic Whaling Expedition Co., [c. 1893]. 46 pp.

Coffin sailed on the *Charles Phelps* of Stonington on whaling cruises to the Indian Ocean and North Pacific which embraced several visits to Hawaiian ports, from 1844. The *Charles Phelps* was sold at Hawaii in 1856 to a New London owner. After the Civil War she was rebuilt and named the *Progress*, with New Bedford as home port. This pamphlet was written while the author was on board the *Progress* on his way to the Chicago World's Columbian Exposition, 1893, where the *Progress* was to be an exhibit. (PMB 792, 844)

25   COFFIN, Robert, 1833-1914, *The last of the* Logan; *the true adventures of Robert Coffin mariner in the years 1854 to 1859 wherein are set forth his pursuit of the whale, his shipwreck on Rapid Reef, his life among the cannibals of Fiji, and his search for gold in Australia, as told by himself and now first published*, ed. with intro. by Harold W. Thompson. Ithaca, N.Y., Cornell University Press, 1941. 214 pp. Frontis. port., endp. map, bibliog., appendices, index.

The *Logan* of New Bedford, Captain Moses A. Wells, sailed 27 July 1854, and was wrecked on Rapid Reef (Starbuck: "Sandy Island Reef" = Conway Reef?) on 26 Jan.

1855. Whaling activities described particularly from pp. 29-70. Coffin's reminiscences were written down when he was nearing 80. Introduction, "Bearings and scrimshawing", pp. 3-26, gives details of Coffin family and whaling, Robert Coffin's life, and Fiji and Australia in the 1850s.

26   COLBURN, George L., *Scraps from the log book of George L. Colburn, who was more than twenty years a sailor: an account of the whale fishery: with many thrilling incidents in the life of the author.* Peoria, Ill., Benjamin Foster, 1854. 96 pp.

Includes description of author's experiences whaling in the Pacific aboard an unnamed barque out of New Bedford, sailing in the spring of 1832. Galápagos visited, then Hawaii. Impressions of the Hawaiian Islands given at length. Under the pseudonym of George Lightcraft, author first published this work under the title *Scraps from the log book of George Lightcraft, who was more than twenty years a sailor; an account of the whale fishery.* Syracuse, N.Y., Hall & Dickson, Printed by Barns, Smith and Cooper, 1847. 108 pp. Another ed. of this work pub. Detroit, 1850. (Colburn, Kendall Whaling Museum. Lightcraft, 1847, Widener Library, Harvard University: Kaplan 3499)

27   COMSTOCK, William, 1804-1882, *A voyage to the Pacific, description of the customs, usages, and sufferings on board of Nantucket whale-ships.* Boston, 1838. 72 pp.

28   _____, *The life of Samuel Comstock [1802-1824], the terrible whaleman. Containing an account of the mutiny, and massacre of the officers of the ship Globe, of Nantucket; with his subsequent adventures, and his being shot at the Mulgrave Islands. Also, Lieutenant Percival's voyage in search of the survivors.* By his brother, William Comstock. Boston, James Fisher, Publisher; New York and Philadelphia, Turner & Fisher, 1840. Another edition, Boston, James Fisher, 1849. xvi, 17-115 pp. Illus.

29   _____, *The life of Samuel Comstock, the bloody mutineer.* Boston, N.H. Blanchard, 1845. 36 pp. Illus.

The last two books both contain accounts of the whaling voyage of the *Globe*, of Nantucket, Captain Thomas Worth, which commenced on 20 Dec. 1822 and included visits to Hawaii (Oahu, 1823), Japan grounds and Fanning Island. After the mutiny in Nov. 1824 the ship passed through the Kingsmill Islands, Marshall's Island, Gilbert's Island and the Mulgrave Islands (Mili), where mutineers landed.

30   COULTER, John, M.D., *Adventures in the Pacific; with observations on the natural productions, manners and customs of the natives of the various islands; together with remarks on the missionaries, British and other residents, etc. etc.* Dublin, William Curry, Jun. and Company; London, Longmans, Brown and Co.; Edinburgh, Fraser and Co., 1845. x, [xi], 290 pp.

Coulter was on the English whaler *Stratford*, 1832-36; his Pacific voyage touched on Galápagos and the Marquesas Islands, Tuamotu Archipelago and Tahiti (visited in 1833).

31   ———, *Adventures on the western coast of South America and the interior of California; including a narrative of incidents at the Kingsmill Islands, New Ireland, New Britain, New Guinea, and other islands in the Pacific Ocean*, 2 vols (see vol. 1 only). London, Longman, Brown, Green and Longmans, 1847. xxiv, 288 [+32] pp.

Vol. 1 continues the whaling cruise of the *Stratford* from Tahiti, the earlier part of which was described in the author's *Adventures in the Pacific . . .* , q.v. above. See particularly chaps. 1 and 2 for whaling material.

32   CRAPO, Thomas, Captain, 1842-1899, *Strange, but true: life and adventures of Captain Thomas Crapo and wife*, ed. by William J. Cowin. New Bedford, Captain Thomas Crapo, 1893. 154 pp. Illus., ports. Re-issued by Mrs. Thomas Crapo, after her husband's death in 1899: New Bedford, T. Crapo, 1893 [i.e. 1900?]. 151 pp.

Chap. 1, pp. 7-45, covers period 1857-58, when Crapo was whaling in the Pacific on the *Marcia*, of New Bedford, Captain Randall Billings. Author leaves ship at the Marquesas and stays there three months in 1858. (PMB 267)

33   [CRAWFURD, Frederik, Captain, b. 1815], *Captain Crawfurds dagbog. En norsk hvalfangstferd 1843-1846 og andre europeiske lands deltagelse i Stillehavsfangsten 1800-1860. (Captain Crawfurd's diary. A Norwegian whaling voyage 1843-1846, and other European countries' participation in South Sea whaling, 1800-1860)*, [ed.], with commentaries by Thomas Hauge. Oslo, J.W. Cappelen, 1953. 296 pp. Illus., port., map, facsim., bibliog.

Crawfurd's diary (pp. 9-195) describes whaling voyage of *17 de Mai* of Arendal to Kamchatka, via Hawaii, back to Hawaii, then to Starbuck, Christmas, Fanning and Malden Islands, Hawaii, Kamchatka, Hawaii. Hauge's commentaries: whaling out of the New England states (pp. 196-8); crew of *17 de Mai*, pay arrangements, description of voyage and other information concerning it (pp. 199-239); whaling from Sweden, Denmark, Finland, Holland, Germany, England (useful list of whalers to the Pacific ca. 1849-51), France (detailed information, with list of French whalers 1816-68), pp. 239-93.

34   CUFFE[E], Paul, [Jr.], b. 1796 ?, *Narrative of the life and adventures of Paul Cuffe, a Pequot Indian: during thirty years spent at sea and in travelling in foreign lands*. Vernon, [N.Y.], Printed by Horace N. Bill, 1839. [ii], 21 pp.

Some whaling experiences in the Pacific, including a trip on the *Mechanic* of Newport, R.I., to "Reupore Islands" and "Riotier" (Raiatea), Society Islands, where Cuffe left the ship and lived for about five months. According to Starbuck, the *Mechanic* was built in 1834, and her first whaling cruise was from 22 Sept. 1834 to 6 July 1838, under the command of Captain Edward Harding. Cuffe's narrative should not be confused with the memoir published by his father (*Memoir of Captain Paul Cuffee, a man of colour*, Liverpool, 1811). For further details, see E.J. Lefkowicz, *Catalogue Three*, pp. 2-3, item 20 and R.L. Silveira de Braganza, *The Hill Collection*, 2, 387-8. (PMB 880)

35   CURTIS, Stephen, Jr, *Brief extracts from the journal of a voyage performed by the whale ship M[ercur]y, of New Bedford, Massachusetts, commencing May 25, 1841 and terminating August 1, 1844*. Boston, Samuel L. Dickinson, 1844. 46 pp.

The *Mercury* was commanded by Captain Dennis F. Haskell on this voyage to Pacific Ocean via Cape Horn. The Society Islands (Tahiti and Eimeo), Marquesas and Galápagos Islands were visited. The voyage was "almost exactly the same as Melville's. Curtis describes brutality aboard his whaleship and he also has some interesting details about Nukahiva . . .". - Vincent, *The trying-out of Moby-Dick* (see below, no. 306), p.212, fn. (New Bedford Whaling Museum; Sabin 18063; PMB 363)

36   DAVIS, William M[orris], 1815-1891, *Nimrod of the sea; or, The American whaleman*. New York, Harper & Brothers, 1874. ii, 403 pp. Frontis., illus., pls., appendices. Reprinted Boston, Charles E. Lauriat Co., 1926. xix, 406 pp. Frontis., illus., pls.; also North Quincy, Mass., Christopher Publishing House, [1972]. 405 pp.

Davis sailed on ship *Chelsea*, of New London, William Butler, master, on 1834-38 voyage to the Pacific. His book refers to visits to the Galápagos Islands, Hawaii and the Japan grounds. Davis's original log kept during the voyage covers the period 1 Nov. 1834 to 10 Sept. 1836. (PMB 394, 395)

37   DELANO, Reuben, b. 1809, *Wanderings and adventures of Reuben Delano, being a narrative of twelve years' life in a whale ship. Now first published*. [New York, H. Long & Brother]; Worcester, Thomas Drew, Jr.; Boston, Redding & Co., 1846. [iv], [13]-102 pp. Illus., 3 pls.

"Reminiscences rather than a contemporary journal, and the author was at the time he wrote it a 'guest' of the State of Massachusetts, in their hospital for the insane" - Glen Adams, of Ye Galleon Press, pers. comm. Delano was a member of the crew of the *Stanton* of Fairhaven in 1824-1825. In that period the *Stanton* visited the Galápagos Islands and Hawaii. (PMB 728)

38   DENISON, Charles W. (ed.), "Editor of the 'Sheet Anchor' ", *Old Slade; or, Fifteen years' adventure of a sailor: including a residence among cannibals on Wallace Islands and sketches of the North and South Pacific Oceans*, Stories of the Sea, no. 1. Boston, John Putnam, [c.1844]. 108 pp. Illus.

"The following pages are filled with nothing but facts. The Editor has taken them down from the lips of the narrator, who, though 'a man of sorrow and mystery' is evidently a man of intelligence . . ." (Introduction). Narrator shipped on board the whaler *Canton* of New Bedford, Captain Abraham Gardner, probably on its 1834-38 voyage, to Galápagos, Maui (Hawaii), Japan grounds, returning Hawaii, where discharged, sick. Thereafter joined trading vessel for cruise among Pacific Islands southwards to Samoa and Wallace (Wallis) Islands. Note: A subsequent volume of reminiscences was to have been published, as no. 2 in series "Stories of the Sea", but evidently did not actually appear. (Library of Congress; PMB 804, 842)

39 DENSMORE, David C., b. 1813, *The halo: an autobiography of D. C. Densmore*, vol. 1 (no more pub.). Boston, Voice of Angels Publishing House, 1876. 359 pp. Frontis. port.

Describes a whaling voyage in the *Henry*, Captain George Chase, of Nantucket, 1836-40, with visits to Galápagos and Juan Fernández Islands. The author was a New Englander who later became a shipbuilder. (Kaplan 1522)

40 DIMAN, George Waters, b. 1823, *Autobiography and sketches of my travels by sea and land*. Bristol, R.I., Press of the Semi-Weekly Bristol Phoenix, 1896. [iv], 64 pp. Port., illus.

Diman shipped aboard the *America* of Bristol, R.I., Captain Gilbert Richmond, on a Pacific whaling cruise in Oct. 1840 (Starbuck: 7 Oct. 1840 - 2 July 1844). Islands visited were "Waytaho and Wompor, off the Marques Islands" (possibly Hatutu and Uapu?), Tahiti and "other islands of the Society Isles", Pitcairn and Juan Fernández. At Callao he became ill, and was left at the hospital at Lima. He later rejoined the *America* in Hawaii. *America* left Oahu on her return voyage in Oct. 1843, visiting Pitcairn Island (Jan. 1844) and Juan Fernández *en route*. Diman's other voyages were in trading vessels. (Fonda, Catalogue 10, 105; Lefkowicz, Bulletin 31, 16)

41 DODGE, George A., 1814? - 1889, *A narrative of a whaling voyage in the Pacific Ocean, and its incidents*. Salem, Mass., [Merrill & Mackintire/Salem Gazette Press], 1882. 30 pp. Reprinted Fairfield, Wash., Ye Galleon Press, 1981, as *A whaling voyage in the Pacific Ocean and its incidents*, ed. with intro. and notes by Kenneth R. Martin. 31 pp. Illus., notes, index. (Limited ed. of 500 copies.)

Whaling voyage 1831-35 in the Nantucket ship *Baltic*, Captain William Chadwick, to Pacific Ocean - Juan Fernández, Sandwich and Society Islands ("Uhana" = Huahine) and Galápagos. Account includes descriptions of whaling activities.

[42] DUFOUR, Paul-François, Captain, 1813-1885. See under André Manguin, no. 55 below.

43 ENDICOTT, William, Third Mate, 1809-1881, *Wrecked among cannibals in the Fijis; a narrative of shipwreck & adventure in the South Seas*, by William Endicott, third mate of the ship *Glide*, Publications of the Marine Research Society, no. 3; notes by Lawrence Waters Jenkins. Salem, Mass., Marine Research Society, 1923. 76 pp. Port., pls., illus.

After trading vessel *Glide* of Salem wrecked at Fiji in March 1831, author succeeded in reaching Wallis Island, where he took passage on whaler *Braganza*, Captain Wood, of New Bedford Nov. 1831. Whaling voyage "about the Equator" lasted from 29 Nov. to 1 Feb. 1832. Endicott reached Eimeo in the Society Islands on 23 Feb. where he shipped on board the whaler *Atlantic*, Capt. Elihu Fisher, returning to Nantucket in June 1832. Some descriptions of whaling activities included (see partic. pp 51-4).

44   FAULKNER, Joseph P., *Three years on a whaler*. Bath, N.Y., A.L. Underhill, Book and Job Printer, 1875. iv, 72 pp. [+ pp. 73-6 adverts].

Includes a voyage in the *"Tidy Addly"*, of New Bedford (unidentified), probably in the early 1860s, with references to Galápagos, Juan Fernández and Marquesas Islands. (Kaplan 1887)

45   FISK, J.H., b. 1833?, *Two years before the mast, and ten behind it. How I came to Portland. A true narrative of exciting adventures on land and sea*. Portland, Oregon, Madden & Crawford, Printers, 1892. 48 pp.

Describes whaling voyage of New London sailor in the bark *"Tenedous"* (*Tenedos*), Captain Nat Middleton, to Pacific, commencing 3 Sept. 1850, via Cape of Good Hope, Tasmania, southern New Zealand to Mangaia, Rarotonga, Ocean and Pleasant Islands, Tongatapu and North Pacific - Arctic whaling grounds. Fisk and other crew members deserted off coast of Mexico (pp 4-22). Author tells of the later fate of Captain Middleton, p.44, and of the *Tenedos*, p.48. (University of Washington Libraries)

46   FOSDICK, W.L., b. 1823, *My voyage around the globe; portraying life on the ocean as it was sixty years ago. Interesting and instructive reminiscences of travel and adventure on land and sea, extending over a period of seven and one-half years, including a description of whaling, and experiences of three years spent with the natives of the South Pacific*. Shawano, Wis., Wiegand & Esser, Printers, 1897. 112 pp.

According to Fosdick, he embarked on the whaler *Margaret Scott* of New Bedford, Captain William Plaskett, on 6 Oct. 1838. Tubuai was visited in April 1839. *Margaret Scott* then sailed to Papeete, where Fosdick deserted. This particular voyage of the *Margaret Scott* is not documented. An interesting aspect of Fosdick's account is his statement that this vessel carried four Mormon missionaries on board, bound for the South Pacific, one of whom he named as "Parley B. Pratt". Another died after four weeks at sea. As the date of the departure of the Mormon missionaries is known to be 1843, and their ship the *Timoleon* of New Bedford (Starbuck: left port on 9 Oct. 1843, commanded by Captain W. Plaskett), doubt must be attached to the accuracy of this section of Fosdick's work.

47   FOSTER, Henry, "Trinity pilot, Dover", *Recollections of a South Sea whaler*, bound with *Memoir of James Anderson* by G[eorge] Newman. Gravesend, Printed by Smither Brothers, 1877. 45-70 of 70 pp.

Foster shipped aboard the London whaleship *Sussex*, Captain Hammer, on voyage to the Pacific Ocean, 1840-44. Reference is made in the text to Samoa, Kingsmill Islands, Japan grounds, Hawaii and the Ladrones. (British Library)

48 FROUIN, Charles, Surgeon, 1827-1891, *Journal de bord 1852-1856: Charles Frouin, chirurgien du baleinier "L'Espadon"*. Paris, Éditions France-Empire, [1978]. 340 pp. Pls, illus., maps, annexes, gloss. of whaling terms.

Voyage from Le Havre included New Zealand (Akaroa), Sandwich Islands ("Karakakoa", i.e. Kealakekua Bay, and Honolulu), Marianas and Guam, and also North Pacific - Kuriles and Aleutians. Full crew list of *L'Espadon* from Archives Maritimes de Rouen is appended. Biography of author pp. 7-8.

49 GARDNER, Edmund, Captain, 1784-1875, *Captain Edmund Gardner of Nantucket and New Bedford. His journal and his family*, ed. and comp. by John M. Bullard. New Bedford, Mass., 1958. [Printed by the Cabinet Press, Milford, New Hampshire.] [8], 109 [+ 8] pp. Frontis. ports, pls., facsims., index.

Gardner made several whaling voyages into the Pacific Ocean, the first as first officer of the *Maria*, Captain David Coffin, in 1808 and later in command of the *Winslow* (pp. 17). On the *Winslow*'s 1815-17 voyage Gardner sustained terrible injuries from attack by whale off the coast of Peru. After recovering ashore for several months, he rejoined the *Winslow* for whaling off Galápagos (pp. 29-31). While in command of the *Balaena* of New Bedford, Gardner put in to Kealakekua Bay, Hawaii, for refreshments on 19 Sept. 1819 - one of first whaleships to visit Hawaiian group (pp. 34-6, 77-8). Gardner also had interests in whaleships which visited the Pacific from the mid-1820s - e.g. *Hector*, *Rodman*, *Roman* and *Tobacco Plant* (which was set on fire by crew member at Hawaii and destroyed - pp. 46-9).

50 GELETT, Charles Wetherby, Captain, b. 1813, *A life on the ocean: autobiography of Captain Charles Wetherby Gelett. A retired sea captain whose life trail crossed and recrossed Hawaii repeatedly*, The Advertiser Historical Series, no. 3; intro. by Lorrin A. Thurston. Honolulu, Hawaiian Gazette Co. Ltd, 1917. 119 pp. Port.

"Reprinted by permission from *The Ojai*, a little country California newspaper of the early 90s." Gelett commanded such ships as the *India* and *Uncas* of New Bedford and the *Arctic* of Fairhaven on whaling cruises to the North Pacific and Hawaii in the 1840s and 1850s; he also refers to whaling off "Aitutahi" (Aitutake) in the Cook Islands.

51 HALEY, Nelson Cole, Harpooner, 1832-1900, *Whale hunt: the narrative of a voyage by Nelson Cole Haley harpooner in the ship Charles W. Morgan 1849-1853*. New York, Ives Washburn, Inc., 1948. 304 pp. London, Robert Hale, 1950. 319 pp. Illus. N.Y. ed. has endp. map and illus. by contemporary whaleman who drew them as decorations for his journal of bark

Clara Bell of Mattapoisett; also "Note of Introduction" by "The Publishers", pp. 9-18.

Orig. MS. of Nelson Cole Haley journal on the *Charles W. Morgan*, Captain John D. Sampson, is in the G. W. Blunt White Library of Mystic Seaport Museum, Inc., of Mystic, Conn. On 1849-53 voyage, *Charles W. Morgan* visited, or cruised in the area of, Bay of Islands, Tonga, "on the Line", Byron, Sydenham and Strong's Islands, northern islands of Fiji Group, N.Z. whaling grounds, again to Bay of Islands, "on the Line", Fijis, "Farewell" Island, Rotuma, Kingsmills, returning via Bay of Islands and Cape Horn.

[52]   HAMBLEN, Herbert Elliott, b. 1849. See under Frederick Benton Williams, no. 103 below.

53   HARTSHORN, Edmund F., b. 1843, *Experiences of a boy, by his father's son*. Newark, N.J., Baker Printing Co., 1910. 131 pp.

Author's whaling voyage on the *Mount Wollaston*, of New Bedford began during the Civil War and ended in 1866 (Starbuck: 24 Nov. 1862 - 13 June 1867). It included several visits to Hawaii, as well as to Juan Fernández and Ladrones Islands. Author later settled in Hawaii. (Kaplan 2522)

54   HEMPLEMAN, George, Captain, 1799-1880, *The Piraki log* (E Pirangi ahau koe) *or diary of Captain Hempleman, with introduction, glossary, illustrations and map by the present owner . . .* [F.A. Anson]. London, New York, Toronto and Melbourne, Henry Frowde, Oxford University Press, [1911]. 171 pp. Pls., fold. map, glossary-index, with 4 pp. insert, "Notes and corrections to the glossary" and port.

Refers particularly to shore whaling from Akaroa, Banks Peninsula, but also has general whaling material, and includes "Remarks on board the brig 'Bee' on a whaling voyage", 1835-36, from Sydney to "Piraki" (Akaroa district), pp. 11-27.

55   HEUSTIS, Daniel D., Captain, b. 1806, *Narrative of the adventures and sufferings of Captain Daniel D. Heustis and his companions, in Canada and Van Dieman's* [sic] *Land, during a long captivity: with travels in California, and voyages at sea*. Boston, Published for Redding & Co., by S.W. Wilder & Co., 1847; 2nd ed., Boston, Silas Wilder & Co., 1848. vi, 168 pp. Frontis. [On cover: *The remarkable adventures of Captain Heustis*, with port.]

Chap. 13, pp. 131-41 includes experiences on board whaleship "Steiglitz" (i.e. *Stieglitz*) from Tasmania with visits to Society Islands and Hawaii. Starbuck has *Stieglitz* of Bridgeport, Conn., on voyage 7 Aug. 1844-20 June 1849: "sold 1,200 barrels whale at Hobart Town" (no precise date). See also Samuel Snow, no. 87 below.

56   HOLDEN, Horace, 1810-1904, *A narrative of the shipwreck, captivity, and sufferings of Horace Holden and Benj. H. Nute; who were cast away in the American ship Mentor, on the Pelew Islands, in the year 1832; and for two years afterwards were subjected to unheard of sufferings among the*

{15}

barbarous inhabitants of Lord Norths Island. Boston, Russell, Shattuck, and Co., 1836; xii, 133 pp. Frontis. pl. Boston, Weeks, Jordan, 1839. 133 pp.; Cooperstown, N.Y., H. & E. Phinney, 1841, 1843. 120 pp. Reprinted Fairfield, Wash., Ye Galleon Press, 1975. 149 pp. (ed. by Keith Huntress).

The whaleship *Mentor*, of New Bedford, Captain Edward Barnard, which left port 20 July 1831, was wrecked on reef off Palau. For details, see F. Hezel, *Foreign ships in Micronesia* (no. 120, below), pp. 5-6. See also Edward C. Barnard, *"Naked and a prisoner"* . . . , (no. 2) above.

57   HOPKINS, Robert B., M.D., *Seventeen years from home; or, the adventures of Andrew Jackson Pettyjohn* . . . , "Written and illustrated by Rbt. B. Hopkins, M.D.". Milford, Delaware, "Excelsior" Book, and Job Print, 1897. 167 pp. Pls.

Pettyjohn's (b. 1818) experiences in the Pacific are described in chaps 8 and 9, pp. 116-53, "Whale fishing" and "An entertainment by aboriginese" (sic), of the section "Whaling in Pacific Ocean"; he sailed in the whaleships *Scotland* (of Glasgow), *Boy* (of Warren, R.I.) and *Matilda* (of London). (Mitchell Library)

58   HOPKINS, William John, b. 1863, *She blows! And sparm at that!*, illus. from paintings by Clifford W. Ashley. Boston and New York, Houghton Mifflin Co., 1922; London, Constable & Co. Ltd., n.d. [1922?]. [v], 361 pp. Frontis., pls. Another ed., Boston, Houghton Mifflin Co., "Riverside Bookshelf" ser., 1926. Col. pls.

Relates Hopkins's whaling experiences on the *Clearchus*, Captain Nelson, of New Bedford: chaps. 31 onwards have Pacific whaling descriptions - Japan grounds, New Zealand, Tahiti in 1874.

59   HUNT, Levi, *A voice from the forecastle of a whale ship: being a narrative of incidents of a voyage around the world.* Buffalo, G. Reese & Co. Printers, 1848. iv, 133 pp.

Voyage in the *Huntress* of New Bedford, Captain E.T. Shearman from June 1844 to May 1847, visiting Pitcairn Island (Feb. 1845), Hawaii (March 1845, and again in 1846), Tonga and Samoa (Oct. 1845). (PMB 247)

60   JARMAN, Robert [B.], *Journal of a voyage to the South Seas, in the "Japan", employed in the sperm whale fishery, under the command of Captain John May.* Beccles, R.B. Jarman, 1838. Another ed. London, Longman and Co. and Charles Tilt, n.d. [1838?]. vi, 242 pp.

The voyage of the *Japan*, an English whaler from Gravesend, took place between 1831 and 1834. It included visits to Japan grounds, via Halmahera Islands, Hawaii (Oahu), Kingsmill Islands, Sydney, Tongatapu, Sydney, Fiji, Rotuma, "Duprester's" Group, Tamana, Simpson's and Dundas Islands, "Orrori", Pylstaarts Island, Eua and Tongatapu, New Zealand (Bay of Islands). Many references to other whaleships. (Ferguson 2526).

61   [JONES, John D.?], *Life and adventure in the South Pacific.* By a roving printer. New York, Harper & Bros.; London, Sampson Low, Son, & Co., 1861. x, 361 [+10] pp. Illus., map, pls.

Account of a whaling voyage out of New Bedford in the whaleship *Emily Morgan*, Captain Prince W. Ewer, 1849-54. Visits were made to Guam, Strong's Island, Hawaiian Islands, Tonga, Cook Islands and Juan Fernández. Many ships' names are mentioned in the text.

62   LAWRENCE, Mary Chipman, *The captain's best mate: the journal of Mary Chipman Lawrence on the whaler* Addison *1856-1860*, ed. by Stanton Garner. Providence, R.I., Brown University Press, 1966. xxi, iii, 311 pp. Illus., appendices, notes with bibliog. refs., index.

Addison of New Bedford had seven cruises in the Pacific between 25 Nov. 1856 and 14 June 1860. The journal is specially concerned with shipboard life and whaling, but also gives detailed descriptions of life ashore in Hawaii and notes on contacts with the Marquesas, Aitutake and Kermadec Islands. (See no. 328, below.) (PMB 71, 572, 772)

63   LAY, William, b. 1805?, and Cyrus M. HUSSEY, 1805-1828, *A narrative of the mutiny, on board the ship Globe, of Nantucket, in the Pacific Ocean, Jan. 1824. And the journal of a residence of two years on the Mulgrave Islands; with observations on the manners and customs of the inhabitants.* New-London, [Conn.], Published by Wm. Lay and C. M. Hussey, 1828. x, 168 pp. Reprinted [New York, Abbey Press, 1901]. xiv, 163 pp. Also reprinted, with minor corrections, New York, Corinth Books, [1963], in the "American Experience" series (AE 20), with intro. by Edouard A. Stackpole. xxvi, 109 pp. Illus., map, facsims.

Lay of Saybrook, Conn. and Hussey of Nantucket, "the only survivors from the massacre of the ship's company by the natives", were taken from two neighbouring islands in the Marshall group by Lieut. Paulding of the U.S. Schooner *Dolphin* late in 1825. The whaleship *Globe*'s company had mutinied Jan. 1824 and eventually sailed the ship to Mili. See William Comstock, *The life of Samuel Comstock . . . ,* above, and Hiram Paulding, *Journal of a cruise of the . . . Dolphin*, below.

[64]   LIGHTCRAFT, George (pseud.). See under G. L. Colburn, no. 26 above.

65   MANGUIN, André, *Trois ans de pêche de la baleine, d'après le journal de pêche du Capitaine Dufour et des documents de l'époque 1843-1846*, with pref. by Marcel Hérubel. Paris, J. Peyronnet et Cie, 1938. 200 pp. Port., pls., fold. map, appendices, bibliog.

Captain Paul-François Dufour, 1813-1885, was a well-known whaling master of Le Havre. The information about the whaling voyage of the *Faune* of Le Havre from 15 June 1843 - 10 June 1846 to the Pacific Ocean via Indian Ocean, returning via

Cape Horn, comes from his *Journal de bord*, with additional information on the practice of whaling, equipment on board, provision, discipline, surgeons, etc. interspersed in the text. Appendices contain much material from Jules Lecomte's *Pratique de la pêche de la baleine dans les Mers du Sud* (q.v. no. 212, below), together with data about Le Havre whalers, e.g. departures between 1836-37. The *Faune* visited New Zealand (Akaroa), Hawaii (Oahu), Kamchatka, Sydney, Japan grounds and Hawaii (Maui) before returning to France.

66 MAYNARD, Félix, Dr., 1813-1858, *Les baleiniers, voyage aux terres antipodiques: journal du docteur Maynard*, "publié par Alexandre Dumas". Paris, A. Cadot, 1858 (3 vols). 987 pp. Other French eds: Paris, Michel Lévy frères, 1861 (2 vols). 633 pp.; Poissy, Impr. de Bouret, 1864 (1 vol. in 4to). 98 pp.; Paris, Calmann-Lévy, 1877 and [1889] (2 vols). Pp. n.a.

Maynard's journal relates to more than one voyage in the whaleship *Asia*, Captain Thomas Jay, of Le Havre, from 1837 to about 1846. The areas visited were mainly in New Zealand waters and in the region of the Chatham Islands. See also entry below.

67 _____, and Alexandre Dumas, *The whalers*, trans. by F.W. Reed, with intro. and notes by Johannes C. Andersen. London, Hutchinson & Co., [1937]; New York, Hillman-Curl, Inc., 1937. [vi], 414 pp. (London ed. contains 16 extra pp. of adverts.)

Translation of Maynard's *Les baleiniers . . .* , cited above. In his introductory note, "Alexandre Dumas and Dr. Felix Maynard", F.W. Reed writes that Dumas originally received some of Maynard's whaling material, a series of articles, when he was editor of *Le Mousquetaire*. Later Maynard collected together all his whaling reminiscences, which Dumas "edited". *Les baleiniers* first appeared as a serial in a Parisian daily paper before its publication in three vols. in 1858.

68 MILLER, George, *A trip to sea from 1810 to 1815*. Long Sutton, [Eng.], John Swain; London, Messrs Simpkin, Marshall and Co., 1854. iv, 92 pp.

Describes whaling off New Zealand, 1810-11. Miller's ship visited Sydney in 1811 and was wrecked off New Guinea in the same year. (National Library of Australia - Ferguson 12598)

69 MULLETT, J.C., b. 1830, *Five years on the Pacific Ocean*. Cleveland, Ohio, E. Cowles & Co., 1858. [3], 45 pp. 2nd ed. pub. with title *A five years' whaling voyage 1848-1853*. Cleveland, Ohio, Fairbanks, Benedict & Co., Printers, 1859. 68 pp. This ed. reprinted Fairfield, Wash., Ye Galleon Press, 1977. 58 [+2] pp. Illus. (Limited ed. of 423 copies.)

Account of voyages in various ships, principally whalers -- in particular the *George and Susan*, Captain White [Wight], of New Bedford, to Juan Fernández and Hawaii; the *Champion*, Captain Waterman, of New Bedford, to Polar regions, and the *Empire*, captain unnamed (Starbuck: Captain William Upham), of Nantucket, from

Hawaii to "Neukeheva" (Nukuhiva), coast of Tahiti (*en route* called at an island "on which the inhabitants were very savage"), Pitcairn, "Terrapin Island" (in Galápagos group?) and coast of Peru. (PMB 328: *George and Susan*.)

70   MUNGER, James F., 1830-1852, *Two years in the Pacific and Arctic Oceans and China, being a journal of every day life on board ship, interesting information in regard to the inhabitants of different countries, and the exciting events peculiar to a whaling voyage*, with biography of author by L.H. Stanley. Vernon, [N.Y.], J.R. Howlett, Printer, 1852. viii, 79 [+1] pp. Reprinted Fairfield, Wash., Ye Galleon Press, 1967. [7], 79 [+1] pp., with intro. by Glen Adams, pp. [5-7]. (Limited ed. of 401 copies.)

Munger on the New Bedford whaleship *St. George*, Captain W. Hawes, between 1850 and 1852, visiting Hawaiian ports (Hilo, Lahaina, Honolulu), Fanning, Jarvis, Hope, Ocean and Pleasant Islands, Ladrones, Raven's Island and Guam. Pp. 56-71 contain correspondence from Hawaii, 1851. In 1852 Munger shipped aboard the merchant vessel *Annie Buckman* from Canton to New York. He died in July 1852, when he fell from the rigging off the coast of Florida. (PMB 773: *St. George*)

71   MURPHEY, Charles, Third Mate, *A journal of a whaling voyage on board ship Dauphin, of Nantucket*, "composed by Charles Murphey, 3rd mate, on the voyage" (on cover: *Thrilling whaling voyage journal, in poetry . . .*). Mattapoisett, Mass., Atlantic Publishing Company, 1877. 39 pp. Note: There were two 1877 eds: Mitchell Library copy has small illus. on cover and vignette on verso of title; another ed. has title vignette and 5 pls.

Dauphin, Captain Zimri Coffin, sailed on 4 Sept. 1820, returning in July 1823. Voyage included Galápagos and Hawaiian Islands (1822). Poem recounts the finding of boat from the *Essex* with two survivors aboard. An officer list also provided. (Mitchell Library; PMB 772, 890)

72   NEL, [J.-B. Généreux], Dr., b. 1797, *Voyage et désordres à bord du navire baleinier Albatros, Capitaine Hurtel, de 1837 à 1840 par le Dr Nel, chirurgien de ce navire, ouvrage dédié à la marine française*. Ingouville, Le Petit, 1840. 139 pp. Port.

Albatros, Captain A. Hurtel left Le Havre on 16 Oct. 1837, returning 18 Apr. 1840. Visited Honolulu and Bay of Islands, New Zealand and in 1839 was at Tahiti. Dr. Nel wrote his account to protest against the captain's brutality. (Bibliothèque Nationale, Paris; O'Reilly 1033, see also no. 425)

73   NEVENS, William, b. 1781, *Forty years at sea: or, A narrative of the adventures of William Nevens. Being an account of the vicissitudes, hardships, narrow escapes, shipwrecks and sufferings in a forty years' experience at sea*. Portland, [Maine], Thurston, Fenley and Co., Printers, 1846. 314 pp. Pls. Another (3rd) ed., Portland, S.H. Colesworthy, 1850. 314 pp. Frontis., pls.

Nevens sailed on the *"Rosellic"* (*Rosalie*), Captain Gardner, of Warren, R.I., August 1825, on a three-year voyage visiting Japan grounds, Sandwich Islands and Off-shore grounds. Returned June 1828. In May 1829 he shipped aboard the *Magnet*, also of Warren, with same captain, visiting Galápagos (James and Charles Islands), and Off-shore grounds. In November 1832 Nevens joined the *Isaac Howland*, Captain Austin, of New Bedford (Starbuck: *Isaac Howland*, Capt. William Austin, sailed 28 November 1831), which cruised on the Off-shore grounds and to Galápagos. On voyage Nevens contracted scurvy and was discharged, sick. Later he joined the *Hobomok*, in January 1835, Captain Barnard, of Falmouth, visiting Sandwich Islands and Japan grounds. *Hobomok* returned July 1836 and Nevens shipped out again in September of that year in the *Boy*, of Warren, R.I., with the same Captain Barnard (Starbuck has "Barton") calling at Juan Fernández, Galápagos, Sandwich Islands, Japan grounds, Marquesas, Christmas and Fanning Islands, returning in November 1839. (PMB 890: *Rosalie*)

74　NEWHALL, Chas. [Charles] L., b. 1834, *The adventures of Jack: or, A life on the wave*. Southbridge, [Mass.], "Printed by the Author", 1859. [iv], 134 pp. Reprinted Fairfield, Wash., Ye Galleon Press, 1981. 92 pp. Frontis. port., illus., bibliog., index, ed. with notes, introduction and afterword by Kenneth R. Martin.

Whaling experiences in the Pacific Ocean aboard the *Copia*, of New Bedford, Captain C.M. Newell (see no. 836, Helen P. Hoyt, for note on Newell), from Jan. 1853-Jan. 1854 (Hawaiian Islands, North Pacific, Ladrones), *Bowditch*, of Warren, R.I., Captain Waldron, from March to late 1854 (Bonin Islands, North Pacific, Hawaii) and *Dover* of New London, late 1854 to Feb. 1855 (Hawaii, Marquesas). Newhall's account also includes whaling in the Indian Ocean and merchant marine service in northern hemisphere. (PMB 577: *Bowditch*)

75　NICHOLSON, Paul C. (ed.), *Abstracts from a journal kept aboard the ship Sharon of Fairhaven on a whaling voyage in the South Pacific, 1841-1845*. [Providence, R.I., Privately Printed and Published by Paul C. Nicholson, 1953.] [1-6], 7-14, [15] pp.

The *Sharon*, Captain Howes S. Norris, left Fairhaven in May 1841. *En route* to New Zealand from Ascension Island in the Carolines, Captain Norris was murdered by three crew members. This journal was probably kept by the cooper, Andrew White of Tiverton, R.I., and is now in the Paul C. Nicholson collection of logbooks in the Free Public Library, Providence, R.I. The *Sharon's* cruise in the Pacific embraced Nauru, Tuvalu, Ocean Island, Gilbert Islands, Caroline Islands, Sydney, and Loyalty Islands (1842), Samoa - Upolu and Savaii, Fiji and Rotuma (1843); New Zealand (Bay of Islands) and Hawaii (Maui) (1844). She returned to Fairhaven on 10 Feb. 1845. (PMB 674, 893)

76　OLMSTED, Francis Allyn, 1819-1844, *Incidents of a whaling voyage: to which are added observations on the scenery, manners and customs, and missionary stations of the Sandwich and Society Islands accompanied by* *numerous lithographic prints.* New York, D. Appleton and Co., 1841. x, 360 pp. Illus.; London, John Neale, 1844. vi, 104 pp. Illus. New ed., with preface by W. Storrs Lee, Rutland, Vermont & Tokyo, Charles E. Tuttle Co.; New York, Bell Publishing Company, [1969], "with the cooperation of Friends of the Library, Maui, Hawaii". xiii, 360 pp. Illus.

Voyage in the *North America*, Captain Richards, of New London, (a "Temperance ship"), 1839-40. Whaling off the coast of South America - Galápagos; passage to Hawaii - Honolulu; life in Honolulu; visit to Hawaii Island. Aug. 1840 embarkation on trading vessel *Flora* to Tahiti. Much information on life on a whale-ship.

77   OSBORN, Burr, Captain, *Reminiscences of a voyage around the world in the forties.* Union City, Mich., The Union City Register, 1892. 150 pp. (doub. col.).

According to Osborn's account, his whaling experiences in the Pacific included voyages in the New London whaler *Tenedos*, Captain Comstock, and the *Magnolia* of New Bedford, Captain Simmons, in the 1840s, in New Zealand waters and with visits to Hawaii (Maui and Oahu). The author shows himself to be scholarly and well-read, but because some of the events described in his narrative have proved difficult to authenticate, doubts must be expressed as to its complete reliability as a true record of actual events. (New Bedford Whaling Museum)

78   OXX, Thomas H., b. 1821?, *History of a whaling voyage in the Pacific Ocean.* Pelham Manor, N.Y., [1892.] 39 pp.

Oxx was a native of Rhode Island, and was "13 years old" at the time of his voyage in the *Mechanic*, of Newport, R.I., Captain Edward Harding, which took place from 22 Sept. 1834 to 6 July 1838. Oxx refers to Galápagos, Raiatea - Society Islands, and Sydney. On this voyage the *Mechanic* also visited Aitutake, New Zealand, Rurutu, Lord Howe Island and Solomon Islands. (Kaplan 4382; PMB 880)

79   PADDACK, William C., Captain, b. 1831, *Life on the ocean: or thirty-five years at sea. Being the personal adventures of the author, William C. Paddack for twenty-eight years captain in the merchant service of the United States.* Cambridge, [Mass.], Printed at the Riverside Press, 1893. xii, [2], 242 pp. Frontis. port., pls., ports.

Written in journal form. Includes reminiscences of whaling in the Pacific, 1848-51, in the whaleship *Planter*, Captain Isaac B. Hussey, of Nantucket. Three cruises to the Gilbert Islands are described, with visits to Ocean and Pleasant Islands and Sydney. The *Planter* took "King Amannook" of "Morgan Island" (in the Gilbert group), on a visit to Sydney in 1849. Captain Hussey elected to stay at Strong's Island following his shooting of a mutinous crew member on the brig *William Penn* (unidentified) at Woodle's Island in 1853 while on another whaling cruise.

80   PAULDING, Hiram, Lieutenant, U.S. Navy, 1797-1878, *Journal of a cruise of the United States schooner Dolphin, among the islands of the Pacific Ocean; and a visit to the Mulgrave Islands, in pursuit of the mutineers* *of the whale ship Globe.* With a map. New-York, G. & C. & H. Carvill, London, C. Hurst & Co., 1831. iv, 258 pp. Reprinted, Honolulu, University of Hawaii Press; Sydney, Melbourne and Singapore, Australia & New Zealand Book Co. Pty Ltd, 1970. xxi, iv, 258 pp., with new intro. by A. Grove Day and list of sources.

See William Comstock, *The life of Samuel Comstock . . .* (no. 28) and William Lay and Cyrus M. Hussey, *A narrative of the mutiny, on board the ship Globe . . . ,* (no. 63) above.

81 PERKINS, Edward T., *Na motu* [The islands]: *or, Reef-rovings in the South Seas. A narrative of adventures at the Hawaiian, Georgian and Society Islands; with maps, twelve original illustrations, and an appendix relating to the resources, social and political condition of Polynesia, and subjects of interest in the Pacific Ocean.* New York, Pudney & Russell, J.H. Colton & Co., 1854. xvi, [17]-456 pp. Pls, maps, appendices. Another ed., condensed, without appendices, pub. New York, Garrett & Co., 1854. 370 pp.

Perkins describes his experiences in the Pacific, which took place between 1848-53. In this period he embarked on the whaleship *Planet* (unidentified), Captain Peter Smith Buck, for a six month cruise. The first of three parts the book is entitled "The whale-ship", and relates specifically to whaling. Pt. 2 relates to the Hawaiian Islands. Pt. 3 relates to the Society Islands and Tubuai. Apppendix IV refers to "American whaling interests in the Pacific". It is possible that Perkins used fictitious names for his ship and its captain. It is also possible that the voyage he describes is not authentic, and further research is needed to identify it.

82 RHODES, W.B., Captain, 1807-1878, *The whaling journal of Captain W.B. Rhodes: barque Australian of Sydney 1836-1838*, with intro. and notes by C.R. Straubel. Christchurch [N.Z.], Whitcombe and Tombs Ltd, [1954]. xxxviii, [ii], 123 pp. Pls, appendices, index.

Rhodes's whaling cruise lasted from 14 June 1836 to 10 June 1838. The journal covers the period 14 June 1836 to 6 March 1838. The voyage embraced New Zealand - Cloudy Bay, Kermadec Islands, Tonga group - Eua, back to the Kermadecs, northeast New Zealand - Bay of Islands, southern New Caledonia, Loyalty Islands - Walpole Island, northeast coast of Australia, Niue, Tonga group - Vavau and Eua, returning to the Kermadec Islands and New Zealand. Rhodes mentions many other whaleships cruising in these regions (see Appendix 21, "Ships mentioned in the journal").

83 RICKETSON, Annie Holmes [Anna], *The journal of Annie Holmes Ricketson on the whaleship A.R. Tucker, 1871-1874, from the original in the Kendall Whaling Museum*, with foreword by Philip F. Purrington. (Cover title: *Mrs. Ricketson's whaling journal.*) New Bedford, Mass., Old Dartmouth Historical Society, 1958. 79 pp. Illus.

The *A.R. Tucker*, Captain D.L. Ricketson, of New Bedford left port on 2 May 1871, returning 18 Oct. 1874, and was at New Ireland, Green Islands and Bougainville in November 1872; sighted Admiralty Islands in December 1872. (PMB 274,307,803)

84   ROBBINS, Charles Henry, Captain, 1822-1903?, *The gam, being a group of whaling stories*. New Bedford, Mass., H.S. Hutchinson & Co., 1899. 203 pp. Frontis., pls., illus. Rev. ed., Boston, A.J. Ochs & Co., 1899. 238 pp. Frontis., pls. Another rev. ed., Salem, Mass., Newcomb & Gauss, 1913. xxviii, 242 pp. Frontis., pls.

First section contains anecdotes based on the author's "own earlier experiences" on the New Bedford whaler *Swift*. The *Swift*, Captain Lewis Tobey, sailed on a whaling voyage to the Pacific on 22 Feb. 1837, returning 31 Aug. 1841. Robbins refers to visiting the Society, Navigators, and Marquesas groups, and Pitcairn Island between 1837 and 1839. 1913 ed. has foreword which includes brief history of New Bedford whaling industry and section at end, "A typical whaleman", by "Z.W.P." [i.e., Zephaniah W. Pease], on life of Capt. Robbins (pp. 240-2).

85   SAMPSON, Alonzo D., b. 1831, *Three times around the world, or life and adventures of Alonzo D. Sampson*. Buffalo, N.Y., Express Printing Co., 1867. 170 pp.

Sampson's voyages round the world were on whale ships. He sailed on the *Junior* of New Bedford, Captain Silas Tingham (or Tinkham) on a cruise to the North Pacific from 1 July 1850 to 10 July 1853, via Cape of Good Hope, to Van Diemen's Land, New Zealand, Friendly Islands, Bering Strait and Arctic Ocean, Honolulu, Society Islands, Ladrones and Sea of Okhotsk. From 1853 to 1857 he was on board the *Rebecca Sims* of New Bedford, Captain Samuel B. Gavett (or Gavitt) which also cruised to the North Pacific via Cape Horn, to Hawaii, Sea of Okhotsk, Baja California, Sea of Japan, Bering Strait, Arctic Ocean and Cook Islands. Sampson's last voyage was again on the *Junior*, Captain Archibald Mellen, from 21 July 1857 via Cape of Good Hope to North Pacific. In December 1857 a mutiny took place near Van Diemen's Land, led by Cyrus B. Plummer, during which the captain and most of the officers were killed. Eventually the mutineers, including Sampson, left the *Junior* in two boats and landed not far from the site of the present town of Merimbula, on the east coast of Australia, south of Sydney. All but two of the mutineers were picked up by police and returned to the United States to stand trial. Sampson was freed and later published this narrative in his native state of New York, after a stay in California where he had been accidentally blinded. (PMB 816: *Rebecca Sims*; 340: *Junior*, 1857-58)

86   SMITH, Thomas W., *A narrative of the life, travels and sufferings of Thomas W. Smith: comprising an account of his early life, . . . his travels during eighteen voyages to various parts of the world, during which he was five times shipwrecked . . .* Written by himself. Boston, Wm. C. Hill; New Bedford, Thomas W. Smith; Portsmouth, W.B. & T.Q. Lowd; Exeter, A.R. Brown, 1844. 240 pp. List of contents at end.

Smith made whaling voyages to the Pacific Ocean in the English whalers *Spring Grove* and *Hibernia* of London in the 1820s. These are the 11th and 12th voyages, described in chaps. 14 and 15, partic. pp. 164-70 and 190-216. The areas visited were the Galápagos Islands, Easter Island, Samoa, Kingsmill Islands, Matthew's Island, New Hebrides, Solomon Islands (with refs. to the *Alfred* and *John Bull* of Sydney: in Dec. 1827 the captain and several sailors of the *Alfred* were killed by Malaitans), Caroline Islands, Guam, Japan grounds and Rotuma.

87   SNOW, Samuel, *The exile's return: or narrative of Samuel Snow, who was banished to Van Dieman's* [sic] *Land, for participating in the patriot war, in Upper Canada, in 1838.* Cleveland, [Ohio], [J.B. Fellowes, Arcade News-Room], Printed by Smead & Cowles, 1846. 32 pp. 4th ed., Smead & Cowles Steam Press, 1851. 32 pp. Cover illus.

On 15 Jan. 1845 Snow and 28 other American prisoners took passage at Hobart on the whaleship "Steiglitz" (i.e. *Stieglitz*), Captain Selah Youngs (or Young?), of Bridgeport, Conn. (Snow gives Sag Harbor, N.Y., as home port), after being granted free pardons. Among those pardoned was Daniel D. Heustis, q.v. above. The *Stieglitz* on its way to N.W. Coast grounds passed New Zealand and called at "Rematura" (Rimatara, Tubuai) and "Tahita". Then sailed to "Owhyhee" Island and reached Oahu and Honolulu 27 April 1845. Snow returned to U.S. on whaleship *Canton*, Captain Dyke, from Honolulu, passing Society Islands again and reaching New Bedford 2 May 1846. Descriptions of whaling operations, contact with people of "Rematura", the French at "Tahita", background sketch of Hawaiian Islands and impressions of Honolulu are given (pp. 24-32). (Sabin 85537)

88   SØDRING, Thomas [Jepsen], Captain, *Capitain Thomas Sødrings Dagbog, fort paa den første Danske Sydhavs-Expedition*, udgiven og bearbeidet af J. Holbech. Kjøbenhavn, Forlagt af Universitetsboghandler C.U. (A?) Reitzel, 1841. iv, 5-55 pp.

The *Concordia*, commanded by Captain Sødring, left Copenhagen on 11 May 1839, returning at the end of 1841, after whaling in New Zealand waters and on the Chatham Islands grounds.

89   SPARSHATT, Charles, "of Stoke Newington, one of the crew", *A narrative of the loss of the ship Harriet, (whaler) of London, which was wrecked on a reef of coral rocks off the Fejee Islands, in the South Pacific Ocean, on the sixteenth of July, 1837 . . . Together with some account of their providential escape in the boats, and their landing on Wallis's Island, after eight days of intense suffering. There they remained among savages for three months, when he, with six of his fellow sufferers, was taken on board a Sydney whaler, and left at Port Jackson in August 1838.* London, Printed by the Philanthropic Society, 1839. 28 pp.

"This narrative is published from his own dictation, almost verbatim, with a view of raising, by its sale, a small sum to meet his expenses while under medical treatment for deafness, and also to provide an outfit for a future voyage." Sparshatt's account contains some interesting information on whaling activities. (National Library of Australia - Ferguson 2845)

90   SPENCER, Thomas, Captain, 1812-1884, *Narrative of the events attending the massacre of part of the crew belonging to the whaleship* Triton, *of New-Bedford, by the natives of Sydenham's Island.* Honolulu, Oahu, E.A. Rockwell, Printer, Sandwich Islands News Press, 1848. 17 pp. (Also published in *The Friend*, Sept. 1848, pp. 70-1 and Oct. 1848, pp. 73-6.)
See no. 497, Thomas G. Thrum, "Captain Thomas Spencer". The *Triton* sailed from New Bedford on 21 July 1846 and was attacked at Nonouti in 1848, when five of the crew were killed and seven wounded. According to Starbuck, Captain Spencer was rescued by the whaleships *Alabama* and *United States* of Nantucket and the *Triton* returned to New Bedford on 31 May 1850. (Sabin 89389)

91   TABER, Charles S[pooner], Captain, 1809-1892, *A narrative of a shipwreck in the Fiji Islands 1840.* [New Haven, Conn.], "Privately Printed" (Press of Tuttle, Morehouse & Taylor), 1894. 50 pp. Frontis. port., illus.
Published from author's MS. after his death, probably by his wife. Taber, born in Fairhaven, Mass., was master of the whaleship *Shylock* of Rochester, which left port (New Bedford) on 26 May 1839, bound for N.Z. whaling grounds. Sailed from Hobart 8 Feb. 1840 and at Bay of Islands, N.Z., early May. On 20 May wrecked on reef south of Fiji. Crew split up. Some were picked up later after stay on Turtle Island. Taber sailed boat to Tofua (23 May), then moved on to Lifuka in the Ha'apai group, where met missionaries. Reaching Ha'ano, Taber picked up by missionary schooner *Triton*, which took him to Hobart.

92   THIERCELIN, [Louis], Dr., b. 1809, *Journal d'un baleinier. Voyages en Océanie*, 2 vols. Paris, L. Hachette et Cie, 1866. [iv], 352; [iv], 376 pp.
Describes Thiercelin's voyage to the Pacific in the whaleship *Gustave* of Le Havre, commencing 7 April 1863. In the course of the voyage the *Gustave* passed Tasmania, sailed through the Coral Sea and visited New Caledonia. The cruise continued to the Chatham Islands and from thence to Akaroa, N.Z. (Feb. 1864), and Tahiti, where Thiercelin left the ship. (The *Gustave* was condemned at Papeete on 15 Jan. 1866.) Much material on the business of whaling and on the history of the areas visited by the *Gustave*. Thiercelin was already familiar with whaling in some of these regions from his earlier cruise in the whaler *Ville de Bordeaux* between 1837 and 1841. After leaving Tahiti, Thiercelin returned to France on the *Ferdinand de Lesseps*, via Hawaii.

93   _____, *Journal d'un baleinier (1863)*, Les Grandes Aventures Maritimes ser. [Genève], Éditions Vernoy, [c. Éditions Idégraf], 1979. 252 pp. Pls.
Vol. I only of Thiercelin's original *Journal d'un baleinier*. This includes the *Gustave*'s visit to Tasmania, passage through the Coral Sea via Chesterfield and Bampton Islands and sojourn at New Caledonia.

94   THOMAS, Sylvia, *Saga of a Yankee whaleman*. [New Bedford, Mass., Trustees of the Old Dartmouth Historical Society, 1981.] xvi, 132 pp. Illus., ports., bibliog.

Granddaughter of New Bedford whaling captain Albert Alexander Thomas, 1833-1915, has traced his whaling career from 1853-76, using logs, journals and letters, some written by Thomas himself, and also oral history. Thomas made five Pacific whaling voyages, first in the ship *Franklin*, Captain Josiah Richmond, of New Bedford, 1853-57, as carpenter, and again in 1857-59, as fourth mate and boatsteerer. In 1860-64 he was on the ship *Daniel Wood*, Captain Richmond, of New Bedford, as first mate; from 1867-71 he was master of the bark *Albion* from New Bedford (registered in Gibraltar) and from 1872-76 he commanded the bark *Merlin* of New Bedford. The *Franklin's* first voyage embraced Juan Fernández, Maui (Lahaina), Arctic Ocean, Japan and Okhotsk Seas, Guam and Cook Islands (Rarotonga); the second, Chatham grounds (where *Franklin* was wrecked on Pitt Island, Dec. 1859), New Zealand (Bay of Islands) and Rarotonga. The *Daniel Wood's* cruise was mainly on the Chatham and Vasquez grounds, among the Fiji Islands and Northern Cook group, Rarotonga and Bay of Islands. The *Albion's* was in similar regions (sold at Auckland in 1871). The *Merlin* fished on the Chatham and Vasquez grounds with visits to Bay of Islands and Rarotonga. The *Merlin's* cruise also included Norfolk Island, Rapa, the Marquesas, Tuamotu Archipelago, and Society, Cook and Kermadec Islands. (PMB 862: *Franklin* 1; 243: *Daniel Wood*; 572: *Albion*; 254: *Merlin*)

95   THOMPSON, A[bsalom] C[hristopher] C[olumbus], 1821-1877, *Incidents of a whaling voyage by A.C.C. Thompson. Being a true account of the voyage and shipwreck of the author*. Written for the Central Georgian in the year 1859, with foreword by James W. McClendon. [N.p., n.d. (= Austin, Texas, Privately Printed), 1969.] [4], 43 pp. Port., illus.

Describes voyage of the *Cadmus* of Fairhaven, Captain Mayhew, which sailed on whaling cruise 11 Nov. 1841, to Pacific Ocean via Cape Horn. After passing Juan Fernández and Galápagos Islands, reached Marquesas in 1842. *Cadmus* was at Nukuhiva when French took possession of the group in May of that year. In August 1842 ship struck reef about 360 miles northwest of Pitcairn (Morane, formerly Cadmus or Barstow Island) and was wrecked. One boat with crew of eight (including author) was saved and reached Tahiti after 11 days. Other survivors rescued later. Thompson stayed at Tahiti for three months before leaving on English vessel *Zendia*.

96   TORREY, William, b. 1814, *Torrey's narrative; or, The life and adventures of William Torrey, who . . . was held captive by the cannibals of the Marquesas . . .* Written by himself . . . Boston, Press of A.J. Wright, 1848. xii, 300 pp. Pls.

Includes several whaling cruises in the Pacific in the 1830s, with visits to Hawaii, Marquesas, Keppell's Island, Duke of York Island, Fanning Island, Mulgrave's Islands, and "Cohannah" (?) Island. Hezel, *Foreign ships in Micronesia* (see no. 120), p. 118, refers to Torrey's report of visit to Mili in 1837.

97   TREGURTHA, Edward Primrose, Captain, 1803-1880, *The Tregurtha log: relating the adventurous life of Captain Edward Primrose Tregurtha. Napoleonic wars - The East India Company's China run - Whaling in the South Seas - Shipmaster to the Port Phillip District*, ed. by Dan Sprod. [Sandy Bay, Tasmania], Blubber Head Press, 1980. 165 pp. Frontis. port., illus., endp. maps, notes, bibliog., appendices, index. (Limited ed. of 600 copies.)

Captain Tregurtha commanded the barque *Caroline* of Hobart on a whaling cruise in the Pacific, 1831-33. The voyage commenced Nov. 1831 and embraced Lord Howe Island, the Kermadec Islands, New Zealand (Bay of Islands), Kingsmill Islands, Pleasant Island, Solomon Islands (Malaita and Guadalcanal), New Ireland, Santa Cruz Islands ("Mallicolo" = Vanikoro), Banks Islands, New Caledonia, Bay of Islands, and coast of Queensland, concluding in Hobart in July 1833. See Sect. III of the *Log*, "South Seas whaler", pp. 84-105 and Appendix 1, "Remarks on board the barque Sydney *Caroline*, Captain Tregurtha", pp. 115-27 (by unidentified crew member), also pp. 19-25, 147-50, 155-6.

98   [WARD, James, ed.], *Perils, pastimes, and pleasures of an emigrant in Australia, Vancouver's Island and California.* London, Thomas Cautley Newby, 1849. [2, ii], 404 + [12] pp. Appendices.

From internal evidence, this work written by a surgeon [James Ellis?] while on a whaling cruise in the *Jane* of Sydney, 1845-7. Whaling voyage described in chaps. 5-9, pp. 120-97, and embraces fishing "On the line", near Lord Howe Island, off New Zealand, near Cook Islands ("Mangea", "Whytotacke" and "Hervey's Island") and Sandwich Islands; also off Vancouver Island and coast of California. Chap. 12, pp. 274-96 deals with importance of whale fisheries to the Australian colonies. Dedication and introduction signed "J.W." - identified as James Ward. (Ferguson 5237)

99   WATROUS, Charles, 1827-1891, *Written for my grandchildren . . .* New York, Press of W.R. Jenkins, 1892?. 147 pp. Port.

Watrous was a whaler for three years on the *Merrimack*, Captain Destin, of New London, from July 1844 to May 1847, visiting Hawaii, Pitcairn Island, the Mariana Islands and Samoa (in Nov. 1846). (Library of Congress [microfilm copy]; Yale University Library)

100   WEST, Ellsworth Luce, b. 1864, *Captain's papers: a log of whaling and other sea experiences*, as told to Eleanor Ransom Mayhew, with foreword by Henry Beetle Hough. Barre, Mass., Barre Publishers, 1965. viii, 172 pp. Map, illus.

Pt. I, pp. 1-75, contains records of whaling voyages to the Pacific, 1880s - 1900. See partic. the voyage of the *California*, 1893-94, embracing the Marshall Islands, Kusaie, Ponape, Guam, to the Arctic; and the *Horatio*, 1897-98, embracing Gilbert Islands, Hawaii, Marianas Islands and Ocean Island, to the Okhotsk Sea. On her next voyage the *Horatio* was lost off Kusaie in January 1899. (PMB 833: *Horatio* 1897-98)

101   WHITECAR, William B., Jr, *Four years aboard the whaleship. Embracing cruises in the Pacific, Atlantic, Indian, and Antarctic Oceans in the years 1855, '6, '7, '8, '9.* Philadelphia, J.B. Lippincott & Co.; London, Trubner & Co., 1860, 1864. xii, 13-413 pp.

Whitecar was on the whaling barque *Pacific*, Captain John W. Shearman, of New Bedford, on her voyage between 24 July 1855 and 20 Mar. 1859. The *Pacific* sailed through the South Atlantic fishing grounds and across the Indian Ocean to S.W. Australia, then to the New Zealand grounds (early 1857), Tasmanian waters and back to S.W. Australia, before returning to New Bedford via the same route.

102   WILKINSON, David, "Youngest member of the first Victorian Whaling Expedition to the southern and Siberian polar regions", *Whaling in many seas and cast adrift in Siberia. With a description of the manners, customs and heathen ceremonies of various (Tchuktches) tribes of north-eastern Siberia.* London, Henry J. Drane (Ye Olde Saint Bride's Presse), [1906]. [ii], 3-296 pp. Frontis., pls., fold. map "shewing the 'Japan's' track in two hemispheres".

Describes the voyage of the whaling barque *Japan*, owned by Osborne & Cushing of Melbourne, Captain Frederick Allan Barker, master, which commenced in January 1869. In the early part of the voyage, the *Japan* cruised in New Zealand waters, and near Navigators Islands, Hope Island, Gilberts, Pleasant Island, Solomons, Coral Sea, into the Antarctic, via Bay of Islands, then past the Caroline and Marshall Islands to Bering Sea. In October 1870 the *Japan* was wrecked in the Arctic Ocean, and the survivors were cared for by Eskimos until rescued by American whaleships *Contest* and *Henry Taber* in June 1871. These ships, along with the rest of the Arctic whaling fleet, bar seven vessels, were later lost in the ice in September 1871. The *Japan*'s remaining crew eventually reached Melbourne late in 1871, via Hawaii and New Zealand. Illustrations, by the author and J. Dow, are based on incidents and scenes of the voyage.

103   WILLIAMS, Frederick Benton (pseud. of Herbert Elliott Hamblen, b. 1849), *On many seas: the life and exploits of a Yankee sailor*, ed. by his friend William Stone Booth. New York, The Macmillan Co.; London, Macmillan & Co., 1897. x, 417 pp. Reprinted 1898.

Chaps. 26-31, pp. 238-84, describe the author's desertion from a naval vessel in Valparaiso and his shipping aboard a whaler, the *Bahio* (i.e. *Bohio*) of Nantucket, Captain Henry Davis, on a whaling cruise toward the Galápagos grounds. Details of whaling operations given. Author later jailed at Paita, Peru, for mutiny. No dates are given, but it is known that the *Bohio* made only one whaling voyage from Nantucket, from 12 July 1868; she called at Valapraiso at the end of March 1871; the captain's log records the removal of a mutinous crewmember in Nov. 1871. The *Bohio* was sold at Valparaiso in January 1872. (PMB 393)

104   WILLIAMS, Harold (ed.), *One whaling family*. Boston, Houghton Mifflin Company; Cambridge, The Riverside Press, 1964]. London, Victor Gollancz, 1964. x, 401 pp. Illus. (U.S. ed. only), endp. maps, appendices.

Pt. I, "The voyage of the *Florida*", Captain Thomas W. Williams, of Fairhaven, Mass., 1858-61, taken from the journal of Eliza Azelia Williams (1826-1885), to the North Pacific via Atlantic and Indian Oceans and Tasmania, then to New Zealand (Mangonui). Thereafter the cruise included visits to or whaling in the vicinity of Ocean and Strong's Islands, Japan and Okhotsk Seas, Wellington's and Ascension Islands, Mangonui and Bay of Islands, Pleasant, Strong's and MacAskill's Islands, Guam and Hawaii (Honolulu). The crew list and outfitting details of the *Florida* are included. Pt. II, "Destruction of the whaling fleet in Arctic Ocean in 1871" by William Fish Williams (1902). Pt III, "The voyage of the *Florence*", Captain Thomas W. Williams, of San Francisco, 1873-74, from MS. by William Fish Williams (1859-1929), son of Eliza and Thomas Williams, member of crew and boatsteerer. Voyage embraced Ocean and Pleasant Islands, New Ireland, Bougainville and New Britain, Ponape, Saipan, Guam, Japan and Okhotsk Seas, San Francisco. Appendix 1 contains biographical details of the Williams whaling family. (PMB 301: *Florida*)

105   WILLIAMS, John G., b. 1824?, *The adventures of a seventeen- year-old lad and the fortunes he might have won*. Boston, Printed for the Author by the Collins Press, 1894. x, 11-308 pp. Frontis. port., illus.

Williams, born in Canada, sailed in 1841 on "a Duxbury whaler" (the *Sophia and Eliza*, Captain Rufus Coffin) which he deserted in S.W. Australia. He made his way to Hobart where he joined the *Kingston* of Fairhaven, Mass., Captain T. Ellis, on a whaling cruise (Starbuck: 14 Sept. 1844 - 26 May 1848). Williams describes visits to Fiji (Ovalau) and Tonga ("Tongaboo") and gives details of the inhabitants. The *Kingston* sailed to Sydney, then to Lord Howe Island and south to Hobart, where Williams left the ship. See chap. 4, partic. pp. 97-130. (Ferguson 18598; PMB 342)

106   WOOD, George C. (ed.), *In a sperm whale's jaws: an episode in the life of Captain Albert Wood of Nantucket, Mass.*, illus. by J.J. Lankes. Hanover, N.H., Friends of the Dartmouth Library, Dartmouth College, 1954. [iv], 17 pp. 14 vignettes and photo of Capt. Wood. (Limited ed. of 1000 copies.)

Contains excerpts from a journal kept by Henry A. Phelon, a crew member of the *Ploughboy* of New Bedford, and son of the captain, Henry Phelon, Jr. It also includes personal narrative of Captain Wood, who was mate on the vessel, dictated to his eldest son, Charles. *Ploughboy* left port on 16 June 1848. Journal's first entry is dated 4 March 1849. Incident with whale, when Wood was gored in its jaws, took place on this date at lat. 4° S., while ship was on the Off-shore grounds, bound for the Society Islands; on 1 April *Ploughboy* reached Tahiti and Wood was put ashore for medical treatment. Note: *Ploughboy* was lost near Tumbes, Peru later in 1849.

107   WOODHOUSE, James H., Captain, b. 1820, *Autobiography of Captain James H. Woodhouse. Compiled between Dec. 3rd 1896, and Dec. 10th 1896, principally from memory, but with facts and dates verified by reference to the author's journals and ship logs*. New Haven, W.H. Hale, Typewriter and Mimeographer, 1897. 174 pp.

Woodhouse embarked on *Columbus* of Fairhaven (i.e. New Bedford), Captain Tristram D. Pease, 20 May 1840, on cruise to Pacific Ocean via Cape Horn. Voyage encompassed Juan Fernández, Off-shore grounds, Easter Island, Galápagos, Marquesas (where author sees tapa-making and describes trading with islanders), Sandwich Islands, Pearl Islands, "Otaheite". Narrative has comments on French and English missionaries at Tahiti, description of meeting with Queen Pomare and of being tattooed. *Columbus* cruised again to Off-shore grounds, returning to Tahiti in Feb. 1842 (1843?). Voyage ends on 25 Dec. 1843. (PMB 674, 675, 795)

108　ZOLLERS, George D[ehaven], *Thrilling incidents on sea and land: the prodigal's return*. Mount Morris, Ill., The Brethren's Publishing Company, 1892. viii, [9]-400 pp. Frontis., pls., illus., index. First 4 eds. pub. 1892; 5th ed. 1903. Other later rev. eds., 6th, Mount Morris, Ill., Kable & Rittenhouse Co.; 7th, Elgin, Ill., Brethren Publishing House, 1909.

Zollers was converted to Christianity by the Rev. G.H. Wallace while a member of the crew of the whaleship *Oriole*, Captain Jared Jernegan, of New Bedford (formerly of Fairhaven), cruising in the Pacific 3 June 1863 - 3 Apr. 1866. Juan Fernández, the Marquesas and Hawaiian Islands were visited on the voyage.

II.

General Works

(A) Bibliography, shipping lists, source material, indexes.

109 ADAMS, James Truslow, 1878-1949, *History of the town of Southampton (east of Canoe Place).* Bridgehampton, L.I., Hampton Press, 1918. xx, 424 pp. Frontis., pls., ports., maps, facsims., bibliog. Reprinted Port Washington, N.Y., Ira J. Friedman, Inc., 1962, Empire State Historical Pubs. series, no. 14. Limited ed. of 300 copies.
Includes list of whaling voyages from Sag Harbor based on Starbuck's tables, with additions and corrections.

110 AUSTRALIA, COMMONWEALTH OF, *Historical records of Australia,* Series I, vols. 1-26: "Governors' despatches to and from England", [1788-1848]. [Sydney], Library Committee of the Commonwealth Parliament, 1914-25.
See entries under "Whale fishery" and "Whaling" in indexes. Note: Another set of *Historical records* was issued in 1971 (Canberra, W.G. Murray, Government Printer), partly reprinted and partly made up of unbound sheets remaining from the first edition.

111 CARMICHAEL, Henry, b. 1862, *Hints relating to emigrants and emigration, embracing observations and facts, intended to display the real advantages of New South Wales . . . ,* 2nd and 3rd eds. 2nd ed., Sydney, W. M'Garvie, 1836. iv, 102 pp.; 3rd ed., London, Smith Elder and Co. and D. Walther, 1839. 102 pp. 3rd ed. has title *Useful hints relating to . . . .*
See data relevant to Sydney-owned vessels engaged in sperm whaling Jan. 1833 - Dec. 1835, pp. 26-7, 81-6 (1836 ed.); pp. 30-1, 84-9 (1839 ed.). (National Library of Australia - Ferguson 2105, 2727)

112 COFFIN, Marie M. (comp.), *The history of Nantucket Island: a bibliography of source material with index and inventory,* limited ed. Nantucket, Mass., [Nantucket Historical Trust, 1970]. viii, 65 pp. Illus., maps.

113   COLBY, Barnard L., *New London whaling captains*, Publications of the Marine Historical Association Inc., Mystic, Mass., vol. 1, no. 11 (reprinted also as no. 12). [Westerly, R.I., The Utter Company, Printers], 1936. Pp. 187-225. Illus., ports., bibliog.

114   CUMPSTON, J.S., *Shipping arrivals and departures Sydney, 1788-1825.* Canberra, The Author, 1963. 164 + 26 pp. Frontis., pls., maps, index to ships and vessels. Reprinted 1964, with Part III (Index to persons) added. (164 + 66 pp.)
Major source of information on whalers in and out of Sydney.

115   ———, *Shipping arrivals and departures Sydney*, 1788-1825, Roebuck Society Publication no. 22. Canberra, A Roebuck Book, 1977. vii, 164 + 66 pp. (Rev. and expanded ed. of 1963 ed.) Frontis., illus., maps, index to ships and vessels, and to persons.

116   FEDERAL WRITERS' PROJECT, Works Progress Administration of Massachusetts (comp.), *Whaling masters*, "American Guide" series. New Bedford, Mass., Old Dartmouth Historical Society/Reynolds Printing, 1938. 314 pp. Frontis., pls.
Alphabetical list of American whaling masters, 1731-1925.

117   HEGARTY, Reginald B. (comp.), *Returns of whaling vessels sailing from American ports: a continuation of Alexander Starbuck's "History of the American whale fishery", 1876-1928*, with additions by Philip F. Purrington. New Bedford, Mass., Old Dartmouth Historical Society and Whaling Museum, 1959. 58 pp. Tables.

118   ———, *A list of log books of whaling voyages in the collection of the Melville Whaling Room in the Free Public Library*, New Bedford, Massachusetts. New Bedford, Mass., Reynolds-De Walt Printing Inc., 1963. 28 pp. Illus.
About 450 items listed. Note: This library possesses handwritten abstracts of 2,500 whaling voyages 1831-73, covering more important aspects, compiled by Dennis Wood, q.v. no. 155 below.

119   ———, *Addendum to "Starbuck" and "Whaling Masters": New Bedford Customs District*. New Bedford, Mass., Melville Whaling Room, New Bedford Free Public Library, [1964]. 110 pp.

120   HEZEL, Francis X., *Foreign ships in Micronesia: a compendium of ship contacts with the Caroline and Marshall Islands 1521-1885*. Saipan, Mariana Islands, Trust Territory Historic Preservation Office and U.S.

Heritage Conservation and Recreation Service, 1979. vi, 185 pp. Bibliog., index.

Major source of information on whalers in Micronesia.

121   [HILL, Laurence G.], *Index to whaling ship logs on microfilm at the New Bedford Free Public Library.* (Cover title: *Whaling logs.*) [New Bedford, Mass., Free Public Library], 1951. 9 pp.

122   HUNTRESS, Keith G., *A checklist of narratives of shipwrecks and disasters at sea to 1860, with summaries, notes and comments.* Ames, Iowa, Iowa State University Press, 1979. xiv, 194 pp. Frontis., index.

See partic. entries from 1821, p. 110 ff., for material on whaling - *Essex, Globe,* etc.

123   HUSSEY & ROBINSON, *Catalogue of Nantucket whalers and their voyages from 1815 to 1870.* Nantucket, Hussey & Robinson, Printers and Publishers, 1876. [vi], [7]-54 pp.

Also includes list of Nantucket ships sailing for the Californian gold rush and "Names of Nantucket men who commanded ships engaged in the Whale Fishery from French and English ports prior to 1812".

124   INTERNATIONAL MARINE MANUSCRIPT ARCHIVES, formerly THE WHALING AND MARINE MANUSCRIPT ARCHIVES, *A compilation of the holdings of the Whaling and Marine Manuscript Archives.* Nantucket, Mass., I.M.M.A., [1971]. iv, 36 pp. Indexes. 1-6 Addenda, 1972-1977/78. Various pagings. Note: Title changes in 1974.

Now at the New Bedford Whaling Museum.

125   JUDD, Bernice, *Voyages to Hawaii before 1860. A record, based on historical narratives in the libraries of the Hawaiian Mission Children's Society and The Hawaiian Historical Society, extended to March 1860,* enlarged and edited by Helen Yonge Lind. Honolulu, University Press of Hawaii for Hawaiian Mission Children's Society, [1974]. xviii, 129 pp. Index of vessels and persons, bibliog.

This ed. is revision of that originally published in 1929 by Hawaiian Mission Children's Society. Chronological list of vessels commences 1778. Many whaling refs.

126   LANGDON, Robert (ed.), *American whalers and traders in the Pacific: a guide to records on microfilm.* Canberra, Pacific Manuscripts Bureau, Research School of Pacific Studies, Australian National University, 1978. ix, [161] pp. Illus., maps.

Indexes to ships, captains and logkeepers, places visited.

127   _____, *Thar she went: an interim index to the Pacific ports and islands visited by American whalers and traders in the 19th century, being* *a supplement to "American whalers and traders in the Pacific: a guide to records on microfilm".* Canberra, Pacific Manuscripts Bureau, Research School of Pacific Studies, Australian National University, 1979. ix, 158 + 1 pp. Illus.

[128]   LEYDA, Jay (ed.), *The Melville log: a documentary life of Herman Melville.* See no. 301 below.

129   McCORMICK, Edgar L. and Edward G. McGEHEE (eds.), *Life on a whaler: selected source materials for college research papers.* Boston, D.C. Heath and Co., [1960]. xii, 112 pp. Illus., bibliog.
Passages from Bullen, Melville, Macy, Cheever, Delano, Chase, etc.

130   McNAB, Robert (ed.), *Historical records of New Zealand,* 2 vols. Wellington, John McKay, Government Printer, 1908-14. xvi, 779 pp.; xxii, 650 pp. Indexes. Reprinted Wellington, A.R. Shearer, Government Printer, 1973.
See refs. to "Whale-fishery", "Whalers" and "Whaling" in index to Vol. I, and to "United States Consular Records", Vol. II.

131   MAGNOLIA, L.R. (comp.), *Whales, whaling and whale research: a selected bibliography,* Pub. no. WM-1. Cold Spring Harbor, Long Island, N.Y., The Whaling Museum, 1977. [iii], 91 + 4 pp.

132   MARTIN, R. Montgomery, 1803?-1868, *History of the British colonies,* 5 vols. Vol. IV - *Possessions in Africa and Austral-Asia.* London, James Cochran and Co., 1835. xii, 624 [+60] pp. Appendices, index.
Data on Australian sperm whale fishery, pp. 363, 365, 368. (Ferguson 1818)

133   _____, *History of Austral-Asia: comprising New South Wales, Van Diemen's Island, Swan River, South Australia, &c.* London, John Mortimer, 1836. [vi], 371 [+10] pp. 2nd ed. London, Whittaker & Co., 1839. viii, 416 pp.
See chap. 8 of 1st ed. relating to N.S.W., "Finance - monetary system, and commerce" for whaling information, and chaps. 9 and 10 of 2nd ed.: "Finances and monetary system" and "Staple products and commerce", partic. pp. 238-41 on "Fisheries". (Ferguson 2144, 2801)

134   MAURY, M[atthew] F[ontaine], Lieutenant, U.S. Navy, 1806-1873, *Whale chart (preliminary sketch). Series F* [of *Wind and current charts. Series A-F*]. Published . . . by authority of Commo. L. Warrington, Chief of Bureau of Ordinance & Hydrography. [Washington, U.S. Navy Dept.], 1851. 23 3/4 inches x 36 5/8 inches.

135   MILLER, Pamela A., *And the whale is ours: creative writing of American whalemen.* Boston, Mass., David R. Godine, Publisher; Sharon,

Mass., Kendall Whaling Museum, 1979. ix, 201 [+2] pp. Illus., footnotes, bibliog., index.

Examination of some 3500 whaling logs: contents include short stories, poetry, novellas, songs, paintings, drawings.

136   [NASH, Howard P., Jr (comp.)], *Logbooks of the Old Dartmouth Historical Society and Whaling Museum, New Bedford, Mass.* New Bedford, Old Dartmouth Historical Society, 1959. 29 pp.

Lists 700 items.

137   NEW BEDFORD, Mass., Free Public Library, *A collection of books, pamphlets, log books, pictures, etc. illustrating [whales and] the whale fishery, contained in the . . . Library.* [New Bedford, Mass.], Free Public Library, 1907. 13 pp. Illus. Reprinted, with addition to title, 1920; 24 pp. Pls.

138   NEW BEDFORD WHALING MUSEUM, *Checklist of logbooks in the collection of the Old Dartmouth Historical Society and Whaling Museum.* New Bedford, Mass., New Bedford Whaling Museum, 1976. 34 pp.

139   [NEW BEDFORD WHALING MUSEUM], *Whaling exhibits of the Old Dartmouth Historical Society, New Bedford, Mass.*, Old Dartmouth Historical Society Publication no. 53. New Bedford, Mass., Old Dartmouth Historical Society, 1924. 47 pp. Illus. Also later eds. - 1926, "prepared by Arthur C. Watson", 51 pp., and 1930.

140   NICHOLSON, Ian Hawkins, *Shipping arrivals and departures Sydney. Volume II 1826 to 1840.* Parts I, II and III, Roebuck Society Publication no. 23. Canberra, A Roebuck Book, 1977. vi, 258 + 93 pp. Endp. maps, illus., maps, indexes to ships and vessels, and to persons.

141   ———, *Gazetteer of Sydney shipping 1788-1840: being a geographical index of ports of origin and destination, and places discovered, visited or remarked upon by Sydney shipping of the period*, Roebuck Society Publication no. 26. [Canberra], A Roebuck Book, [1981]. x, 217 pp. Illus., maps.

Gazetteer based on J.S. Cumpston's *Shipping arrivals and departures, Sydney, 1788-1825* and the author's *Shipping arrivals and departures Sydney. Volume II 1826 to 1840*, q.v. no. 114 above. Much of whaling interest.

142   ———, *Shipping arrivals and departures: Tasmania. Volume 1: 1803-1833.* Parts I, II and III, Roebuck Society Publication no. 30. [Canberra], A Roebuck Book, [1983]. viii, 224 + 94 pp. Endp. maps, illus., maps, indexes to ships and vessels and to persons.

Comprehensive record of shipping movements, partic. for Hobart and Launceston. Much of whaling interest.

143   PARSONS, Ronald (comp.), *Tasmanian ships registered 1826-1850 . . . (Full details of every ship enrolled by the Registrar of British Ships at the ports of Hobart Town and Launceston).* Magill, South Australia, Ronald H. Parsons, 1980. ii, 102 pp.

144   [PEABODY MUSEUM OF SALEM], *The whaling industry, exhibition of objects illustrating the whaling industry and the natural history of whales . . . List of Essex County whaling vessels. List of pictures of whaling vessels in the Marine Room. List of log-books of whaling vessels in the library of the Essex Institute. List of books on whales and whaling in the Salem Public Library . . .* [Salem, Mass., Peabody Museum of Salem, 1908.] 10 pp. Pls.

145   SCHULTZ, Charles R. (comp.), *Inventory of the logbooks and journals in the G.W. Blunt White Library.* Mystic, Conn., Marine Historical Assoc. Inc., 1965. 60 pp.
775 items of which 265 relate to whaling. Destinations given.

146   SHERMAN, Stuart C., *Logbooks and leviathans: an account of the Nicholson Whaling Collection.* [Hanover, N.H., 1962.] 8 pp.
Reprinted from *Polar Notes: Occasional Publication of The Stefansson Collection, Dartmouth College.* The Nicholson Whaling Collection is in the Providence, R.I., Public Library.

147   _____, *The voice of the whaleman. With an account of the Nicholson Whaling Collection.* Providence, R.I., Providence Public Library, 1965. 219 pp. Ports., facsims., bibliog., index.

148   STARBUCK, Alexander, 1841-1925, *History of the American whale fishery from its earliest inception to the year 1876.* Waltham, Mass., The Author, 1878. 779 pp. Illus., indexes. Reprinted in 2 vols., New York, Argosy-Antiquarian Ltd, 1964, with new preface by Stuart C. Sherman. vii, 407; [ii], 408-779 pp. Frontis., endp. maps. First pub. in Part IV of the *Report of the U.S. Commission on Fish and Fisheries* (Washington, 1878).
See 1964 ed., Vol. I, pp. 168-407, Vol. II, pp. 408-767 for returns and tables of whaling vessels sailing from American ports and other whaling data including index to voyages by vessels' names. See also no. 256.

149   TABER, Gordon, and Company, *Outfits for a whaling voyage.* New Bedford, [1856]. 64 pp.
Printed checklist for supplies. Similar lists were published by other outfitters.

150   UNITED STATES - SURVEY OF FEDERAL ARCHIVES [Bristol-Warren, R.I.], *Ship registers and enrollments, ship licenses issued to vessels under twenty tons, ship licenses on enrollments issued out of the port of Bristol-Warren, Rhode Island, 1773-1939,* prepared by the Survey of Federal Archives, Division of Community Service Programs, Work Projects Administration . . . Providence, R.I., National Archives Project, 1941. vii, 354 + 72 + 9 pp. Illus., tables, index.

Note: Whale ship data also included in following Survey of Federal Archives publications.

[Dighton-Fall River, Mass.], *Ship registers of Dighton-Fall River, Massachusetts, 1789-1938,* compiled by the Survey of Federal Archives, Division of Women's and Professional Projects, Work Projects Administration; National Archives, cooperating sponsor. Boston, Mass., National Archives Project, 1939. xii, 178 pp. Index.

[New Bedford, Mass.], *Ship registers of New Bedford, Massachusetts,* compiled by the Survey of Federal Archives, Division of Professional and Service Projects, Work Projects Administration; National Archives, cooperating sponsor; 3 vols. Boston, Mass., National Archives Project, 1940. pp. n.a. Index. Vol. 1, 1796-1850, vol. 2, 1851-1865, vol. 3, 1866-1939.

[Newport, R.I.], *Ship registers and enrollments of Newport, Rhode Island, 1790-1939,* prepared by the Survey of Federal Archives, Division of Professional and Service Projects, Work Projects Administration. State of Rhode Island, Department of State, Division of Archives, sponsor; National Archives, cooperating sponsor; 2 vols. Providence, R.I., National Archives Project, 1938-41. vii, 810; viii, 332 + 36 pp. Index. Vol. 1 consists of lists of vessels over 20 tons with descript. of vessels, owners, and masters (includ. whaleships). Vol. 2 includes ship licenses on enrollments issued out of Newport.

[Plymouth, Mass.], *Ship registers of the district of Plymouth, Massachusetts, 1789-1908,* compiled by the Survey of Federal Archives, Division of Women's and Professional Projects, Works Progress Administration; National Archives, cooperating sponsor; two parts in one vol. Boston, Mass., National Archives Project, 1939. ix, 171; xv, 172-209 pp. Index.

[Providence, R.I.], *Ship registers and enrollments of Providence, Rhode Island, 1773-1939,* prepared by the Survey of Federal Archives, Division of Community Service Programs, Work Projects Administration . . . , 2 vols. in 3. Providence, R.I., National Archives Project, 1941. pp. n.a. Index. Vol. 2 has title: *Ship licenses issued to vessels under twenty tons and ship licenses on enrollments issued out of the port of Providence, Rhode Island, 1793-1939.*

151   VAN METER, Elizabeth L. (comp.), Whaling logbooks and journals in the Kendall Whaling Museum collection. Sharon, Mass., Kendall Whaling Museum, [1977]. Xerographic typescript, [2], 48 pp. [Irregularly updated by various hands through 1984.]

152   WACE, Nigel and Bessie LOVETT, *Yankee maritime activities and the early history of Australia,* with foreword by Lady Hasluck; Research

School of Pacific Studies Aids to Research ser., no. A/2. Canberra, Australian National University, 1973. xiv [+ ii], 131 pp. Figs., refs., bibliog.

American maritime contacts with Australia up to 1850, including whaling.

153   WALTON, John, *Twelve months' residence in New Zealand; containing a correct description of the customs, manners, &c., of the natives of that island, with other information valuable to emigrants.* Glasgow, W.R. M'Phun; London, N.H. Cotes; Edinburgh, W. Wite & Co., 1839. v, 80 pp.

Author in N.Z. 1837-38. Pp. 23-4 gives list of whalers arriving Bay of Islands from Sydney and Hobart during this period. (National Library of Australia - Ferguson 2891)

154   WARD, R. Gerard (ed.), *American activities in the Central Pacific, 1790-1870: a history, geography and ethnography pertaining to American involvement and Americans in the Pacific taken from contemporary newspapers etc.*, with introduction by Ernest S. Dodge; 8 vols. Ringwood, N.J., Gregg Press, 1966-67. 316; xiii, 596; xiii, 655; xiii, 695; xiii, 578; xi, 572; xiii, 545; vii, 295 pp. Illus. Maps in separate slip case.

Important source book on American whaling activities in the Central Pacific. Entries listed by island - Abaiang to Zephyr Shoal. Vol. 1 includes explanatory "Editorial preface"; Vol. 8 has appendix and index.

155   WOOD, Dennis, d.1878, Abstracts of whaling voyages, 1831-1873. (Manuscript - unpublished. Original journals in New Bedford Free Public Library.) 5 vols.: 1, 1831-47; 2, 1845-53; 3, 1854-61; 4, 1862-73; 5, 1843-62

Detailed abstracts, indexed by ship's names. Vol. 5 includes "Register of Whaling Ships", Mutual Marine Insurance Co., and list of whaling vessels lost or condemned since 1815, to 1862. PMB 299 concludes with a list of ship arrivals from, and departures to, the whale fisheries, including Pacific Ocean grounds, at various U.S. ports, 1823–32, from original in New Bedford Whaling Museum.

(B) General works which relate wholly or partly to whaling in the Pacific Ocean.

156   *ABSTRACT OF REPORTS from the Commissioner of the Southern Whale Fishery Company to the Directors.* London, Printed by Pelham Richardson, 1850. 24 pp. Illus., map.

Report on the settlement at Port Ross, Auckland Islands, and whaling off the islands. (British Library)

157   ALLEN, Everett S., *Children of the light: the rise and fall of New Bedford whaling and the death of the Arctic fleet*, 1st ed. Boston, Little, Brown and Co., [1973]. viii [+ iv], 302 pp. Illus., list of refs., index.

158   ANDERSON, Florence Bennett, *Through the hawse-hole: the true story of a Nantucket whaling captain.* New York, Macmillan Co., 1932. x, 277 pp. Frontis. port., illus., facsims.

Life of Captain Seth Pinkham, 1786-1844, whose whaling voyages to the Pacific Ocean were in the Nantucket whaleships *Dauphin*, 1815-17, 1817-19, *Galen*, 1820-23 and *Henry Astor*, 1840-44. See partic. chaps. 16 and 17 "South of the Equator" and "A whaleman's spy-glass", pp. 229-53, for information about Pinkham's experiences on *Henry Astor*, which visited the Marquesas in 1842. Pinkham was one of a number of whaling captains who sent a memorial to the French governor at "Naoshenah" (Nuku Hiva ?), asking him to put a stop to the activities of "Irish Jemmy", who was encouraging American seamen to desert (26 Sept. 1842). Pinkham's letter to Barker Burnell, Congressman for Massachusetts District, urging need for U.S. naval protection of American whaleships in the Pacific, dated June 1841, is also included.

159   ANSEL, Willits D., *The whaleboat: a study of design, construction and use from 1850 to 1970.* [Mystic., Conn., Mystic Seaport Museum Inc., 1978.] vi, 147 pp. Illus., fold. plans, index.

Includes historical accounts and details of construction.

160   ASHLEY, Clifford W., *The Yankee whaler*, with intro. by Robert Cushman Murphy and preface to pictures by Zephaniah W. Pease; 1st ed. of 1625 copies of which 156 numbered and signed, with orig. drawings by author. Boston and New York, Houghton Mifflin Co., London, Martin Hopkinson & Co. Ltd, 1926. xxiv, 379 pp. Frontis., illus., pls., diagrs., bibliog., index. Second pop. ed. with additions and corrections, Boston, Houghton Mifflin Co., 1938; London, George Routledge & Sons Ltd., [1938]. xxviii, 156 + 111 pp. (pls.). Col. pls., glossary of whaling terms, bibliog., index. This ed. reprinted: Garden City, N.Y., Halcyon House, [1942].

Much information on whaling techniques and equipment, and on scrimshaw and sailors' arts.

161   BULLARD, John M., *Joseph Rotch in Nantucket and Dartmouth, an address by . . . at a meeting of the Old Dartmouth Historical Society. Delivered at Friends Meeting House, New Bedford, December 12, 1931.* New Bedford, Mass., Old Dartmouth Historical Society, [1931?]. 32 pp. Illus.

162   CAULKINS, Frances Manwaring, 1796-1869, *History of New London, Connecticut. From the first survey of the coast in 1612, to 1852.* New London, The Author; [Hartford, Ct., Press of Case, Tiffany and Co.], 1852. xi, [13]-679 pp. Illus. 2nd ed., continued to 1860. xi, [13]-692, [673]-679 pp. Illus. New ed., with memoir of the author, New London, H.D. Utley, 1895. xviii, 696 pp. Illus., port., maps.

Index to the above, [Cecelia Griswold (comp.), New London, 1950]. 134 pp.

163   CHATTERTON, E. Keble, *Whalers and whaling: the story of the whaling ships up to the present day.* London, T. Fisher Unwin Ltd., New York, W.F. Payson, [1925]. 248 pp. Frontis., pls. Reprinted London, Philip Allan & Co. Ltd, 1930 ("Nautilus Library"). 251 + 4 pp.; Detroit, Mich., Gale Research Co., 1974.

164   CHISHOLM, Jocelyn, *Brind of the Bay of Islands: some readings and notes of thirty years in the life of a whaling captain,* limited ed. of 400 copies. Wellington, J. Chisholm, 1979. 92 pp. Port., illus., refs.
Refs. to whaling in the Pacific - partic. Tonga, Gilbert Islands, 1820-50.

165   CHURCH, Albert Cook, *Whale ships and whaling.* New York, W.W. Norton & Co., [1938]. 179 pp. Illus., endp. facsims. Reprinted New York, Bonanza Books, n.d.
Pt. 1, "Whaleships and whaling"; Pt. 2, "Illustrations" (over 200 photos of whale ships and whaling accessories); Pt. 3, "Whaleship plans and specifications".

166   COWAN, James, *A trader in cannibal land: the life and adventures of Captain Tapsell.* Dunedin and Wellington, A.H. and A.W. Reed, 1935. 158 pp. Illus.
Life of Philip (Hans) Tapsell, of Danish origin, who was whaling in the Pacific before he began life as trader in N.Z. From 1809, sailed in British whalers - the *New Zealander, Catherine, Asp* (Capt. Brind), *The Sisters* (Capt. Duke) and *Minerva.* See partic. pt. 1, pp. 5-66.

167   CRAIG, Adam Weir, *Whales and the Nantucket Whaling Museum,* designed and illus. by Barbara Melendy. Nantucket, Mass., Nantucket Historical Association, 1977. iii, 26 pp. Illus., bibliog.

168   DAKIN, W[illiam] J[ohn], 1883-1950, *Whalemen adventurers: the story of whaling in Australian waters . . .* Sydney, Angus & Robertson, 1934. rev. ed., 1938; a "Sirius Book", 1963. xx, 263 pp. Illus., appendices, bibliog., index. Reprinted London, Angus & Robertson, 1977 ("Non-Fiction Classics"). 252 pp.

169   DARDEN, Genevieve M. (comp. and ed.), *My dear husband.* [Taunton, Mass., William S. Sullwold Publishing, Inc., 1980.] A project of The Descendants of Whaling Masters, Inc. [xii], 84 pp. Illus.
A collection of heretofore unpublished letters of the whaling era.

170   DECKER, Robert Owen, *The whaling city: a history of New London.* Chester, Conn., Pequot Press for the New London County Historical Society, 1976. [xvi], 415 pp. Illus., index, bibliog., appendices.
See esp. chap. 5, "New London in whaling days," & App. 12, "Whaling firms".

171 _____, *Whaling industry of New London*. York, Pa., Liberty Cap Books (imprint of G. Shumway Publisher), [1973]. 202 pp. Illus., bibliog., index.

172 DODGE, Ernest S., *New England and the South Seas*. Cambridge, Mass., Harvard University Press, 1965. xv, 216 pp. Illus., endp. map, bibliog., index.
See partic. chap. 2, "Hunting the cachalot", pp. 27-56.

173 _____, *Baleiniers à Tahiti / Whaling off Tahiti*, Société des Océanistes Dossier 11 (in Fr. and Eng.). [Paris, Société des Océanistes, 1971.] 31 [+ 1] pp. Illus., bibliog.

174 Dow, George Francis, *Whale ships and whaling: a pictorial history of whaling during three centuries. With an account of the whale fishery in colonial New England*, with intro. by Frank Wood; Marine Research Society Pub. no. 10. Salem, Mass., Marine Research Society, 1925. xi, 446 [+ 11] pp. (pp. 43-439 pls.). Index. Reprinted, New York, Argosy Antiquarian, 1967.
Includes section "The whaler 'Charles W. Morgan' of New Bedford, Mass.", pp. 331-87.

175 DULLES, Foster Rhea, *Lowered boats: a chronicle of American whaling*, 1st ed. New York, Harcourt, Brace and Co., [1933]; London, George G. Harrap & Co. Ltd., [1934]. [x], 292 pp. pls., endp. maps, bibliog., index.

176 DU PASQUIER, Thierry, *Les baleiniers français à XIXe siècle (1814-1868)*. Grenoble, Terre et Mer/4 Seigneurs, 1982. 256 pp. Illus., pls., appendices, bibliog.
Includes section on the renaissance of French whale fishery 1817-32, led by Americans such as Jeremiah Winslow, and the taking over of the French whaling industry by the French 1832-68, with records of over 60 captains of French whalers and chronological list of all known French whaling voyages 1814-68, using official and other primary French sources.

177 EARLE, Walter K., *The ships "Richmond" and "Edgar" of Cold Spring*. Cold Spring Harbor, Long Island, Whaling Museum Society, 1948. 13 pp. Bibliog. footnotes.
Richmond made at least one voyage into the Pacific to N.W. Coast via Hawaii, 1843-46. *Edgar* lost in the Sea of Okhotsk 1855.

178 ENDERBY, Charles, 1798?-1876, *Proposal for re-establishing the British Southern Whale Fishery, through the medium of a chartered company, and in combination with the colonization of the Auckland Islands, as* *the site of the company's whaling station,* 3rd ed. London, Effingham Wilson, 1847. 67 pp. Map, appendix. (Kendall Whaling Museum; National Library of Australia - Ferguson 4503)

179 _____, *British Southern Whale Fisheries - statement, explanatory of the necessity and means of re-establishing the above important branch of the national industry.* No imprint [London, 1848]. 4 pp.

Printed statement on profit to be made in southern whaling, and soliciting financial support from shareholders. "Being in reply to a letter addressed to him on behalf of certain parties connected with the British shipping interest, inviting the expression of his sentiments on the first-named subject." (National Library of Australia - Ferguson 4760)

180 _____, *The Auckland Islands: a short account of their climate, soil & productions; and the advantages of establishing there a settlement at Port Ross for carrying on the Southern Whale Fisheries.* London, Pelham Richardson, 1849. vi, 57 pp. Appendix, map. (National Library of Australia - Ferguson 5036)

181 _____, *Proceedings at a public dinner given to Charles Enderby, Esq., F.R.S., at the London Tavern, Bishopsgate Street, on Wednesday, the 18th of April, 1849.* London, Pelham Richardson, 1849. 24 pp.

Farewell on C.E.'s departure to Auckland Islands. Enderby's speech gives some account of the Southern Whale Fishery: "In this year, whilst the United States had 596 whale-ships, of 190,000 tons and 18,000 seamen, English whale-ships were only 14. Revival of trade was imperative". (Hocken, *Bibliography*, p. 143)

182 [FERGUSON, Robert, 1806-75], *Affecting intelligence from the South Sea Islands. A letter addressed to the directors and friends of Bible and missionary institutions in Great Britain and America.* London, Printed by W. Tyler, 1839. 8 pp.

Pamphlet written to warn of the backsliding of recently converted Pacific Islanders as a result of unlimited availability of liquor from whaling and merchant vessels and licentiousness of their crews. (R. L. Silveira de Braganza, *The Hill Collection*, 1, 103).

183 FINCKENOR, George A., *Whales and whaling, port of Sag Harbor, New York.* Sag Harbor, N.Y., W. Ewers, 1975. 159 pp. Illus.

184 FORBES, R[obert], B[ennet], 1804-1889, *Loss of the Essex, destroyed by a whale. With an account of the sufferings of the crew, who were driven to extreme measures to sustain life.* Cambridge, [Mass.], J. Wilson and Son, 1884. 14 pp.

185 FRENCH, Thomas, *The missionary whaleship.* New York, Vantage Press, [1961]. 134 pp. Illus., bibliog.

Whaler *Thames* of New Haven, owned by the Whalefishery Company, carried
A.B.C.F.M. missionaries to Hawaii in 1822, then went whaling, returning to New
Haven in 1825. The Whalefishery Company made a loss on the voyage and went
out of business.

186   GARDNER, Will[iam Edward], *Three bricks and three brothers: the
story of Nantucket whale-oil merchant, Joseph Starbuck*, with foreword by
Austin Strong; Nantucket Whaling Museum Publication. Boston, Houghton
Mifflin Co., [1945]; Cambridge, [Mass.], Riverside Press, 1945. xi, 113 pp.
Illus., pls., ports., endp. map.

"Three brothers" in title refers to Joseph Starbuck's ship *Three Brothers* as well as
to his three sons. *Three Brothers*, under Starbuck ownership, made a number of
successful whaling voyages to the Pacific from 1833 onwards, bringing home 2212
barrels of sperm oil on first voyage.

187   _____, *The Coffin saga: Nantucket's story, from settlement to
summer visitors*, Nantucket Whaling Museum Publication. Cambridge,
[Mass.], Riverside Press, [1949]. ix, 321 pp. Illus., ports., maps.

188   GILBRETH, Frank B., Jr., *Of whales and women: one man's view of
Nantucket history*, illus. by Donald McKay. New York, Thomas Y. Crowell
and Co., 1956. 242 pp. Melbourne, Heinemann, [1957]. ix, 231 pp. List of
sources (in foreword).

See partic. chaps. 6-10 for popular history of Nantucketers and whaling, partic. in
the Pacific.

189   GRANT, Gordon, *Greasy luck: a whaling sketch book*. New York,
William Farquhar Payson, [1932]; repr. Jamaica, N.Y., Caravan Maritime
Books, 1970. xiv, 127 pp. Illus.

Outline of a typical mid-19th century whaling voyage and preparations for it in pictures.

190   HARE, Lloyd C.M., *Salted tories: the story of the whaling fleets of
San Francisco*, Marine Historical Association Pub. no. 37. Mystic, Conn.,
Marine Historical Association, Inc., 1960. ix, 114 pp.

Some South Pacific material.

191   HAWES, Charles Boardman, *Whaling: wherein are discussed the first
whalemen of whom we have read; the growth of the European whaling industry, and of its offspring, the American whaling industry* . . . London,
William Heinemann Ltd; Garden City, N.Y., Doubleday, Page & Co., 1924.
ix [iii], 358 pp. Illus., pls., appendices, index.

192   HEFFERNAN, Thomas Farel, *Stove by a whale: Owen Chase and the Essex.* Middletown, Conn., Wesleyan University Press (distrib. by Columbia University Press), [1981]. xiii, 273 pp. Illus., appendices, notes, index. A detailed study of the *Essex* story and its sources.

193   HIGGINS, Joseph T., *The whale ship book: the distinguishing details of old time whale ships with a complete description of a typical whaler and working plans of the famous Alice Mandell.* New York City, Rudder Publishing Co., [1927]. 36 pp. Frontis., illus., pls., fold. diagrs.

194   HIRSHSON, G. Warren, *The whale ship Charles W. Morgan.* New Bedford, Mass., Reynolds Printing Co., 1926 ("2nd ed." 1st ed. also copyrighted 1926). 14 [+8] pp. Frontis., port., illus. Reprinted several times, with 5th ed. pub. in 1941.

195   HODGKINSON, R[ichard], *Eber Bunker of Liverpool. "The father of Australian whaling",* Roebuck Society Publication no. 15. Canberra, A Roebuck Book, 1975. viii, 64 pp. Illus., pls., maps, bibliog., index.

196   HOHMAN, Elmo Paul, *The American whaleman: a study of life and labor in the whaling industry.* New York, London, Toronto, Longmans, Green and Co., 1928. xiv, 355 pp. Illus., appendices, bibliog., index. Reprinted Clifton, N.J., Augustus M. Kelley, 1972; London, Macdonald and Jane's in "Macdonald Maritime History" series, 1974; New York, Gordon Press, 1977; Cranbury, N.J., A.S. Barnes & Co., Inc., n.d. (See no. 416.)

197   HOYT, Edwin P., *Mutiny on the Globe.* New York, Random House, [1975]; London, Arthur Barker, 1976. x, 203 pp. Illus., endp. map, biog. note.

198   _____, *Nantucket: the life of an island.* Brattleboro, Vt., Stephen Crane Press, 1978. vi, 209 pp. Illus., bibliog., index.
See partic. chaps. 12-18, pp. 90-154 for Pacific material. Includes refs. to sinking of the *Essex* (chap. 13) and mutiny on the *Globe* (chap. 14).

199   HOWLAND, Chester, *Thar she blows!* New York, Wilfred Funk, [1951]. xv, 304 pp. Illus., bibliog.
Partial list of logbooks consulted 1835-89, pp. xiii-xiv. Includes accounts of events on *Globe, Junior* and *Essex.*

200   HUGILL, Stan, *Sailortown.* London, Routledge & Kegan Paul Ltd.; New York, E.P. Dutton & Co., Inc., 1967. xxii, 360 pp. Illus., maps, bibliog., index.
Refs. throughout to whalemen (see index), but see partic. chap. 1, "On the beach", pp. 3-30.

201   HUNT, Cornelius E., "One of her officers", *The Shenandoah; or, The last Confederate cruiser.* New York, G.W. Carleton & Co.; London, S. Low, Son, & Co., 1867. 275 pp. Frontis. Reprinted New York, W. Abbatt, 1910. 135 pp. Frontis., pl. (In "The Magazine of History with Notes and Queries", extra number, no. 12.)

The *Shenandoah*, Captain Waddell, attacked and sank four whaleships at Ponape in 1865, and caused other damage to the New England whaling fleet.

202   IMLAY DISTRICT HISTORICAL SOCIETY (comp.), *Death on the Junior 1857: a saga of early Merimbula. Murderous mutineers filled ship's log with details of their crime aboard an American whaler.* N.p. [Merimbula, N.S.W.?], Imlay District Historical Society, with acknowledgment to the Sydney *Daily Mirror*, 1958. [7] pp.

203   JACKSON, Gordon, *The British whaling trade.* London, Adam & Charles Black; Hamden, Conn., Shoe String Press, [1978]. xvi, 310 pp. Appendices, bibliog., index.

See partic. pt. 1, chaps. 5 and 7 on the Southern Whale fishery, ca. 1776-1840, pp. 91-116, 132-42.

204   JENKINS, J.T., *A history of the whale fisheries from the Basque fisheries of the tenth century to the hunting of the finner whale at the present date.* London, H.F. & G. Witherby, 1921. 336 pp. Frontis., pls., appendices (tables), bibliog., index. Reprinted Port Washington, N.Y., London, Kennikat Press, [1971].

See partic. chaps. 6 and 7, "The Southern fishery" and "The American whale fisheries", pp. 207-55.

205   JENKINS, Thomas H., Captain, *Bark* Kathleen *sunk by a whale, as related by the captain, Thomas H. Jenkins, to which is added an account of two like occurrences, the loss of the ships* Ann Alexander *and* Essex. New Bedford, Mass., H.S. Hutchinson & Co., [1902]. 40 [+2] pp., incl. pls.

The *Kathleen* was sunk by a sperm whale in the South Atlantic on 17 March 1902. *Ann Alexander* and *Essex* were lost in the Pacific.

206   KERR, Margaret and Colin, *Australia's early whalemen*, "Pageant of Australia" series. Adelaide, Rigby, 1980. 64 pp. Illus., bibliog.

207   LACROIX, Louis, *Les derniers baleiniers français. Un demi-siècle d'histoire de la grande pêche baleinière en France de 1817 à 1867*, with pref. by Émile Gabory. Nantes, Imprimerie de Bretagne in "Librairie Nautique du 'Yacht' " series., [1938]; reprinted Nantes, Aux Portes du Large, 1947. viii, 373 pp. Reprinted under title *Les derniers baleiniers français*, with pref. by Jean Randier, [Paris], Éditions Maritimes et d'Outre-Mer, [1968]. xvi, 379 pp. Illus., pls., ports., maps, appendices. This ed. reprinted 1974.

Comprehensive history of 19th century French whaling with details of whaling techniques, social life on board whalers, whaling ports and ships. Appendix II contains selection of French whaling songs.

208   LAFOND [DE LURCY], Gabriel, 1802-1876, *Rapport à la Société de Géographie . . . sur l'ouvrage intitulé* Journal d'un baleinier *et exposé, relatif au continent polynésien, par le capitaine Gabriel Lafond (de Lurcy) . . .* Paris, A. Bertrand; Guillaumin & Cie, 1867. 64 pp. (O'Reilly 1248)

209   [LANCE, William], *Address to the owners of ships engaged in South Sea fishery, and to capitalists generally, on the decline of the fishery,* by a member of Lloyd's. London, Printed by G. M'Kewan, 1844. vi, 11 pp. (National Library of Australia - Ferguson 3848)

210   LAWSON, Will, *Harpoons ahoy! Fighting the great sperm whales.* Sydney, Angus & Robertson Ltd, 1938. ix [+ iii], 219 pp.
Whaling in the late 19th century - partic. around Auckland Islands and in New Zealand waters. Based on experiences of Captain McKillop.

211   LEAVITT, John F., *The Charles W. Morgan.* Mystic, Conn., Marine Historical Association, Inc., [1973]. xvi, 131 pp. Illus., index.
History of the *Charles W. Morgan,* built in 1841. 37 recorded voyages, including several to Pacific grounds. Crew lists, log book lists, summary of voyages and glossary included.

212   LECOMTE, Jules, b. 1813, *Pratique de la pêche de la baleine dans les Mers du Sud.* Le Havre, J. Morlent; Paris, Lecointe et Pougin, 1833. xvi, 280 pp.
Contains much practical information on the techniques of whaling and equipment of whaleships, with some refs. to Pacific. Chap. 19 contains "Lois et ordonnances sur la pêche de la baleine".

213   LIVERSIDGE, Douglas, *The whale killers.* Chicago, Rand McNally; [London], Jarrolds, [1963]. 191 pp. Illus., bibliog.
Whaling history, 19th and 20th centuries. Includes Pacific material.

214   McLAREN, Fergus B., *The Auckland Islands: their eventful history,* with intro. by Angus Ross. Wellington, A.H. and A.W. Reed, [1948]. 109 pp. Illus., pls., endp. map, appendices, bibliog.
See partic. chaps. 3-5, pp. 39-74 for material relating to Charles Enderby and the British Southern Whale Fishery Company.

215   McNAB, Robert, 1864-1917, *Murihiku: a history of the South Island of New Zealand and the islands adjacent and lying to the south, from 1642-1835.* Limited ed. of 515 copies. Wellington, Whitcombe & Tombs,

1909. xiv, 499 pp. Frontis., pls., maps, refs. See partic. chap. 2 ff., pp. 379-443 for Pacific whaling refs.

Earlier eds.: *Murihiku: some old time events*. Gore, N.Z., Printed at "Southern Standard" Office, 1904. 46 pp. (doub. col.). Appendix pp. [45]-46; *Murihiku: some old time events. Being a series of twenty-five articles on the early history of the extreme southern portion of New Zealand. Written for the "Southern Standard"*. Gore, N.Z. Printed at the "Southern Standard" Office, 1905. [iv], 97 pp. No appendix; *Murihiku and the southern islands: a history of the west coast sounds, Foveaux Strait, Stewart Island, The Snares, Bounty, Antipodes, Auckland, Campbell and Macquarie Islands, from 1770 to 1829*. Invercargill, William Smith Printer, 1907. xii, 377 pp. Maps, facsims., chap. refs.; reprinted Auckland, Wilson Horton, 1970.

216 _____, *The old whaling days: a history of Southern New Zealand from 1830 to 1840*. Christchurch, Whitcombe & Tombs, 1913. xvi, 508 pp. Reprinted in the "New Zealand Classics" series, Auckland, Golden Press, 1975. xiii, 508 pp.

217 MACY, Obed, *The history of Nantucket; being a compendious account of the first settlement of the island by the English, together with the rise and progress of the whale fishery; and other historical facts relative to the said island and its inhabitants*. In two parts. Boston, Hilliard, Gray and Co. 1835. xii, 300 [+8] pp. Pl., map. 2nd ed., Mansfield, [Mass.], Macy & Pratt, 1880. xiv, 313 pp, "with a concise statement of . . . events from 1835 to 1880, by William C. Macy". Map, pls. 1835 ed. reprinted New York, Research Reprints Inc., [1970]. xii, 300 pp.; 1880 ed. reprinted Clifton, N.J., A.M. Kelley, 1972. xiv, 313 pp.

See partic. pt. 2 for refs. to Pacific whaling by Nantucket whalemen and loss of Nantucket whalers in Pacific Ocean.

218 MAREC, [Théophile-Marie], *Dissertation sur la pêche de la baleine, faisant suite à celle sur la pêche de la morue; pour servir à la discussion du projet de loi présenté, sur l'une et l'autre pêches, à la Chambre des Députés*. Paris, Impr. de Guiraudet, 1832. 39 pp. (Bibliothèque Nationale, Paris)

219 MARTIN, Kenneth R., *Delaware goes whaling, 1833-1845*. Greenville, Del., Hagley Museum, [1974]. 64 [+1] pp. Illus., bibliog.

220 _____, *Whalemen and whaleships of Maine*. Brunswick, Maine, Harpswell Press, 1976. 72 pp. Illus.

221 [MATTHEWS, Leonard Harrison (ed.), et al.], *The whale*, 1st ed. New York, Simon and Schuster, Inc.; London, George Allen & Unwin Ltd, [1968]. 287 pp. Illus., bibliog., index. Reprinted New York, Crescent Books, 1974.

See partic. pp. 126-58 for Pacific whaling refs.

222   MORTON, Harry, *The whale's wake*. Dunedin, University of Otago Press, [1982]. 396 pp. Illus., notes and refs., sources, bibliog., index.
Account of whaling in the southwest Pacific, which discusses whales, whaling techniques, whalers, and whaling from shore stations in New Zealand. The role of whaling in the development of early New Zealand examined.

223   MRANTZ, Maxine, *Whaling days in old Hawaii*. Honolulu, Aloha Graphics and Sales, 1976. 39 pp. Illus., list of "suggested reading".

224   MURDOCK, W.B., *The Murdock whaling voyages: [a story of the Murdocks of South Carver]*. New Bedford, Mass., Reynolds Printing, [1938]. 66 pp. Illus.
First pub. in serial form in *Middleboro Gazette* "many years ago". Includes voyages between 1838 and 1856, many to the Pacific.

225   MURPHY, Robert Cushman, *The founding of the Whaling Museum at Cold Spring Harbor, L.I., N.Y. Address at Cold Spring Harbor on September 15, 1967*, Pamphlets on Biography of APS Members, no. 6. Cold Spring Harbor, L.I., [Whaling Museum Society, 1968]. 7 pp. Port., illus.

226   OESAU, Wanda, *Die deutsche Südseefischerei auf Wale im 19. Jahrhundert*. Glückstadt, New York, J.J. Augustin, [1939]. 137 pp. pls., map.

227   O'MAY, Harry (comp.), *Whalers out of Van Diemen's Land*. Tasmania [sic], L.G. Shea, Government Printer, n.d. 101 [+3] pp. Index. Reprinted Hobart, T.J. Hughes, Government Printer, 1978. (Bound with *Wooden hookers of Hobart Town*.)
Contains material on offshore whaling *inter alia*.

228   PEASE, Zephaniah W. (ed.), b. 1861, *History of New Bedford*, 3 vols. New York, Lewis Historical Publishing Co., 1918. Frontis., pls., ports. 1200 pp.
Much material on the whale fishery. Vols. 2 and 3 are made up chiefly of biographical sketches.

229   _____, *A visit to the Old Dartmouth Museum*, Old Dartmouth Historical Sketches no. 60. [New Bedford], Reynolds Printing, 1932, and later eds. 64 pp. Illus.
Refs. to Pacific whaling. First published as a series of articles in the *New Bedford Mercury and Sunday Standard*.

230   PHILP, J.E., *Whaling ways of Hobart Town*. Tasmania [sic], J. Walch & Sons Pty Ltd, [1936]. 95 pp. Illus., appendix.
Pacific whaling refs. - see partic. pt. 3, "The sperm oil quest 1840-1860", pp. 28-46.

231 PICKERING, H.J., "Editor of 'Old Countryman' Newspaper, New-York", *A concise, yet perfect detail of the sperm whale fishery, as carried on in ships of the United States, in the North and South Pacific, and South Atlantic Oceans; to which is added a complete description of the different species of whales. With the method pursued in their capture, and the dangers attendant upon it. An appropriate accompaniment to the plate, representing the capturing of a sperm whale, by Cornelius B. Hulsart.* New-York, Cornelius B. Hulsart, at the Office of the Seaman's Friend's Society, 1835. 11, [1] pp.
Author describes himself as having been "for considerable time. . . engaged in the whale fishery in the Pacific Ocean". (Sterling Memorial Library, Rare Book Room - Yale University Library)

232 PORTER, David, Captain, 1780-1843, *Journal of a cruise made to the Pacific Ocean . . . in the United States frigate Essex, in the years 1812, 1813, and 1814. Second edition. To which is now added . . . an introduction, in which the charges contained in the Quarterly Review, of the first edition of this journal, are examined . . .* , 2 vols. New-York, Wiley & Halsted, 1822. [ii], lxxvi, 247; [iv], 256 pp. Frontis. port., maps (some fold.), illus. Reprinted Upper Saddle River, N.J., Gregg Press, 1970.
First pub. Philadelphia, Bradford & Inskip; New-York, Abraham H. Inskip, 1815. 2 vols. in 1, with extra title: *Containing descriptions of the Cape de Verd Islands, coasts of Brazil, Patagonia, Chili, and Peru, and of the Gallapagos Islands . . . .* A condensed version pub. London, Sir Richard Phillips & Co., 1823; 126 pp. + 3 engravings (inc. fold. map), with title *A voyage in the South Seas, in the years 1812, 1813, and 1814. With particular details of the Galipagos and Washington Islands.* In 2nd ed. see partic. vol. 1, chaps. 5-9, for refs. to whaling and whalers in area of the Galápagos Islands, but many other whaling refs. scattered throughout both vols. See pp. 29 ff. in condensed ed.

233 REYNOLDS, J[eremiah] N., 1799-1858, *Address on the subject of a surveying and exploring expedition to the Pacific Ocean and South Seas delivered in the Hall of Representatives on the evening of April 3, 1836 . . . with correspondence, and documents.* New York, Harper & Brothers, 1836. 300 pp.
Much whaling information in address, and in documents included in book, particularly Document 9: "Letter from the Secretary of the Navy, transmitting a report of J.N. Reynolds, in relation to islands, reefs, and shoals in the Pacific Ocean, &c.", pp. 93-230. Cf. author's "Report on islands discovered by whalers in the Pacific", no. 696. (National Library of Australia - Ferguson 2173aa)

234 RICHARDS, Rhys, *American whaling on the Chatham grounds: viewed from an antipodean perspective.* Nantucket, Mass., Nantucket Historical Association, 1971. 70 pp.
1st pub. as two articles in *Historic Nantucket* (1970 and 1971). See no. 697.

235   ———, *Whaling and sealing at the Chatham Islands*, Roebuck Society Publication no. 21. [Canberra], A Roebuck Book, [1982]. 74 + 90 pp. Illus., maps, tables, bibliog., index.
2nd section of book, entitled "Whaling on the Chathams [sic] grounds: an historical and quantitative assessment", comprises 15 chaps. 1st section deals with sealing only.

236   RICKARD, L.S., *The whaling trade in old New Zealand*. Auckland, Minerva Ltd., [1965]. [xi], 163 pp. Illus., pls., endp. maps, bibliog., index.
See partic. chaps. 1-3 and 9, pp. 1-48, 126-42 for refs. to Pacific whaling in general.

237   RICKETSON, Daniel, 1813-1898, *The history of New Bedford, Bristol County, Massachusetts: including a history of the old town of Dartmouth and the present townships of Westport, Dartmouth, and Fairhaven, from their settlement to the present time*. New Bedford, For the Author, 1858. xii, 412 pp.
Much on the whale fishery.

238   RIGGS, Dionis Coffin, in collab. with Sidney Noyes RIGGS, *From off island: the story of my grandmother*. New York, London, Whittlesey House, McGraw-Hill Book Co. Inc., [1940]. xvi, 347 pp. Frontis. port., pls., endp. map, appendix, bibliog. Pub. as *Martha's Vineyard: the story of my grandmother*, London, Bodley Head, [1941]. [vii], 308 pp.
Account of Cleveland whaling family - voyages in the Pacific, with visits to Hawaii in the 1850s.

239   ROBOTTI, Frances Diane, *Whaling and old Salem: a chronicle of the sea, with an account of the seal fisheries, excerpts from whaling logs and whaling statistics*, with intro. by Carleton D. Morse. Salem, Mass., Newcomb & Gauss Co., 1950. xvi, 193 [+9] pp. Illus., bibliog., index. New edition, with intro. by Henry Beetle Hough, with title *Whaling and Old Salem. (A chronicle of the sea)*, New York, Fountainhead Publishers, 1962. xxi, 292 pp. Illus., bibliog., appendices, index. This ed. reprinted New York, Bonanza Books, n.d.

240   [RODMAN, Samuel, 1792-1876], *The diary of Samuel Rodman: a New Bedford chronicle of thirty-seven years, 1821-1859*, ed. by Zephaniah W. Pease. New Bedford, Reynolds Printing Co., n.d. 349 pp. Frontis., illus., pls., ports.
Reprinted from the *Morning Mercury*, 1927. Many references to Pacific whaleships scattered throughout diary.

241   RUSPOLI, Mario, *À la recherche du cachalot*, "Conquêtes" series. Paris, Éditions de Paris, [1955]. 310 [+11] pp. Illus., ports, maps, charts, fascims.

242 SANDERSON, Ivan, *Follow the whale*, with maps and charts by the author, illus. by F. Wenderoth Saunders. Boston, Toronto, Little, Brown & Co., [1954]. xx, 423 pp. London, Cassell & Co., [1958]. xxiv, 423 pp. Illus., maps, diagrs, bibliog., appendices, index. Another ed., New York, Bramhall House [C.N. Potter, Inc.], [1956]. xvii, 423 pp.
See partic. pt. 5, pp. 197-264.

243 SAWTELL, Clement Cleveland, *The ship* Ann Alexander *of New Bedford 1805-1851*, Marine Historical Association Pub. no. 40. Mystic, Conn., Marine Historical Association, Inc., [1962]. 103 pp. Illus., ports, facsims., bibliog. notes, appendices, indexes.

244 SCHMITT, Frederick P., *Mark well the whale! Long Island ships to distant seas*, Empire State Historical Publications series, no. 97. Port Washington, N.Y., Ira J. Friedman Division, Kennikat Press, [1971]. xix, 149 pp. Illus., endp. maps, glossary, bibliog., appendices, index.
Whalers from Cold Spring Harbor, N.Y.

245 ———, *The whale's tale, as told with postage stamps*, with intro. by Edouard A. Stackpole. Chippenham, Wilts, Picton Publishing, 1975. xi, 69 pp. Illus., ports, facsim., maps, plan, bibliog.

246 SEWARD, William H., 1801-1872, *The whale fishery, and American commerce in the Pacific Ocean. Speech of William H. Seward, in the Senate of the United States, July 29, 1852*. Washington, Buell & Blanchard, Printers, 1852. 8 pp.
See also no. 715.

247 SLEIGHT, Harry D., *The whale fishery on Long Island*. Bridgehampton, N.Y., Hampton Press, 1931. 231 [+xi] pp.
History of Sag Harbor whale fishery.

248 SPEARS, John R[andolph], *The story of the New England whalers*. New York, Macmillan Co., 1908. ix, 418 pp. Frontis., pls.

249 SPENCE, Bill, *Harpooned: the story of whaling*. Greenwich, [Lond.], Conway Maritime Press, 1980. 192 pp. Illus., bibliog., index.
See partic. "The great days of American whaling", pp. 99-125.

250 SPENGEMANN, Friedrich, *Südseefahrer*. Bremen-St. Magnus, The Author, 1952. 162 + 1 pp. Pls.
Contains information about German Pacific whaling operations *inter alia*, with details of many of the whaleships involved. Activities in Hawaii of Captain Hinrich Hackfield (1816-1887), which included whaling, discussed (see, e.g., "Unter ha-

waiischer Flagge", pp. 112-14). Pacific whaling voyages of Captain Eduard Dallman (1830-1896) also described, pp. 152-61.

251   [STACKPOLE, Edouard A.], *The loss of the 'Essex': a thrilling tale of the sea when a Nantucket ship was sunk by a whale in mid-ocean; the suffering of the crew as related by the survivors of the tragedy; the horrors of cannibalism that any might live.* Nantucket, Mass., Inquirer and Mirror Press, 1935. [32] pp. Reprinted 1950, 1958, under Edouard A. Stackpole's name. New ed., extensively revised, pub. Falmouth, Mass., Kendall Printing, Inc., 1977, with title *The loss of the 'Essex': sunk by a whale in mid-ocean. The true story of the destruction of a whaleship by a bull whale in mid-Pacific, and the sufferings of the survivors during a ninety-day voyage in open boats, with a last resort to cannibalism to survive.* 36 pp.
Based on Owen Chase's 1821 account.

252   STACKPOLE, Edouard A., *William Rotch (1734-1828) of Nantucket, America's pioneer in international industry.* New York, Newcomen Society in North America, 1950. 36 pp. illus.

253   _____, *The sea-hunters: the New England whalemen during two centuries 1635-1835.* Philadelphia, New York, J.B. Lippincott Co., [1953]. 510 pp. Illus., notes with bibliog. information, index. Reprinted Westport, Conn. and London, Greenwood Press, Inc., 1973.

254   _____, *The Charles W. Morgan; the last wooden whale ship*, a Duell, Sloan and Pearce Book. New York, Meredith Press, [1967]. 179 pp. Illus., facsims., plans, ports.

255   _____, *Whales & destiny: the rivalry between America, France, and Britain for control of the Southern Whale Fishery, 1785-1825*, pub. with support of the Nantucket Historical Trust. [Amherst], University of Massachusetts Press, [1972]. xii, 427 pp. Illus., appendices, footnote refs., index.

STARBUCK, Alexander, 1841-1925, *History of the American whale fishery.*
See no. 148.

256   _____, *The history of Nantucket, county, island and town, including genealogies of first settlers.* Boston, C.E. Goodspeed & Co., 1924. viii, 871 pp. Frontis., illus., tables, fold. maps, bibliog., footnotes. Reprinted Rutland, Vt., Charles E. Tuttle, [1969], and Nantucket, Mass., Nantucket Historical Association, 1980.

257   STATE STREET TRUST COMPANY [Boston], *Whale fishery of New England: an account, with illustrations and some interesting and amusing* *anecdotes, of the rise and fall of an industry which has made New England famous throughout the world,* [comp., arranged under the direction of the Walton Advertising and Printing Company . . .]. Boston, Mass., Printed for the State Street Trust Company, [1915]. 63 pp. List of refs. in foreword, illus. Reprinted with intro. by Philip F. Purrington, New Bedford, Mass., Reynolds-De Walt Printing Inc. [1968], in coop. with State Street Bank and Trust Co., Boston and Old Dartmouth Historical Society of New Bedford. Also reprinted Taunton, Mass., William S. Sullwood, 1975.

258   STEVEN, Margaret, *Merchant Campbell 1769-1846: a study of colonial trade.* Melbourne, Oxford University Press in association with the Australian National University, 1965. xv, 360 pp. Frontis., pls., refs., bibliog., index.
Information relating to formation of whale fishing industry in early N.S.W. See index refs. to "Whaling", "Whale oil", "Fishing trade".

259   ————, *Trade, tactics and territory: Britain in the Pacific 1783-1823.* [Carlton, Vic.], Melbourne University Press, 1983. xi, 155 pp. Appendices, bibliog. notes, index.
See partic chap. 4, "A degree of madness", for history of the southern whale fishery up to the beginning of the 19th century, and other refs. to whaling passim (see index under "Whale fishery"). Appendices relate wholly to southern whale fishery: vessels employed, catch, owners. App. IV includes list of vessels employed in southern whale fishery from France, 1803.

260   SWAN, R.A, *To Botany Bay . . . if policy warrants the measure: a re-appraisal of the reasons for the decision by the British government in 1786 to establish a settlement at Botany Bay in New South Wales on the eastern coast of New Holland,* Roebuck Society Publication no. 8. Canberra, A Roebuck Book, 1973. ii, 189 pp.
Study of reasons for British government's subsidy of British south sea whaling industry after American War of Independence.

261   TAPP, E.J., *Early New Zealand: a dependency of New South Wales, 1788-1841.* [Melbourne], Melbourne University Press, [1958]. xi, 192 pp. pls., maps, appendices, bibliog., index.
See partic. chaps. 1 "Early contacts", pp 1-23, and 3 "Trade and commerce", pp. 53-64, and see index for other whaling refs.

262   TASMANIAN MUSEUM AND ART GALLERY, *Whaling out of Hobart Town,* Tasmanian Museum and Art Gallery Information Leaflet ser. 3/ 1976. [Hobart], Tasmanian Museum and Art Gallery, 1976. [3] pp. Illus., bibliog.
See pp. [2-3] for deep-sea whaling refs.

263   TOD, Frank, *Whaling in southern waters.* Dunedin, [Frank Tod, Printed by New Zealand Tablet Co. Ltd], 1982. 158 pp. Endp. maps, ports., illus., appendices, bibliog., index.

Of partic. interest for material on shore-based whaling in the Otago area 1831-48, but also has information on deep-sea whalers and whaling. Includes "Songs and verses of the whalers", pp. 124-30.

264   TOWER, Walter S., *A history of the American whale fishery*, Publications of the University of Pennsylvania, "Political Economy and Public Law" series, no. 20. Philadelphia, University of Pennsylvania, 1907. x, 145 pp. Appendices, bibliog., index.

265   VERRILL, A. Hyatt, *The real story of the whaler: whaling, past and present.* New York, London, D. Appleton and Co., 1916. [iv], xv, 248 pp. Frontis., illus., pls., maps. Other eds., 1923, 1926. xv, 295 pp.

Pacific material included - e.g., refs. to New Bedford vessels *Alexander*, 1835, and *Barclay*, 1834-7. Includes section on scrimshaw.

266   WATSON, Arthur C., *The long harpoon, a collection of whaling anecdotes*, with sketches by the author. New Bedford, Mass., G.H. Reynolds, 1929. 165 pp. Illus.

Includes material on Pacific whaling, based largely on whalemen's own accounts - e.g., the loss of the *Essex*, the *Triton* story, the sinking of the *Ann Alexander* and the development of scrimshaw.

267   ———— (comp.), *Logbook tales, mostly about Galapagos tortoises which provided "turtle soup" to vary whalemen's diet.* New Bedford, Mass., Reynolds Printing, 1936. [32] pp.

Mainly reprints from New York Zoological Society publications.

268   WAYLAND, Francis, Reverend Dr., 1796-1865, *The claims of whalemen on Christian benevolence, a discourse delivered in the Baptist Church, William Street, at the request of the New Bedford Port Society, on the evening of November 20th, 1842.* New-Bedford, Press of Benjamin Lindsey, 1843. 26 pp.

Problems of the whaleman's life, his temptation by drink ashore, his influence on the inhabitants of the Pacific Islands, bringing profligacy and disease, and suggested remedies to improve his moral well-being.

269   WHIPPLE, A.B.C., *Yankee whalers in the South Seas.* Garden City, N.Y., Doubleday & Co., Inc., 1954. 304 pp. Illus., endp. map, bibliog. notes. Reprinted, Rutland, Vt., C.E. Tuttle Co., [1973].

Stories of whaling in the Pacific, e.g., sinking of *Essex*, "Mocha Dick", escape of *Charles W. Morgan* from "cannibals" of Nonouti in 1851.

270   _____, and eds. of Time-Life Books, *The whalers*, "The Seafarers" ser., Alexandria, Va., Time-Life Books, 1979. 176 pp. Illus., pls., endp. maps, bibliog., index. Also pub. as *Les chasseurs de baleines*, Paris, Time-Life, 1980. 240 pp.

271   WHITEHILL, Walter Muir, *The East India Marine Society and the Peabody Museum of Salem: a sesquicentennial history*. Salem, Mass. Peabody Museum of Salem, 1949. xvi, 243 pp. Illus.

The East India Marine Society, founded in 1799, encouraged its members, which included whaling masters, to keep detailed journals during their voyages, to be handed over "for the use of" the Society on their return.

272   WHITING, Emma Mayhew and Henry Beetle HOUGH, *Whaling wives*. Boston, Houghton Mifflin Co.; Cambridge, [Mass.], Riverside Press, 1953. xx, 293 pp. Illus., ports., endp., map, index.

Experiences of Martha's Vineyard whaling families who accompanied whalemen, many into the Pacific Ocean.

273   WILLIAMS, E.C., Captain, "Deleniator [sic] of Williams' panorama of a South Sea whaling voyage", *Life in the South Seas: history of the whale fisheries, habits of the whale, perils of the chase and method of capture. Startling incidents - graphic deleneations* [sic] *- thrilling scenes in the life of the American whaleman, compiled from various writers and the authors* [sic] *personal experience of the scenes described*. New York, Polhemus & De Vries, Printers, 1860. 32 pp. New York, J.F. Trow, Printer, 1862. 68 pp. Frontis., pls.

Includes portions of *Moby-Dick* and Hart's *Miriam Coffin*, accounts of the loss of the *Essex* and *Ann Alexander* and other short pieces about whales and whaling. (Houghton Library, Harvard University - 1860 ed.)

274   WINSLOW, J[érôme], "Négociant-Armateur", *Faits et observations sur l'état actuel de la pêche de la baleine en France, soumis à la Commission de la Chambre des Députés chargée de faire le rapport du projet de loi concernant les primes sur les pêches*. [Le] Havre, Imprimerie du Commerce, Alphonse Lemale, 1831. 24 pp.

Much on Winslow's contribution to the French whaling industry. Lists ordinances ("Ordonnances du Roi") passed in France since 1816 relating to the whale fishery, and includes copy of author's "Projet pour la naturalisation en France de la pêche de la baleine, dans les Mers du Sud", dated 28 Dec. 1830. (Bibliothèque Nationale, Paris)

(C) Scrimshaw and marine art, including catalogues, check lists, etc.

275   BARBEAU, Marius, *"All hands aboard scrimshawing"*. Salem, Mass. Peabody Museum of Salem, 1973. 26 pp. Illus.

Reprinted from *American Neptune* (1952). See no. 778.

276   BREWINGTON, M.V. (comp.), *A check list of the paintings, drawings & prints at the Kendall Whaling Museum.* Sharon, Mass., Kendall Whaling Museum, 1957. 58 pp. Pls.

277   _____, and Dorothy Brewington, *Kendall Whaling Museum paintings.* Sharon, Mass., Kendall Whaling Museum, 1965. xiv, 138 pp. (mainly illus.). Bibliog., refs., index.
A catalogue of paintings in the Museum.

278   _____, *Kendall Whaling Museum prints.* Sharon, Mass., Kendall Whaling Museum, 1969. vii, 209 pp. Illus., pls.
Illustrates 597 of Museum's whaling prints.

279   BURROWS, Fredrika Alexander, *The Yankee scrimshanders.* Taunton, Mass., William S. Sullwold Publishing, [1973]. 79 pp. Illus., "additional reading" list. Reprinted [1976].
Pacific refs. throughout, but see partic. chap. 6, "Explorers in the South Pacific", pp. 33-4.

280   [COLONIAL WILLIAMSBURG, INC.], *Abby Aldrich Rockefeller Folk Art Collection presents an exhibition of scrimshaw from the collection of The Mariners Museum April 1 - May 30, 1965.* Williamsburg, Va., 1965. [16] pp. Illus.
"Introduction" by Bruce Etchison gives brief outline of relationship between whaling and the art of scrimshaw.

281   CREIGHTON, Margaret S., *Dogwatch and liberty days: seafaring life in the nineteenth century.* [Salem, Mass.], Peabody Museum of Salem, [1982]. [viii], 88 pp. Illus., index.
Descriptions of shipboard life and art culled from ms. journals, diaries, and logs.

282   CROSBY, Everett U., *Susan's teeth, and much about scrimshaw.* [Nantucket Island, Mass., Tetaukimmo Press, 1955.] 62 pp. Illus.
Includes reprints of papers on scrimshaw by Frank Wood, Arthur C. Watson and Marius Barbeau, as well as author's own work.

283   EARLE, Walter K., *Scrimshaw: folk art of the whalers*, illus. by Jane Davenport. Cold Spring Harbor, Long Island, N.Y., Whaling Museum Society, [1957]. 36 pp.

284   FLAYDERMAN, E. Norman, *Scrimshaw and scrimshanders; whales and whalemen*, ed. by R.L. Wilson. New Milford, Conn., N. Flayderman, [1972]. 291 [+14] pp. Illus., bibliog.

285 FORBES, Allan, *Whaleships and whaling scenes as portrayed by Benjamin Russell. Presenting reproductions in color of the paintings of the foremost artist in that field*, ed. by Ralph M. Eastman, assisted by K.G. Rogers. Boston, Printed for the Second Bank - State Street Trust Co., 1955. 79 pp. Illus.
The Forbes Collection is at MIT Museum, Cambridge, Mass.

286 FRERE-COOK, Gervis (ed.), *The decorative arts of the mariner.* Boston & Toronto, Little, Brown and Co., [1966]. [8], 296 pp. Illus.
Includes a chapter on scrimshaw by Edouard A. Stackpole.

287 GILKERSON, William, *The scrimshander [: the nautical ivory worker and his art of scrimshaw, historical and contemporary]*, with intro. by Karl Kortum. San Francisco, Troubador Press, [1975]. 119 pp. Illus., bibliog., index. Revised edition, [1978].

288 MALLEY, Richard C., *Graven by the fishermen themselves: scrimshaw in Mystic Seaport Museum.* Mystic, Conn., Mystic Seaport Museum, Inc., 1983. 155, [1] pp. Illus., bibliog.; index.

289 MARTIN, Kenneth R., *Whalemen's paintings and drawings: selections from the Kendall Whaling Museum Collection.* Sharon, Mass., Kendall Whaling Museum; Newark, University of Delaware Press; London and Toronto, Associated University Presses, [1983]. 172 pp. Illus., pls., biog. notes, index.

290 MEYER, Charles R., *Whaling and the art of scrimshaw.* New York, Henry Z. Walck, Inc., A Division of David McKay Company, Inc., [1976]. x [+ii], 271 [+2] pp. Illus., glossary, bibliog., index.

291 [PEABODY MUSEUM OF SALEM], *Special exhibition of whaling pictures from the collection of Allan Forbes Esq. from July first to October first 1919. Peabody Museum, Salem, Massachusetts.* Salem, Mass., Newcomb & Gauss, 1919. 24 pp. Illus., pls.

292 PINCKNEY, Pauline A., *American figureheads and their carvers.* New York, W. W. Norton & Co., Inc., [1940]. 223 pp. 30 pls., illus. in text.

293 PURRINGTON, Philip F., *4 years a-whaling*, illus. by Charles S. Raleigh. Barre, Mass., Barre Publishers for the New Bedford Whaling Museum, 1972. 56 pp. Illus., ports., endp. plans of ships.
Illustrated record of Charles S. Raleigh's "Panorama of a whaling voyage in the ship *Niger*", a series of 17 paintings executed 1878-80, owned by New Bedford Whaling Museum. *Niger's* voyage took place 1870-74 to Pacific and N.Z. grounds.

294   STACKPOLE, Edouard A., *Scrimshaw at Mystic Seaport, featuring objects from the Kynett, Howland, Townshend, and White Collections.* Mystic, Conn., Marine Historical Association, Inc., 1958. x, 53 pp. Illus.

295   TASMANIAN MUSEUM AND ART GALLERY, *Scrimshaw*, with preface by Alfred W. Pedder and foreword by W. Bryden. Hobart, Tasmanian Museum and Art Gallery, [1963?]. 23 [+1] pp. Illus.
Catalogue of scrimshaw items, mainly in Tasmanian Museum, with artistic and historical background.

VERRILL, A. Hyatt, see no. 265.
WATSON, Arthur C., see no. 266.

(D) Herman Melville and whaling.
See also WORKS OF FICTION, sect. A.

296   ALLEN, Gay Wilson, *Melville and his world.* New York, Viking Press, ("A Studio Book"), [1971]. 144 pp. Illus., bibliog., index.
See partic. pp. 43-77 for Pacific whaling refs.

297   ANDERSON, Charles Roberts, *Melville in the South Seas.* New York, Columbia University Press, [1939] (and later eds.). [x], 522 pp.; New York, Dover Publications, Inc., [1966], 514 pp. Bibliog., index.
See partic. chaps. 2-4, pp. 22-65.

298   CLUB OF ODD VOLUMES, Boston; [Watson, Arthur C.], [Meeting of the Club of Odd Volumes, January 15, 1936, containing Mr Watson's talk on "The origins of Moby Dick". Boston, 1936]. 6 pp. No title page; title from text; typewritten. On cover: *The origins of Moby Dick*, by Arthur C. Watson.

299   HILLWAY, Tyrus, *Melville and the whale.* Stonington, Conn., Stonington Publishing Company, 1950. Folcroft, Pa., Folcroft Press, Inc., 1969. [2], 12 pp. Notes.
Comments on Melville's use of cetological data in *Moby-Dick*.

300   JAFFÉ, DAVID, *The stormy petrel and the whale: some origins of Moby-Dick*, with foreword by Jay Leyda. [Baltimore, Md., Copyright David Jaffé, Printed by Port City Press, Inc., 1976.] vii, 76 pp. Illus., notes, bibliog.
See partic. sect. 1, "The captain who sat for the portrait of Ahab", for influence of Wilkes's *Narrative of the U.S. Exploring Expedition* on Moby-Dick. See also no. 838.

301   LEYDA, Jay (ed.), *The Melville log: a documentary life of Herman Melville 1819-1891*. New York, Harcourt, Brace and Co., [1951], 2 vols. xxxiv, 494; vii [+16 pp. pls.], 899 pp. Endp. maps, illus., pls., list of sources, index. New ed., New York, Gordian Press, 1969, with new supplementary chapter.
See partic. vol. I, sect. 3, 1840-44, sect. 5, 1850-54, for refs. to Melville's whaling experiences and publication of *Moby-Dick*.

302   OLSON, Charles, *Call me Ishmael: a study of Melville*. New York, Reynal and Hitchcock and Grove Press; [San Francisco], City Lights Books, [1947]. 119 pp. Reprinted, London, Jonathan Cape, [1967]. 111 [+3] pp.
Discusses at length Melville's annotations of Owen Chase's narrative.

303   PARKER, Hershel and Harrison HAYFORD (eds.), *Moby-Dick as doubloon: essays and extracts (1851-1970)*. New York, W.W. Norton & Company, Inc., [1970]. xxi, 388 pp.
See partic. "An annotated bibliography", listing material on *Moby-Dick* written 1921-1969, pp. 367-88.

304   SOULAIRE, Jacques, *À la recherche de Moby Dick*, "À la Recherche de" series. Paris, Hachette, [1959]. 95 pp. pls., maps.

305   STANONIK, Janez, *Moby-Dick: the myth and the symbol. A study in folklore and literature*. [Ljubljana], Ljubljana University Press, 1962. 215 pp. Notes, appendices, indexes, résumé in Yugoslavian.
Study of the "great white whale" legend; brings together many scattered reports.

306   VINCENT, Howard P., *The trying-out of Moby-Dick*. Boston, Houghton Mifflin Co., 1949; Carbondale and Edwardsville, Southern Illinois University Press, [1965], London and Amsterdam, Feffer & Simons, Inc., [1967]. xiv, 400 pp. Bibliog., footnotes, index. 1949 ed. only, illus., maps.

(E) Books for young readers.

307   *THE CHILD'S BOOK ABOUT WHALES*, "New and amusing toys. Series no. 2, or Two cent toys, no. 10". Concord, N.H., Rufus Merrill and Co., 1843. 16 pp. Woodcuts.
Contains account of wreck of the *Essex*, including abridgement of Owen Chase's account, with woodcut of boat's crew harpooning a whale, pp. 12-16.

308   EARLY, Eleanor, *An island patchwork*, illus. by Virginia Grilley. Boston, Houghton Mifflin Co.; Cambridge, Riverside Press, [1941]. Endp., maps, illus.

Concerns Nantucket. Sections relate to the wreck of the *Oeno*, the sinking of the *Essex*, the *Globe* mutiny and Samuel Comstock, Laura Jernegan Spear's journal kept on the *Roman*. See partic. chaps. 6-9, pp. 111-201.

309   ECKERT, Allan W., *In search of a whale*, with intro. by Martin Perkins and illus. by Joseph Cellini. Garden City, N.Y., Doubleday, [1970]. 108 pp.

310   FRANK, R., Jr. (pseud. of Frank Xavier Ross), *Flashing harpoons: the story of whales and whaling*, illus. by John O'Hara Cosgrave II; a "Horn Book". New York, Thomas Y. Crowell and Co., 1958. 183 pp. Illus., bibliog., index.
History of whaling industry told through experiences of three generations of a Nantucket whaling family.

311   GIAMBARA, Paul, *Whales, whaling and whalecraft*. Centreville, Mass., Scrimshaw Publishing, 1967. 127 pp. Illus., map.

312   GARDINER, Alice Cushing and Nancy Cabot OSBORNE, *Father's gone a-whaling: adventures in Nantucket a hundred years ago*, illus. by Erick Berry. Garden City, N.Y., Doubleday, Page & Co.; Sun Dial Press Inc., 1926. 198 pp. Frontis., illus., map, pls. Reprinted Garden City, N.Y., Doubleday, Doran & Co., 1935 in "Young Modern Books" series.

313   [GOODRICH, Samuel Griswold, 1793-1860], *Uncle Philip's conversations with the young people about the whale fishery, and polar regions*. London, Printed for Thomas Tegg and Son; Tegg and Co., Dublin; R. Griffin & Co., Glasgow; J. and S.A. Tegg, Sydney and Hobart Town, 1837. xii, 402 pp.
General account of whaling in both hemispheres, with partic. reference to the fate of the *Essex*. (Ferguson 2268)

314   HOUGH, Henry Beetle, *Great days of whaling*, illus. by Victor Mays; a "North Star" Book. Boston, Houghton Mifflin Co., 1958. 184 pp. Illus., bibliog., index.

315   MEADOWCROFT, Enid LaMonte, *When Nantucket men went whaling*, illus. by Victor Mays; "How They Lived" series. Champaign, Ill., Garrard Pub. Co., [1966]. 96 pp. Glossary, index.

316   PHELAN, Joseph (illus.), *The whale hunters in pictures . . .* , [with text by George Constable]. New York, Time-Life Books, [1969]. 52 pp. Illus., diags, index.
History and description of whaling, partic. in period 1820-50.

317   REINFELD, Fred, *The real book about whales and whaling*, illus. by W.N. Wilson. Garden City, N.Y., Garden City Books, [1960]. 214 pp. Illus., bibliog.

318   SHAPIRO, Irvin (narr.), *The story of Yankee whaling*, by the Editors of American Heritage; narrative by Irvin Shapiro in consultation with Edouard A. Stackpole. "American Heritage Junior Library" series. New York, American Heritage Pub. Co., Inc., 1959. 153 pp. Illus., "further reading" list, index. American Heritage paperback ed., New York, Harper & Row, [1965]. 128 pp. Illus. ("selected" from orig. ed.), index, etc.

319   SHEBAR, Sharon Sigmond, *Whaling for glory!* illus. by Paul Frame. New York, Julian Messner, [1978]. 92 pp. Map, illus., index.
Describes whaling industry of Cold Spring Harbor, Long Island, New York, and includes information about a typical whaling cruise in the mid-19th century to Atlantic, Indian and Pacific Oceans.

320   STEIN, R. Conrad, *The story of the New England whalers*, "Cornerstones of Freedom" ser. Chicago, Ill., Childrens Press, 1982. 31 pp. Illus.

STONES, William. See no. 737.

321   VERRILL, A. Hyatt, *The boys' book of whalers*, illus. by the author. New York, Dodd, Mead and Company, 1922. 210 pp. Frontis., pls.

322   WHITTAM, Geoffrey, *The whale hunters*, illus. by author. Cleveland, World Pub. Co., [1955]. 182 pp.
History of whaling industry told through experiences of a Nantucket whaleman and his descendants.

III.

Works of fiction, including short stories

When an item in this section is particularly rare, a library location and/or bibliographic reference has been provided, if possible.

(A) Adult fiction

323   BAKER, Louis A., Doctor, *Harry Martingale; or, adventures of a whaleman in the Pacific Ocean*. Boston, F. Gleason, "Flag of Our Union Office", 1848. 100 pp.

324   BARNACLE, [Robert], Captain (pseud. of Charles Martin Newell, q.v. below), *Leaves from an old log. Péhe Nú-e, the tiger whale of the Pacific*. Boston, D. Lothrop and Co., 1877. 112 pp. Frontis., illus.

Story of a fierce whale known to sailors as Mocha Dick. Introduces the *Fleetwing*, which appears in Newell's later novels in the "Fleetwing" series.

325   BECKE, Louis, 1855-1913, "Rodman the boatsteerer", pp. 2-20 in his *Rodman the boatsteerer and other stories*. London, T. Fisher Unwin, 1898. vii, 331 pp.

326   ———, "John Frewen, South Sea whaler", pp. 107-231 in his *Chinkie's Flat and other stories*. London, T. Fisher Unwin, 1904. [vi], 336 pp.

327   ———, *The adventures of Louis Blake*. London, T. Werner Laurie, 1909, 1913. [iv], 307 [+9] pp. Also later eds.: Philadelphia, J.B. Lippincott Co., 1926. 307 pp. Sydney, N.S.W. Book Stall Co., n.d. [1914]. [iii], 307 pp.

Semi-autobiographical novel which deals partly with whaling experiences in the Pacific.

328   BROWN, Mrs. Helen E., *A good catch; or, Mrs. Emerson's whaling-cruise.* Philadelphia, Presbyterian Board of Publication, [1884]. 300 pp.

Based on experiences of Mary Chipman Lawrence, q.v. no. 62, above.

329   BULLEN, Frank T[homas], 1857-1915, *The cruise of the "Cachalot": round the world after sperm whales by . . . First Mate.* London, Smith, Elder & Co., 1897. xx, 379 pp. Pls., fold. map. New York, Crowell, 1897. 257 pp. London, Macmillan & Co. Ltd, in Macmillan's Colonial Library series, no. 375, 1899. xx, 379 [+8] pp. Frontis., pls., fold. map. New York, D. Appleton and Co. and International Book and Publishing Co., 1899. xx, 379 pp. Frontis. pls., fold. map. Many later eds. Recent reprints include: New York, Dover Publications, 1962. 271 pp.; Christchurch, N.Z., Capper Press, 1976. xx, 365 pp. Pls, map, illus.; New Haven, Conn., Leete's Island Books (paper), 1980. 379 pp.

Description of a cruise from New Bedford through the Atlantic and Indian Oceans to Pacific whaling grounds - Japan, Hawaii, Christmas Island, Futuna, Vavau, New Zealand. As a young man Bullen shipped out on a New Bedford whaler, and later used his experiences in this fictionalised work. See also no. 496.

330   _____, *The cruise of the "Cachalot": round the world after sperm whales*, with a chapter on modern whaling by Dr J. Travis Jenkins; Modern English series [abridged ed.]. London, John Murray, 1923. 188 pp. Illus., endp. maps, glossary.

Includes intro., which discusses Bullen, by "R.B.L." and "R.B.M.".

331   _____, *La croisière du* Cachalot. *Voyage autour du monde.* [Genève, M. Reymond, 1901]. 250 pp. Pls., map. Reprinted as *La croisière du Cachalot*, trans. by Jean Dufour, Paris, Èditions Sulliver, [1950]. 344 pp.; Paris, Club Français du Livre, in the "Récits" series, 39, 1962. 296 pp. Pl., map, illus. in col.

332   _____, *"Kaskelottens" togt: jorden rundt efter spermhvaler.* Kjøbenhavn, G.E.C. Gad, 1903. xiii, 474 pp. Illus.

333   _____, *Kreuz und quer durch die Südsee: Segelfahrten und Walfischjagden. Erlebnisse des Steuermannes Frank T. Bullen von ihm selbst erzählt*, trans. from English and ed. by A. Feinberg and A. Fuchs, with orig. illus. by A. Bersa. Vienna, Schulbücher-Verlag, 1915. 336 pp. Illus., pl. Reprinted Vienna, Österreichischer Bundesverlag, n.d. [1926]. 320 pp. Illus.

334   _____, " 'Humpbacking' in the Friendly Islands", illus. by Arthur Twidle, *Colonial Good Words* (Sept. 1895), 627-34.

Later appeared in *The cruise of the "Cachalot"*.

335   _____, "Some incidents of the sperm whale fishery", *Cornhill Magazine*, 75, ns 3: 2 (Jan.-June 1897), 642-51.

336   _____, "At Futuna recruiting", *Cornhill Magazine*, 77, ns 3: 4 (Jan.-June 1898), 496-508.
From *The cruise of the "Cachalot"*.

337   _____, "Life on a South Sea whaler", *Appleton's Popular Science Monthly*, 54 (Nov. 1898-Apr. 1899), 818-34.
From *The cruise of the "Cachalot"*.

338   _____, "A day in the Solander whaling-ground" in his *Idylls of the sea and other marine sketches* (London, Grant Richards; New York, D. Appleton & Co., 1899; xvii, 266 pp.), 238-44. Later eds., 1900, 1902 and 1904. Also pub. London, Thomas Nelson, 1909?, 261 pp.

339   _____, "A nineteenth-century Jonah" in his *Idylls of the sea and other marine sketches*, q.v. above, 219-29.
Anecdote telling of loss of whaler's boat crew in encounter with giant squid which was being eaten by a sperm whale; the narrator had been taken into the whale's stomach.

340   _____, "The calling of Captain Ramirez" in his *A sack of shakings* (London, C. Arthur Pearson Ltd.; London and Bombay, George Bell and Sons, in Bell's Indian and Colonial Library; New York, McClure, Phillips & Co., 1901; viii, 389 pp.), 302-12. Another ed., London and Glasgow, Collins' Clear-Type Press, [1908] (Collins' Modern Fiction series, [vol. 30]). 264 pp. Col. frontis.
The whaler *Salem*, Captain Ramirez, off the Kingsmill Islands, and the captain's death on one of the group.

341   _____, "Country life on board ship" in his *A sack of shakings*, q.v. above, 110-68.
Story based on "southern-going" whalers in the Pacific, describing keeping of sheep, pigs and raising of plants on board.

342   _____, "The debt of the whale" in his *Deep-sea plunderings: a collection of stories of the sea* (London, Macmillan and Co., Macmillan Colonial Library series, no. 435, 1901; [v], 350 [+8] pp.), 90-112. Frontis., illus.
"The spotted whale of the Bonins", pursued by Captain Elisha Cushing.

343   _____, *A whaleman's wife*. London, Hodder and Stoughton, 1902. viii, 379 [+5] pp. New York, D. Appleton and Co., 1903. ix, 372 pp. Frontis., pls.
Story concludes with a whaling cruise in the Pacific Ocean.

344 _____, "Whales at home. II" in his *Sea-wrack* (London, Macmillan & Co. Ltd, in Macmillan Colonial Library series, no. 470, 1903; [vi], 321 [+7] pp.), 147-70.

345 _____, "The romance of whaling" in his *Told in the dog watches* (London, Smith, Elder & Co., 1910; viii, 332 [+10] pp.), 57-63. Frontis., illus.

346 _____, "A ride on a whale" from *The cruise of the "Cachalot"*, in *Master sea stories. Famous stories by Russell, Jacobs, Bullen, Becke and others* (New York, E.J. Clode Inc., [1929]; vi, 9-330 pp.), 87-92.
An incident while cruising on the Japan grounds.

347 _____, "The lone whale" in his *From wheel and lookout* (London, T. Werner Laurie Ltd, n.d.; vii, 277 pp.), 171-80.

348 _____, "Une nuit blanche" in his *From wheel and lookout*, q.v. above, 129-36.
Chase at night between Tonga and Futuna after a "whale with a twisted jaw all overgrown with . . . barnacles". This incident is also described in *The cruise of the "Cachalot"*.

349 [CAHOON, Daniel, Captain], "Hell hath no fury—" in Leroy G. Bradford [comp.], *Barnacles and bilge water. A collection of whaling yarns* (New Bedford, Mass., Reynolds Printing, 1941, 1st limited ed.; 50 pp.), 37-42. Illus. (see also "Supplement", July 1941, for additional sketches).
A whaling story featuring Captain Rodney Brightman on his first whaling trip on the *Pantheon*, Captain Caleb Lawrence, set in Hawaii.

350 CARLISLE, Henry, *The Jonah man*. New York, Alfred A. Knopf, 1984. [ii], 260 pp. Illus.
Novel about the life of Captain George Pollard, as told by himself. His narrative includes his account of the *Essex* shipwreck, his second command of the *Two Brothers*, his later failure to obtain another command and his final employment as a night-watchman in Nantucket.

351 COFFIN, R[oland] F[olger], Captain, 1826-1888, "A whaling yarn of the South Seas" in his *An old sailor's yarns: tales of many seas* (New York, Funk & Wagnalls, in the "Standard Library" series, no. 125, 1884; iv, 5-148 [+10] pp.), 5-28.
A fictional story with factual background, more on Pacific Islands than on whaling.

352 COMSTOCK, William, [1804-1882?], "Mark Watch: a tale of the Sandwich Islands", *The Boston Pearl: A Gazette Devoted to Polite Literature*, 5:9 (14 Nov. 1835), 68-71.

Mark Watch aided deserters from whalers in Hawaii, and story concerns the whaling captains' efforts to capture him. Watch's concern over the brutal treatment of crewmen given sympathetic treatment by author, who may be the William Comstock who wrote *The life of Samuel Comstock . . .* (1840) and *A voyage to the Pacific . . .* (1838), q.v. nos. 27, 28, & 29. *The Boston Pearl* apparently changed its title after September 1835. See below, no. 378, under "Whaling in the Pacific".

353   DUBARRY, Armand, b. 1836, *Le roman d'un baleinier: récit maritime*. Paris, E. Dentu, 1869. 318 pp. New ed., rev. and augmented, Paris, Didier & Cie, 1878. [3]-365 pp. Pls., notes.

Fictional narrative, most of which is taken up with whaling voyage from Le Havre to the Pacific Ocean in the early 1820s -- includes visits to, and descriptions of Sandwich Islands, Kamchatka, and Marianas Islands (Guam and "Agagna"). Whaling operations described. (Harvard University Library - 1878 ed.)

354   FOLGER, Isaac H., *Adventures in the Pacific: or, In chase of a wife*, The Novelette series, no. 8. Boston, Office [of the] American Union and Ballou's Monthly Magazine, [1876]. 66 pp. Illus.

The adventures of the whaleship *Rosa Americana* of Nantucket. (Cornell University Library)

355   GERSTÄCKER, Friedrich, 1816-1872, "Die Nacht auf dem Walfisch" in his *Blau Wasser. Skizzen aus See- und Inselleben*, pt. 1 of bd. 3 of his *Gesammelte Schriften. Volks- und Familien-Ausgabe*, 43 vols. (Jena, Hermann Costenoble, 1872; 230 pp.), 208-30. Also pub. as part of his *Seefahrergeschichten*, in *Das Nacht auf dem* Walfisch *und andere Geschichten*, in Schaffsteins Volksbücher, bd. 28. Köln am Rhein, H. Schaffstein, n.d. [191-?]. 168 pp. Illus.

Story concerns English whaler *King Harold* cruising among the Kingsmill Islands. (Library of Congress, 1872 ed.)

356   _____, *Abenteuer der Walfischjäger*, "Sammlung Weltfahrer Bücher der Abenteuer und Reisen" series, bd. 22, ed. by Josef Beira. Reutlingen, Enselin & Laiblins Verlagsbuchhandlung, [1927]. 160 pp.

Whaling adventures of the *Marthas-Vineyard*. (German Society of Pennsylvania, Philadelphia)

357   GOULD, John W., 1814-1838, "The mutiny" in *John W. Gould's private journal of a voyage from New-York to Rio de Janeiro; together with a brief sketch of his life, and his occasional writings*, ed. by his brothers (New York, Printed for Private Circulation Only, 1838, 1839; 207 pp.), 103-16. Fold. map. (Library of Congress). Also pub. in the author's *Forecastle yarns*, ed. by his brother Edward S. Gould (New York, J. Winchester, New World Press, [1843] and [1850?]; Baltimore and New York, W. Taylor & Co., 1845;

New York, Stringer and Townsend, [1854]; 64 pp.), 24-9. (Houghton Library, Harvard University: [1843] ed.)

Gould's stories were originally mostly published in monthly magazines, then published in connected form after his death. "The mutiny" takes place on a whaleship, the *Amazon*, some 500 miles off the coast of Chile, near the uninhabited island of "Cuachos" in "November 183-".

358 HALYARD, Harry (pseud.), *Wharton the whale-killer: Or, The pride of the Pacific. A tale of the ocean.* Boston, F. Gleason, "Flag of Our Union Office", [1848]. 100 pp. (Houghton Library, Harvard University)

359 *HARRY HARPOON: or, The whaleman's yarn. Being adventures in the Pacific Ocean. A thrilling narrative*, by the author of the "Ocean child; or, The lost vessel", De Witt's Stories of the Sea series. New York, Robert M. De Witt, n.d. [185-?]. [2], [9]-107 pp. Illus. (Yale University Library)

360 [HART, Joseph C., d. 1855], *Miriam Coffin, or, The whale-fishermen: a tale*, 2 vols. New York, G. & C. & H. Carvill; Philadelphia, Cary & Hart; Boston, Allen & Ticknor, 1834. xxviii, 209; 206 pp. London, Whittaker and Co., 1834 (3 vols.). 2nd ed., New York, Harper & Brothers, 1835. Reprinted in one vol., "exact and unabridged", San Francisco, H.R. Coleman, 1872. xxviii, 336 pp.

Story of life and whaling in Nantucket. An important source book for *Moby-Dick*.

361 HOUGH, Henry Beetle, *Long anchorage, a New Bedford story.* New York and London, D. Appleton, Century Co., Inc, [1947]. 309 pp.

Novel about the heyday, decline and fall of the whaling industry of New Bedford. Includes adventures of whaling in the Pacific.

362 MACY, W[illiam] H[ussey], Captain, 1826-1891, *There she blows! or, The log of the Arethusa.* Boston, Lee & Shepard; New York, Charles T. Dillingham, 1877. vii, 320 pp. Pls. Later eds. (1889, 1893, 1899) in the "Great and Good" series have title *There she blows! The whales we caught and how we did it.*

Generally accepted as a barely fictionalised account of Macy's whaling experiences on the *Potomac* of Nantucket, first published in serial form in *Flag of Our Union* in 1868. Refs. to Juan Fernández, Marquesas, Byron's Island, Kingsmill Islands, Strong's Island, Japan grounds and Ocean Island.

363 MARTINGALE, Hawser (pseud. of John Sherburne Sleeper), 1794-1878, "A whale adventure in the Pacific" in his *Tales of the ocean, and essays for the forecastle; containing matters and incidents humorous, pathetic, romantic, and sentimental; illustrated with numerous engravings* (Boston, G.W. Cottrell, [1840]; vi, [7]-358 pp.), 329-37. Illus., pls. Other

eds., Boston, S.N. Dickinson, 1841 and 1842. vi, [2], [9]-431 pp. New York, R.P. Bixby, 1844 and Boston, W.J. Reynolds, 1846. 431 pp. Boston, Russell, 1874. 385 pp. Illus., pls.
Story set in the Pacific off the coast of Peru, 1818 or 1819.

364 MELVILLE, Herman, 1819-1891 [*Typee*] *Narrative of a four months' residence among the natives of a valley of the Marquesas Islands; or, A peep at Polynesian life*, Murray's Home and Colonial Library, vol. 15. London, John Murray, 1846. xvi, 285 pp. Map. Published New York, Wiley & Putnam, 1846 (xv, 325 pp.) with title *Typee: a peep at Polynesian life. During a four months' residence among the natives of a valley of the Marquesas*, in the "Library of American Books" series, nos. 13-14. Numerous later eds., with title *Typee . . .*
Chaps. 1-4 are based on Melville's experiences on the whaleship *Acushnet* from which he deserted in July 1842 at Nukuhiva.

365 ———, *Omoo: a narrative of adventure in the South Seas; being a sequel to the "Residence in the Marquesas Islands"*. London, John Murray, 1847. xiii, 321 pp. Frontis., map. New York, Harper & Brothers, 1847. xv, 389 pp. Frontis., map. Numerous later eds., with short title *Omoo: a narrative of adventure in the South Seas*.
Early chaps. describe experiences on the whaleship *Julia* [i.e. *Lucy Ann*] of Sydney, which rescued author from the Typees in 1842. The mutiny of the crew of the *Julia* follows at Papeete.

366 ———, *Moby-Dick; or The whale*. New York, Harper & Brothers, 1851. xxiii, 634 [+1] pp. Published London, Richard Bentley, 1851 in 3 vols. with title *The whale*. viii, 312; iv, 303; iv, 328 pp. with consid. number of textual changes. Bentley's later (1853) ed. is 3 vols. in 1. Many later eds., some with title *Moby-Dick; or, The white whale of the Pacific*.
Based partly on Melville's personal experiences on whaleships in the Pacific. For publishing details of *Moby-Dick*, see G. Thomas Tanselle, *A checklist of editions of Moby-Dick 1851-1976 . . .* (Evanston and Chicago, Northwestern University Press and The Newberry Library, 1975). See also no. 367.

367 ———, *Writings*, uniform edition, ed. by Harrison Hayford, Hershel Parker, and G. Thomas Tanselle, Evanston, Ill., Northwestern University Press, 1968.

368 NEWELL, C[harles] M[artin], 1821-ca.1900, *The voyage of the Fleetwing; a narrative of love, wreck, and whaling adventures*, "Fleetwing" series, [vol. 1]. Boston, De Wolfe, Fiske & Co., 1886. 443 pp. Frontis., pls.
Whaling voyage of the *Fleetwing* to Hawaii. Follows *Fleetwing*'s adventures first described in *Leaves from an old log . . .* (pub. under pseudonym of "Captain Barnacle", q.v. no. 324 above).

369   _____, *The Isle of Palms. Adventures while wrecking for gold, encounter with a mad whale, battle with a devil fish, and capture of a mermaid*, "Fleetwing" series, [vol. 2]. Boston, De Wolfe, Fiske & Co., 1888. vi, [2], 460 pp. Frontis., pls.
Continuation of the voyage of the *Fleetwing* from Oahu, Hawaii. Mocha Dick is encountered and killed. On the "Isle of Palms" Mocha Dick's oil is boiled down and timber from the *Essex* is found in his body. See partic. chaps. 8-11.

370   PRESTON, Hayter and Henry SAVAGE, *The sea beast: the novel of the film (founded on the celebrated classic "Moby Dick")*. London, Readers Library Publishing Co. Ltd, n.d. [193-?]. 253 pp.

371   REYNOLDS, J[eremiah] N., 1799-1858, "Mocha Dick: or the white whale of the Pacific: a leaf from a manuscript journal", *The Knickerbocker, New York Monthly Magazine*, 13:5 (May 1839), 377-92. Also published in *The Sea. Narratives of adventure and shipwreck, tales and sketches illustrative of life on the ocean* (Edinburgh, William and Robert Chambers, 1840, pp. 131-5: "Abridged from the Knickerbocker . . .").

372   _____, " 'Mocha Dick' of the Pacific", *Essex Register*, 39 (May 1839), [1-2].

373   _____, *Mocha Dick, or, The white whale of the Pacific.* London & Glasgow, Cameron & Ferguson, [187-?]. 24 pp. Another ed., with pictures by Lowell LeRoy Balcom, New York, London, Charles Scribner's Sons, 1932. 90 pp. Frontis., illus., pls.

374   _____, "Mocha Dick: or the white whale of the Pacific: a leaf from a manuscript journal", with intro. and annotations by Raymond M. Gilmore and illustrations by Thomas G. Lewis, *Oceans*, 1:4 (1969), 65-80.
Reynolds's narrative tells of the determined pursuit of Mocha Dick, a "renowned monster" by a whaling captain and his final capture.

375   SUFFLING, Ernest R., *Rollin Stone: being the adventures of a young Englishman on a slave estate; during a whaling voyage; on an uninhabited island in the South Pacific, and while living with the natives of Manihiki in the South Seas.* London, Greening & Co., 1908. xii, 308 pp.
Covers the period 1816-24. (British Library)

376   THOMES, Wm [William] H., 1824-1895, *The whaleman's adventures in the Sandwich Islands and California.* Boston, Lee & Shepard, in "Ocean Life" series, 1871; Boston, Lee & Shepard, New York, Lee, Shepard and Dillingham, 1872. [vi], 444 pp. Frontis., pls. Other eds. 1873, 1876. Also published Chicago, H.A. Summer & Co., 1882 and later eds.

Fictitious, but based on the author's experiences. Only a brief section actually deals with whaling in the Pacific on the way to Hawaii.

377   WELLS, Ernest, *Hemp: a story of old landmarks and of yesterday.* Sydney, Angus & Robertson, 1933. [v], 318 pp.

Whaling and South Sea piracy worked into the plot, set in Napoleonic - gold rush eras.

378   "WHALING IN THE PACIFIC", *The Boston Pearl and Literary Gazette*, 4: 47-52 (1 Aug.-5 Sept. 1835), 377-9, 384-5, 392-3, 400-1, 408-9, 415.

Story in six chapters of whaling cruise of the *General S.*, newly purchased from New York by Captain Zenas Coffin, and under command of another Captain Coffin, from Nantucket to the Pacific Ocean, via Cape Horn. Visits "Woahoo" and fishes on the Japan grounds. Encounters ship "painted black from stem to stern", which later proves to have been the *Globe*, just after the mutiny. Thereafter *General S.* pays short visit to Easter Island and then sails for Valparaiso, where *Globe* is met with again, though without the mutineers, who had landed on the Mulgrave Islands.

379   WILLIAMS, Ben Ames, *Once aboard the whaler.* London, Robert Hale Ltd., n.d. [1939]. 319 pp.

Latter section of novel describes whaling cruise of the *Venturer* in the Pacific.

380   WYER, Henry Sherman (ed.), *Spun-yarn from old Nantucket; consisting mainly of extracts of books now out of print, with a few additions.* Nantucket, [Mass.], [Published by H.S. Wyer]; The Inquirer and Mirror Press, 1914. 311 pp. Frontis., illus., pls., map.

Includes excerpts from *Mirian Coffin*, by J.S. Hart, no. 360 and *There she blows!* . . . , by W.H. Macy, q.v. no. 362 above.

(B) Stories for children

381   BALLANTYNE, R[obert] M[ichael], 1825-1894, *Fighting the whales: or, Doings and dangers on a fishing cruise.* London, James Nisbet & Co., n.d., also 1863 and later eds., in the "Ballantyne Miscellany of Entertaining and Instructive Tales" series, vol. I. 126 [+ 12] pp. Frontis., illus. Also pub. New York, D. Appleton & Co.., 1865, in the "Library of Travel and Adventure", series. 169 [+ 10] pp.; London, Blackie & Son Ltd., 1915 as *Fighting the whales*, in "Stories Old and New" series.

Whaling adventures in the South Seas and elsewhere. See also entry following. (Australian National University Library - Mortlake Collection)

382   ———, *Fighting the whales*, in his *Tales of adventure on the sea* (four books bound together with separate pagination). London, James Nisbet & Co., 1884. 124, 124, 124, 126 [+24] pp.

Note also, Ballantyne's *Tales of adventure on the ocean* (London, James Nisbet & Co., n.d.; 366 [+8] pp.) includes "Fighting the whales".

383   BULLEN, Frank T[homas], *A Bounty boy: being some adventures of a Christian barbarian on an unpremeditated trip round the world.* London, Marshall Brothers Ltd., in Marshall's Standard Library no.1, n.d. [1907?]. 361 [+1] pp. Another ed., London, Holden & Hardingham, 1912. 361 pp.

Christmas Bounty Adams's whaling experiences on the *Eliza Adams*, South Sea whaler.

384   BUTMAN, Harry R., *Far islands: being the true story of the adventures of David Snow*, illus. by Rafal Tajpowski. Philadelphia, Venture Press, 1954; London, Independent Press, 1956. 95 pp. Frontis., illus.

Story of David Snow, an American boy who went to sea on a South Sea whaler and during the voyage was influenced by the story of John Williams to become a missionary.

385   COLWELL, Max, *Peter the whaler in southern seas*, illus. by Geoffrey C. Ingleton; "Great Stories of Australia" series, no. 5. Melbourne, London, Toronto, Macmillan; New York, St. Martin's Press, [1964]. 118 pp. Illus., endp. map.

Some Pacific refs.

386   DAVIDSON, Louis B. and Eddie DOHERTY, *Captain Marooner*, with intro. by William McFee. New York, Thomas Y. Crowell Co., [1952]. xiv, 369 pp.

Based on the mutiny on the *Globe* in 1824. "Verifiable sources" used.

387   DULLES, Foster Rhea, *Harpoon: the story of a whaling voyage.* Boston, Houghton Mifflin Co., 1935. 230 pp. Frontis., illus.

Story of David Worth, who shipped aboard a New Bedford whaler in 1846 for a voyage around Cape Horn to Japan grounds and back.

388   EDWARDS, Cecile Pepin, *Luck for the Jolly Gale*, illus. by Harve Stein. New York, Nashville, Abingdon-Cokesbury Press, 1947. 189 pp. Illus., endp. map, glossary.

Story of the *Jolly Gale*, a whaler cruising through the Pacific, Atlantic and Indian Oceans, 1848-51.

389   GERSTAECKER, Frederick [i.e. Friedrich Gerstäcker], *The young whaler: or, The adventures of Charles Hollberg*, illus., by Harrison Weir. London and New York, George Routledge and Sons, n.d. viii, 343 pp. New

ed., London and New York, G. Routledge & Co., 1858. viii, 343 pp. Frontis., pls. Trans. of *Der kleine Walfischfänger* (Jena, Hermann Costenoble, n.d.; viii, 371 pp.). Also pub. in English as *The Little whaler: or, The adventures of* . . . (London and New York, G. Routledge & Co., 1857; viii, 343 pp.).
Charles Hollberg visits Juan Fernández, Hawaii and Tahiti.

390   HENRY, Jan, *Whaleman's world, a novel*. New York, Thomas Nelson & Sons, [1970]. 174 pp.
19th century whaling voyage involving two teenage boys going to sea for the first time. Much information about whales and whalemen.

391   HOLBERG, Ruth Langland, *The wonderful voyage*, illus. by Phyllis Cote; "Junior Books" series. Garden City, N.Y., Doubleday, Doran & Co. Inc., 1945. 208 pp. Illus., endp., maps.
Story of two children who accompany their father on whaling voyage in the 1850s from New England round Cape Horn and into the South Pacific.

392   HOWLAND, Chester Scott, *Whale hunters aboard the "Grey Gold"*. Caldwell, Idaho, Caxton Printers, 1957. 140 pp. Illus., glossary of whaling terms.
Whaling adventures in the Pacific of an Indian boy adopted by a whaling captain.

393   KENYON, Charles M., *First voyage out*. New York, Four Winds Press, [1967]. 173 pp. Frontis.
Story of a boy's search for his father believed killed on one of the Gilbert Islands. He signs on for a South Seas whaling cruise in 1841 for this purpose.

394   KINGSTON, W. H. G., 1814-1880, *Old Jack: a man-of-war's man and South Sea whaler*. London, Edinburgh, New York, Thomas Nelson and Sons, 1859. 296 pp. Pls.
(Cf. *The early life of old Jack: a sea tale*. London, T. Nelson and Sons, 1859. 303 pp.). See below: *Old Jack: a tale for boys*.

395   _____, *Old Jack: a tale for boys*. London, Edinburgh, New York, Thomas Nelson and Sons, 1861 and later eds. viii, 594 pp. Pls. Note: pagination in later 19th century Nelson eds., viii, 507 pp. Also published London, R. Butterworth, [1884?]. 350 pp. London, Ward, Lock & Co. Ltd, 1903. 433 [+ 12] pp. Pls. (Probably other eds. by this publisher, in both "Captain Library" and "The Youths' Library"). London, Thomas Nelson, in "Kingston Library for Boys" series, as *Old Jack*, [ca. 1906?]. viii, 472 pp. Col. frontis. and pls.
See Part 2, chaps. 4 and 5, "Whaling in the South Sea" and "Incidents of whaling".

396   _____, *The South Sea whaler: a story of the loss of the "Champion" and the adventures of her crew*. London and New York, Thomas Nelson and Sons, 1875 and later eds. viii, 363 [+3] pp. Illus. New York, G. Munro in the "Seaside Library", 1882. Also published London and New York, Thomas Nelson, [188-?] and later eds. in the "Kingston Library for Boys" series, with short title *The South Sea whaler*. 304 pp. Col. frontis., pls.

Story of whaling in the South Pacific, with wreck on a Pacific Island and later settlement in N.S.W.

397   _____, *The two whalers: or, Adventures in the Pacific*. London, Society for Promoting Christian Knowledge; New York, Pott, Young & Co., [1879]. 128 [+4] pp.

Published under the direction of the Committee of General Literature and Education appointed by the S.P.C.K.

398   _____, *Peter Trawl: or, The adventures of a whaler*. London, Hodder and Stoughton, 1881, and later eds. 350 [+2] pp. Illus. New York, A.C. Armstrong and Son, 1882. iv, 350 pp. Frontis., pls. London, Henry Frowde & Hodder and Stoughton, 1909. 350 pp. London, Humphrey Milford, Oxford University Press, 1924. 350 pp. This ed. illus. in colour by James Durden.

Covers the Southwest Pacific area, including New Guinea.

399   MEADER, Stephen W., *Whaler 'round the Horn*, illus. by Edward Shenton. New York, Harcourt, Brace & World, Inc., 1950. viii, 244 pp. Illus.

Describes cruise of the whaler *Pelican* from New Bedford to Honolulu, during which a whaleboat is sunk by a whale. The story's hero is marooned on an island with a Hawaiian boy as his only companion. Author acknowledges debt to Melville in foreword.

400   O'BRIEN, Brian (pseud. of Albert Hayward Young-O'Brien), *Scrimshaw and sudden death: a salty tale of whales and men*. New York, E.P. Dutton & Co., 1959. 245 pp. Illus.

Based on the reminiscences and log books of Captain Lester Mosher, who sailed from New Bedford on the whaling bark *Canton* at the age of 15. Covers a two-year period at sea, and includes whaling off Japan.

401   PARLEY, Peter (pseud. of Samuel Griswold Goodrich), 1793-1860, *Tales about the sea, and the islands in the Pacific Ocean*. London, Thomas Tegg and Son; Dublin, Tegg and Co.; Glasgow, R. Griffin and Co.; Sydney and Hobart Town, T. and S.A. Tegg, 1838 (3rd ed.). viii, 360 pp. Illus. Other later eds.

Chaps 33-6 have stories about whales and whaling in the Pacific Ocean.

402 Saint-Aulaire, A., *Récreations instructives: campagne d'un balei-nier autour du monde; croquis et notes d'un officier du bord / Instructive recreations: a trip round the world on board of a whale ship; sketches and notes by one of the officers.* Paris, Aubert et Cie, [ca. 1845]. Title + 18 litho. pls. with 65 vignettes.

In French and English; narrative by lieutenant on board whaleship *Aventure* of Le Havre. (Bibliothèque Nationale, Paris)

403 Shapiro, Irwin, *How old Stormalong captured Mocha Dick.* New York, J. Messner, Inc., 1942. 47 pp. Illus.

404 Stackpole, Edouard A., *Madagascar Jack; the story of a Nan-tucket whaler, being the account of Obed C. Folger, thirteen years of age, who went to the South Seas with whalemen and found there many adven-tures as well as sperm whales,* illus. by Gordon Grant. New York, William Morrow & Co., 1935. ix, 308 pp. Illus., pls.

405 _____, *Mutiny at midnight: the adventures of Cyrus Hussey of Nantucket aboard the whaleship Globe in the South Pacific, from 1822 to 1826,* as told by . . . New York, William Morrow and Co., 1939. viii, 245 pp.

406 _____, *Dead man's gold.* New York, Ives Washburn, [1958]. 212 pp. Illus.

Tale of whaling in the Pacific, involving a treasure of Spanish gold on an uncharted island.

407 Tucker, George F., *The boy whaleman,* illus. in col. by George Avison; "Beacon Hill Bookshelf" series. Boston, Little, Brown Co., 1924. 283 pp. Frontis., pls. Also later eds., 1925, 1929, 1936.

A three-year whaling voyage to Pacific and polar seas.

408 Webb, Christopher, *Quest of the Otter.* New York, Funk & Wag-nalls, [1963]. 180 pp.

Adventures of a Mystic whaleship on a voyage to the Pacific in the 1840s.

409 Westerman, Percy F., *Mystery Island,* "Challenge" series. Lon-don, Humphrey Milford, Oxford University Press, 1927. 159 pp. Another ed. 1928, 190 [+2] pp., illus. by S. Lumley. Also 1929 ed.

Shipwreck of a whaler on a Pacific Island, with survivors taken to Fiji.

IV.

Representative academic dissertations

410 BRADY, Martin, Nineteenth century contact relations in the Gilbert Islands. B.A. (Hons.), Australian National University, 1972. 102 pp.
See partic. chaps. 5-8, pp. 31-57 for information on impact of whalers on southern Gilbert Islands.

411 BUTLER, Martin Joseph, J. & W. R. Wing of New Bedford: a study of the impact of a declining industry upon an American whaling agency. Ph.D., Pennsylvania State University, 1973. 180 pp. DAI, vol. 34/04-A, p. 1811.

412 CANHAM, Paul George, New England whalers in New Zealand waters, 1800-1850. M.A., Victoria University of Wellington, 1959. 265 pp.

413 CARON, Joseph Frederick, Scrimshaw and its importance as an American folk art. Ed.D., Illinois State University, 1976. 152 pp. DAI, vol. 38/01-A, p. 4.

414 CHASE, Oliver Stuart, Owen Chase's narrative of the shipwreck of the whaleship "Essex" and its influence on Melville's "Moby Dick". M.A., Columbia University, 1962. 112 pp.

415 HEFLIN, Wilson Lumpkin, Herman Melville's whaling years. Ph.D., Vanderbilt University, 1952. 495 pp. DA, vol. 12/06, p. 792.

416 HOHMAN, Elmo Paul, The American whaleman: a study of labor conditions in the whaling industry, 1785-1885. Ph.D., Harvard University, 1924. ix, 544 pp.
The predecessor of no. 196.

417 LE, Van, Herman Melville, romancier polynésien et maritime. Doc. en Lettres, Université de Provence (Aix-Marseille I), 1958. 223 pp.

See sect. 3, "Melville, romancier maritime", partic. chap. 8, "La pêche à la baleine".

418   McDEVITT, Joseph Lawrence, Jr., The House of Rotch: whaling merchants of Massachusetts, 1734-1828. Ph.D., American University, 1978. 657 pp. DAI, vol. 39/03-A, p. 1787.

419   MARAN, Michael James, The decline of the American whaling industry. Ph.D., University of Pennsylvania, 1974. 170 pp. DAI, vol. 36/01-A, p. 447.

420   MORTON, Henry [Harry] Albert, Whaling in New Zealand waters in the first half of the nineteenth century. Ph.D., University of Otago, 1978. 459 pp.

421   MUNRO, Doug, The Lagoon Islands: a history of Tuvalu 1820-1908. Ph.D., Macquarie University, 1982. 349 pp.
See "The whaling era" in chap. 2, "Early contact and trade", pp. 30-53.

422   MURRAY, L.C., An account of the whaling and sealing industries of Van Diemen's Land to 1850. Thesis, University Research Scholarship, University of Tasmania, 1927. 41 pp.

423   PALMER, William R., The whaling port of Sag Harbor. Ph.D., Columbia University, 1959. 335 pp. DAI, vol. 20/02, p. 655.

424   REDOR (ROSIÈRE), Florence, Le Docteur Nel, chirurgien-baleinier de l'Albatros, 1837-1840, Le Havre. Doc. en Méd., Université de Nantes, 1879-80. 265 pp.
Contains complete text of no. 72, pp. 161-233. See also chap. 1, sect. C, "Histoire de la pêche à la baleine. Les mers du Sud.", pp. 14-22.

425   STRAUSS, Wallace Patrick, Early American interest and activity in Polynesia 1783-1842. Ph.D., Columbia University, 1958. 328 pp. Map. DA, vol. 19/04, p. 791.
Chap. 2, "Exploration and trade, 1815-1842" contains extensive discussion of whaling in Polynesia (pp. 50-74).

V.

Articles, and chapters in books

(A) Bibliographies, indexes, shipping lists, statistics, source material.

426 ACKERMAN, John, "A whaling library for Massachusetts: report from New Bedford", *Wilson Library Bulletin*, 56: 2 (1981), 100-4.

427 ALBION, Robert Greenhalgh, "Whaling and fishing" in his *Naval and maritime history: an annotated bibliography*, 4th rev. and expanded ed. Mystic, Conn., Marine Historical Association (Munson Institute of American Maritime History), 1972; Newton Abbot, David & Charles, 1973; ix, 370 pp., 201-4. Indexes. 1st ed. 1951; 2nd ed. 1955; 3rd ed. 1963 with supps. 1966, 1968.

428 ANDREWS, Deborah C. (comp.), "Attacks of whales on ships: a checklist", *Melville Society Extracts*, (May 1974), 3-17.
Contains much on *Essex*, but also on other whalers, some in the Pacific (e.g. *Ann Alexander*).

429 CARRICK, R[oderic], "Whale fisheries" in his *Historical records of New Zealand South prior to 1840* (Dunedin, Otago Daily Times and Witness Newspapers Co. Ltd, 1903; vi, 206 pp.), 120-31.
Summaries and extracts from "Sydney Record Office", *Sydney Gazette, London Trade Review*, etc. See also entries in index under "Whales and whaling pursuits".

430 COGHLAN, T[imothy] A[ugustine], Government Statistician, 1855-1926, "The whale fisheries" in "Forestry and fisheries" section of his *The wealth and progress of New South Wales*, issues 8-13 (1894-1901), (Sydney, Government Printer, 1896-1902), various pagings (see index).
Brief history of whaling in Australian colonies, inc. sperm whaling, with statistical data.

431   COOPE, V.T., "Logs and journals at Mystic Seaport", *Log of Mystic Seaport*, 27: 3 (1975), 82-7.

432   GETHER, A., "Übersicht über die von der Weser aus betriebene Grönländische und Südsee-Fischerei", *Petermann's Mittheilungen*, (1863), 311.
Contains statistics on South Sea whalers from Oldenburg, 1855-60.

433   HAINSWORTH, D. R. (ed.), "Sealing and whaling" in chap. 3, "In search of a staple" of his *Builders and adventurers: the traders and the emergence of the colony 1788-1821*, "Problems in Australian History" series ([North Melbourne, Vic.], Cassell Australia, 1968; [iii], 174 pp.), 84-107. List of sources, index.
A documentary survey.

434   HUDSON, Kenneth and Ann NICHOLLS, "Whalers and liners: nineteenth century wooden ships", [chap. 6] of their *The Book of shipwrecks* (London, Macmillan, 1979; [6], 170 pp.), 50-4, 75-7. Pls., illus., facsims., maps, "further reading", index.
Under "Australasia" and "India and the Far East" lists wrecks of ships, including whalers, wrecked in the Pacific area.

435   HUNTRESS, Keith G. (ed.), "Checklist of narratives of shipwrecks and disasters", with supplement, in his *Narratives of shipwrecks and disasters 1586-1860*, with checklist of titles and intro. (Ames, Iowa, Iowa State University Press, 1974; xxxii, 249 pp.), 218-53. Illus.
Particular reference to the destruction of the *Essex*.

436   IM THURN, Everard, 1852-1932, "The whaleships at Pitcairn Island", Appendix 2 in Charles Lucas (ed. - see below), *The Pitcairn Island Register Book*, S.P.C.K. Records 1 (London, Society for Promoting Christian Knowledge, 1929; 181 pp.), 159-64. Map, appendices, bibliog., index.

437   JENKINS, James Travis, "Bibliography of whaling", *Journal of the Society for the Bibliography of Natural History*, 2:4 (1948), 71-166.
About 2000 entries on all aspects of whaling.

438   JENKS, S.H. (ed.), "Compendium of the American whale fishery", *Merchants' Magazine and Commercial Review*, 3:2 (Aug. 1840), 172-82.

439   LUCAS, Charles, (ed.), Shipping lists, 1823-53 in *The Pitcairn Island Register Book*, S.P.C.K. Records 1 (London, Society for Promoting Christian Knowledge, 1929; 181 pp.), 100-45.
Many whaleships included. See also whaling refs. in Lucas's introduction.

440   MCCULLOCH, J.R., "Whale fishery" in his *A dictionary, practical, theoretical, and historical, of commerce and commercial navigation*, vol. 2 (of 2 vols.), ed. by Henry Vethake (Philadelphia, Parry & McMillan, 1856; 803 + 67 pp.), 731-40.
This is the American edition, which includes information about the American whale fishery up to 1838. English ed. first pub. London 1832. Many later eds.

441   MCDONALD, Charles O., "Whaling and whale ships", sect. D of his "Sailing ship technology: some bibliographical and book collecting notes for ship modelers, marine artists, historians, and others. Part I", *Nautical Research Journal*, 26:4 (1980), 184-5. Also of interest: "Mainly contemporary 19th century works on marine technology . . . etc.", sect. C of Part 2 of above, *Nautical Research Journal*, 27:1 (1981), 28-31.

442   M'KONOCHIE (i.e. MACONOCHIE), [Alexander], Captain, R. N., 1787-1860, "Whale fishery" in chap. 2 of his *A summary view of the statistics and existing commerce of the principal shores of the Pacific Ocean . . .* (London, Printed for James M. Richardson and William Blackwood, Edinburgh, 1818; xxi, 365 pp.), 261-3. Frontis. (chart). (National Library of Australia - Ferguson 720)

443   MARTIN, Kenneth R., "An introduction to books on whaling" in George Putz and Peter H. Spectre (eds.), *The mariner's catalog*, vol. 5 (Camden, Maine, International Marine Publishing Company for Marine Annuals, Inc., [1977]), 173-5.

444   MILLER, Pamela A., "What the whalers read" in *Pages: the world of books, writers, and writing*, I (Detroit, Gale Research Co., 1976; 304 pp.), 242-7. Illus.

445   OLD DARTMOUTH HISTORICAL SOCIETY, "Log books: Andrew Snow, Jr., Collection" in "Whaling exhibits of the Old Dartmouth Historical Society", *Old Dartmouth Historical Society Publications*, 53 (1924), 35-47. Reprinted 1926, 1930.

446   RICHARDS, Rhys, "Advice upon using American whaling records in New Zealand research", *Turnbull Library Record*, ns 2 (1969), 24-8.

447   _____, "American whaling records relating to the Pacific Islands", *Journal of Pacific History*, 5 (1970), 151-3.

448   SCHULTZ, Charles R., "Manuscript collections of the Marine Historical Association, Inc. (Mystic Seaport)", *American Neptune*, 25:2 (1965), 99-111.

449   TOWNSEND, Charles Haskins, "The Galápagos tortoises in their relation to the whaling industry: a study of old log books", *Zoologica: Scientific Contributions of the New York Zoological Society*, 4:3 (1925), 55-135. Pls., fold. map, appendix.

Appendix has 152 log book records of tortoises taken at Galápagos Islands, 1831-68, with whaleships' names listed.

450   _____, "The distribution of certain whales as shown by log book records of American whaleships", *Zoologica: Scientific Contributions of the New York Zoological Society*, 19:1 (1935), 1-50. Illus., maps.

The records of 744 ships and 1665 voyages.

451   WALLACE, Frederick William (comp.), "British North American whalers engaged in South Sea whaling, 1833-1850", Appendix A of his *Record of Canadian shipping: a list of square-rigged vessels, mainly 500 tons and over, built in the eastern provinces of British North America from the year 1786 to 1920* (Toronto, Musson Book Company, [1929]; xv, 302 pp.), 296. Frontis., illus., endp., map.

452   WESLEY, Caroline, "A survey of the W.L. Crowther Library, State Library of Tasmania", *Great Circle*, 1:2 (1979), 44-59.

Includes numerous items relevant to Pacific as well as to Tasmanian whaling.

(B) Personal accounts, reminiscences, etc.

453   BENNETT, F[rederick] D[ebell]., 1806-1859, "Extracts from the journal of a voyage round the globe in the years 1833-36" (read June 26, 1837), *Journal of the Royal Geographical Society of London*, 7 (1837), 211-29.

454   BOWERS, W[illiam], Lieutenant, R.N., 1784-1845, The sperm whale-fishery, in chap. 4, vol. 1 of his *Naval adventures during thirty-five years' service* (2 vols.), (London, Richard Bentley, 1833; xxv, 302 pp.), 76-100.

Bowers describes the general state of the sperm whale fishery and gives details of a whaling cruise to the Pacific in the English whaler *Tom* to Galápagos and coast of Mexico in 1803-4. (University of California Library, Berkeley)

455   BROWN, James Temple[man], "Stray leaves from a whaleman's log", *Century Magazine*, 45:4, ns 23 (Feb. 1893), 507-17.

456   BURCHARD, George, 1810-1880, "Excerpts from a whaler's diary", *Wisconsin Magazine of History*, 18:4 (1935), 422-41; 19:1-3 (1936), 103-7, 227-41, 342-55.

Journal kept on board whaleship *Columbia* of Newark, N.J., Captain Hussey, into the Pacific Ocean, 1836-8. Whaling operations mainly in Galápagos-Juan Fernández areas. Many whalers reported on and named. *Columbia* driven ashore on coast of Chile 6 Dec. 1838. Crew shipped on board *John Welles* (i.e. *Wells*), Captain Uriah Russell, of Newark, 25 Dec. 1838 from Talcahuano. Burchard reached New York 10 Apr. 1839. (PMB 378: *John Wells*)

457   CORNELL, E.C., "Whaling voyage of the ship Apollo", chap. 18 of his *Tales of Martha's Vineyard, Cape Cod, and all along the shore. Eighty years ashore and afloat, or, The thrilling adventures of Uncle Jethro* [Ripley]. *Embracing the remarkable episodes in a life of toil and danger, on land and sea* (Boston, A.F. Graves, [1873?]; 253 pp.), 111-71. Frontis. port., pls.

Jethro Ripley, born in 1793, sailed on the whaleship *Apollo*, Captain Daggett, from Edgartown on 5 July (Starbuck: 19 June) 1816, on cruise to Atlantic and Pacific whaling grounds, via Cape Horn. Galápagos Islands were visited. The voyage is said to have lasted 22 months overall, though Cape Horn was not apparently rounded until March 1818. Starbuck does not report date of *Apollo*'s return. (Library of Congress)

458   COULTER, James Wesley, "The journal of Nelson Haley, a whaler", *Forty-Ninth Annual Report of the Hawaiian Historical Society for the year 1940*, (1941), 40-1.

Haley settled down in Hawaii after marriage in 1862. He died in Alaska in 1900. See no. 51, Nelson Cole Haley, *Whale hunt . . .*

[459]   CROCKER, Thomas R. (cooper of whaleship *Columbia* of New London). See under [Joseph] Grinnell, no. 468 below.

460   DUPONT, Ralph P., "The *Holder Borden*", *New England Quarterly*, 27:3 (1954), 355-65.

Holder Borden, a Fall River whaler (Jabeth Pell, master), wrecked in 1844, seven days out of Oahu. Crew, after weeks on a "desert Island" (26° 1'N., 174° 5'W. - probably Lisianski Island), built schooner *Hope* and sailed on it to Hawaii with all but 100 out of 1,500 barrels of oil salvaged. Based largely on extracts of log published in *The Friend* (Honolulu), 1 Nov. 1844, and court records. See also under William Henry Tripp, no. 498 below.

461   EARLE, James A.M., "On the far reaches of the Pacific", *Log of Mystic Seaport*, 2.1 (1975), 17-21.

This relates to a Pacific cruise in 1903, by the *Charles W. Morgan*, which made many earlier voyages to the Pacific.

462   FARWELL, Robert D., "William Eldridge's memorandum: interpersonal conflict in the whaling industry", *American Neptune*, 42:3 (1982), 217-9.

Conflict revealed in log of whaleship *Lewis* of New Bedford, Captain Charles Bonney on 1853-57 cruise to North Pacific. Conflict the result of captain's alleged drunkenness, details of which are given at the end of personal log of first mate, William M. Eldridge, in the form of a memorandum. Original log in the collection of the Cold Spring Harbor Whaling Museum.

463   FORSTER, Honore, "A Sydney whaler 1829-32: the reminiscences of James Heberley", *Journal of Pacific History*, 10:1-2 (1975), 90-104.
Heberley shipped on the Sydney whaler *Caroline*, Captain Swindells, on two cruises, the first 1829 to Kermadec Islands, Kingsmill group, Solomon Islands, New Hebrides and New Zealand, and the second 1830-32 to Kingsmill group, Caroline Islands, Santa Cruz Islands, Japan grounds, New Caledonia and east coast of Australia.

464   FREIDEL, Frank (ed.), "A whaler in Pacific ports, 1841-42", *Pacific Historical Review*, 12:4 (1943), 380-90.
Whaling cruise of the *Braganza*, one of the fleet of William T. Russell, of New Bedford, Captain Charles C. Waterman, to north Pacific with visits to Lahaina, Maui and homewards via Society Islands. Extracts from log kept by James S. Sullivan Purrington, original of which in Shurtleff College Library, Alton, Ill., from 29 Apr. 1841 to 28 Sept. 1842.

465   GERSTAECKER, Frederick [i.e. Friedrich Gerstäcker], "A whaling cruise", chap. 3 in vol. 2 of his *Narrative of a journey round the world, comprising a winter-passage across the Andes to Chili, with a visit to the gold regions of California and Australia, the South Sea Islands, and Java, &c.* (3 vols.), (London, Hurst & Blackett, Publishers, 1853; iv, 343 [+1] pp.), 122-40. Also pub. in 1 vol., New York, Harper & Brothers, 1853, 1854; xii, 624 pp. (specific pagination of chap. 3 in this ed. not known).
Whaling voyage from Honolulu to Maiao, Society Islands, in the Bremen whaler *Alexander Barklay* (or *Barclay*) in, according to the author, 1851. However, according to British Consulate Papers the *Alexander Barclay* was visiting Tahiti from 22-26 Dec. 1848. The *Alexander Barclay* was originally from New Bedford; after a whaling cruise to the Pacific 1840-45, the *A.B.* landed her oil at Bremen and was sold there in 1845 (Starbuck, I, 373). (National Library of Australia)

466   _____, "Kreuzen auf Spermacetifische", chap. 3 in vol. 3, *Die Südsee-Inseln*, of his *Reisen* (5 vols.), (Stuttgart and Tübingen, J.G. Cotta, 1853; [i], 486 pp.), pp. 112 ff.
The whaling episode in the original German version of Gerstäcker's *Narrative of a voyage round the world* . . . appears to be more detailed than the English translation, but actual year of cruise is not apparent. (Australian National University Library)

467   GIESSING, Hans Peter, 1801-1877, The first Danish South Seas whaling expedition, in his *Om Deportationscolonier og Dødsstraffe tilli-*

gemed en historisk Fremstilling af den første Danske Sydhavshvalfangerex-
pedition (Kjøbenhavn, Forlagt af Universitetsboghandler C.U.(A.?) Reitzel,
1841; xi, 165 [+2] pp.), 143-60.

In the section of this work devoted to the first Danish whaling expedition in the
Concordia to the Pacific, 1839-41 (in New Zealand waters and Chatham Islands
grounds), author uses Captain Thomas Sødring's journal extensively - q.v. no. 88.
(Alexander Turnbull Library; British Library)

468   GRINNELL, [Joseph], "Ship Chandler Price, owners and crew of . . .
March 28, 1850. Mr Grinnell, from the Committee on Commerce, made
the following report: The Committee . . . to whom was referred the peti-
tion of the owners of the whaling ship Chandler Price : . . report that . . .".
[Washington, D.C.], United States 31st Congress, 1st Session, House Report 177, [1850]. 8 pp.

Report on rescue of crew of New London whaler *Columbia* (lost 6 Jan. 1846 on
Sydenham's Island with 2700 barrels of oil - Starbuck, II, 417), by crew of whaler
Chandler Price, John H. Pease, master, of New Bedford. Report contains sworn
statements by Pease and crew members, crew list and description of loss of the
Columbia by ship's cooper Thomas R. Crocker, taken from *The Friend* (Honolulu),
1 Dec. 1846.

469   HALL, Daniel Weston, b. 1841, "A peep at the whale fishery", "A
life on the ocean wave" and "A parent's anxiety", chaps. 2, 3 and 5 of his
Arctic rovings: or, The adventures of a New Bedford boy on sea and land.
(Boston, Abel Tompkins, 1861: viii, 9-171 [+5] pp), 26-58, 75-80. Frontis.
port., appendix.

Author was member of the crew of the whaleship *Condor*, which left New Bedford
in 1856. He deserted the ship in Siberia and later joined the *Daniel Wood* of New
Bedford, Captain Thomas Morrison, on which he sailed to Honolulu. The *Daniel
Wood* made several visits to various ports in the Hawaiian Islands on her voyage of
1856-60. Hall eventually returned to New Bedford on the *Frances Henrietta*. The
chapters cited contain references to Hawaii and Honolulu. (Library of Congress;
PMB 914: Daniel Wood)

470   HARTMAN, Howard, Captain, b. 1868, "Shanghaied on the 'Pata-
gonia' ", chap. 3 of his *The seas were mine*, ed. by George S. Hellman (New
York, Dodd Mead & Co., 1935; xv, 330 pp.; London, George G. Harrap &
Co. Ltd, [1936]; 298 pp.), 33-48 (Lond. ed.).

Author describes his abduction in Valparaíso (late 1880s?) for service in the Chilean
whaling barque *Patagonia*, Captain Bob McLaren, which went whaling in Marquesas area and called at Atuan (Atuona) Bay, Hiva Oa. Thereafter sailed to Cocos Island (Costa Rica).

471   HUMPHRIES, "Whaling journals of Edward Cattlin", *Journal of Pacific History*, 5 (1970), 157-8.

Describes contents of MS. journals in Mitchell Library, Sydney, covering period 1827-36, kept by Cattlin on board Sydney whalers *John Bull*, *Alfred*, *Australian* and *Genii* on voyages north to Japan and east to New Zealand.

472 HUNTRESS, Keith G. (ed.), "Destruction of the *Essex*", chap. 17 of his *Narratives of shipwrecks and disasters 1586-1860*, with checklist of titles and intro. (Ames, Iowa, Iowa State University Press, 1974; xxxii, 249 pp.), 164-70. Illus.
Captain George Pollard's narrative.

473 JERNEGAN, Marcus Wilson (ed.), "A child's diary of a whaling voyage", *New England Quarterly*, 2:1 (1929), 125-39.
Journal of Laura Jernegan [Spear] on the *Roman* of New Bedford, 1869-71. The *Roman*, Captain Jared Jernegan, left port 29 Oct. 1868 and visited Honolulu in Sept. 1870; lost in Arctic in 1871.

474 JOHNSON, Barbara E., "The lure of the whaling journal", *Manuscripts* (Pasadena), 23:3 (1971), 159-77.

475 KING, Anna T. (née Stott), 1843-1931, "The infant mariner", *Old-Time New England*, 48:2 (1957), 29-42.
Account of a whaling voyage on which the author accompanied her father, Captain William Stott of the *Northern Light* out of Fairhaven, Mass., which sailed, according to Starbuck, on 18 Nov. 1851 to North Pacific, returning 14 Apr. 1855. Narrative mainly concerned with description of ship; details of whale products and how obtained also included. *Northern Light* cruised off coast of Chile and called at Honolulu.

476 KOBBÉ, Gustav, "The perils and romance of whaling", *Century Magazine*, 40:4, ns 18 (Aug. 1890), 509-25.
"Much of the material for this article was gathered from log-books, old newspapers and records in the possession of F.C. Sanford, of Nantucket, Massachusetts" - author. Relates mainly to Owen Chase's *Narrative*.

477 LAFOND DE LURCY, [Gabriel], Captain, "Journal d'un baleinier, par le Dr Thiercelin. Rapport par le capitaine G. Lafond de Lurcy", *Bulletin de la Société de Géographie de Paris*, 5th ser., 13 (1867), 568-92. (O'Reilly 1247)

478 LONGLEY, Sylvanus S., 1834-1922, "The wreck of the whaler *Canton*", *New England Quarterly*, 13:2 (1940), 324-35.
Narrative of one of the survivors of the *Canton*, commanded by Captain Andrew Wing, of New Bedford, wrecked on Canton Island in 1854. MS. written down when Longley was over 80. After sailing in August 1852, *Canton* called at Hawaii and cruised in Okhotsk Sea before being wrecked. Four boatloads of survivors covered 2900 nautical miles in 42 days before reaching Ladrones and finally Guam.

479   LYMAN, Horace S., "Recollections of Horace Holden", *Quarterly of the Oregon Historical Society*, 3 (1902), 164-217.

See no. 56, Horace S. Holden, A *narrative of the shipwreck, captivity and sufferings of . . .*

480   MACDONALD, Ranald, "Narrative", chap. 5 of his *Ranald Mac-Donald: the narrative of his early life on the Columbia under the Hudson's Bay Company's regime; of his experiences in the Pacific whale fishery; and of his great adventure to Japan; with a sketch of his later life on the western frontier 1824-1894*, ed. and annotated from original manuscripts by William S. Lewis and Naojiro Murakami (Spokane, Wash., Eastern Washington State Historical Society, 1923; 333 [+ 3] pp.), 137-46.

MacDonald shipped aboard the whaler *Plymouth*, probably of Sag Harbor, at "Kalakakna Bay" (Kealakekua Bay, Hawaii) for a whaling cruise, in company with the *David Paddack* of Nantucket, in 1846. The route was to Hong Kong, via the Ladrones. "Gregan" (Agrihan) and "Pegan" (Pagan) were touched at. "Liverpool Jack" and "Spider Jack", two Europeans, were found to be living on Agrihan.

481   MALONEY, Paul R., "Whaler *Ploughboy*", *American Neptune*, 21:3 (1961), 222.

Fragment of log of *Ploughboy*, Captain Nathan Chase, of Nantucket, on Pacific voyage of 1830-34, with list of officers and crew.

482   MARTIN, Kenneth R., "Whalemen of letters", *Oceans*, 12:1 (1979), 20-9. Illus. (facsims.).

Discussion of journals kept in the 1840s by Joseph Eayrs of New Bedford whaler *Gratitude* and John F. Martin of the *Lucy Ann* of Wilmington in the Pacific, and Joseph Hersey of Provincetown schooner *Esquimaux* in the Atlantic. Journals are in the Kendall Whaling Museum.

483   MARTIN, Kenneth R. and Bruce SINCLAIR, "A Pennsylvanian in the Wilmington whaling trade, 1841-1844", *Pennsylvania History*, 41:1 (1974), 27-51.

Voyage of the *Lucy Ann*, recorded by John F. Martin, boatsteerer, to Cape of Good Hope, Indian and Pacific Oceans.

484   MAUDE, H.E., "The cruise of the whaler 'Gypsy' ", *Journal of Pacific History*, 1 (1966), 193-4.

Describes contents of MS. log and private journal in Royal Geographical Society Library, London, of Dr. D. Parker [i.e. John] Wilson, ship's surgeon, on cruise of English whaler *Gypsy*, 1839-43, to Pacific Ocean and Japan grounds, during which many islands and island groups visited, including the Marianas, Carolines and Gilberts, New Guinea and Hawaii.

485   MUNSTERBERG, Margaret, "The journal of a whaling voyage," *Boston Public Library Quarterly*, 7:3 (1955), 156-60.

From "A journal of a voyage from Nantucket towards the South Seas and else-where" by ship *Alexander*, Captain Samuel Bunker, 1827-31 - Japan grounds, Oahu, coast of California, Galápagos, coast of Peru.

486   [NICKERSON, Thomas], "In Nantucket: *Moby Dick* revisited", *Time*, 117:26 (29 June 1981), 46-7.

Excerpts from newly-discovered chronicle of the aftermath of the sinking of the *Essex* by a sperm whale, written by Nickerson, a young crew member. See also Edouard A. Stackpole, "Historic "Essex" manuscript returns after absence of 98 years", be-low.

487   "OF WHALEMEN'S LAMENTS", *Bulletin*, Old Dartmouth Historical Society and Whaling Museum, (Spring 1957), 1-3.

See partic. pp. 2-3 for incidents in Clothier Peirce's voyage in whaler *Rodman* as first officer, 1855-9, to the Pacific and N.Z.

488   PEASE, Henry, 2nd, Captain, 1802-1860, "Adventure on St. Augus-tine Island", *Dukes County Intelligencer*, 3: 4 (1962), 3-13.

From Pease's "An Account of an Adventure of Henry Pease 2nd of Edgartown Mass. Capt. of ship *Planter* of Nantucket on August 18, 1853 on St. Augustine Island Lat. 5.35 South, Lon. 176.12 East, Near Ellis Group", TS, Dukes County Historical So-ciety, Edgartown, Mass. This account relates partic. to appearance and customs of the people of the island, and Pease's reception there. The *Planter* left port 19 May 1852, returning to Edgartown on 7 Aug. 1856. Apart from visit to northern Tuvalu, *Planter*'s whaling voyage embraced New Zealand, Kermadecs (Raoul Island), Tonga (Eua and Vavau) and Samoa (Upolu).

489   [POLLARD, George, Captain, 1789-1870], Narrative of the wreck of the *Essex*, in vol. 2 of Daniel Tyerman and George Bennet; James Mont-gomery (comp.), *Journal of voyages and travels . . . Deputed from the London Missionary Society, to visit their various stations in the South Sea Islands . . . between the years 1821 and 1829*, 2 vols. (London, Frederick Westley and A.H. Davis, 1831; viii, 568 pp.), 24-9. Later eds., Boston, Crocker and Brewster; New York, J. Leavitt, 1832, rev. "by an American editor", in 3 vols. 2nd Eng. ed., London, John Snow, with title *Voyages and travels round the world*, 1840, 1841, in 1 vol.

[490]   [RIPLEY, Jethro, b. 1793]. See under E. C. Cornell, no. 457 above.

491   SCHMITT, Frederick P., Cornelis DE JONG and Frank H. WINTER, "Learning the ropes", chap. 1 of their *Thomas Welcome Roys, America's pi-oneer of modern whaling*, Mariners Museum Pub. no. 38 (Charlottesville, University Press of Virginia for Mariners Museum, Newport News, Va., [1980]; xiv, 253 pp.), 1-10. Illus., appendices, glossary, gazetteer, notes, in-dex.

Describes Roys's early whaling expriences in the Pacific in the *Crescent* of Sag Harbor, 1841-3, based on his MS. journal "The voyages of Thomas Welcome Roys". Mentions Marianas, Bonins, Hawaii, Line Islands, Tonga (Amargura), New Zealand and Chatham Islands.

492   SHERMAN, Susan McCooey, "Lace curtains in the captain's quarters", *Log of Mystic Seaport*, 20:1 (1968), 11-14.
Mrs. William Brewster and her activities on board the whaler *Tiger*, of Stonington, Conn., ca. 1846; the *Tiger* called at Hawaii.

493   SNYDER, Frank (collected and annotated by), "Whaling" in his [*Life under sail.*] *Being a compilation of the adventures, horrors, hardships, delights, and recreations of life under sail*, with foreword by Edouard A. Stackpole (New York, Macmillan Co., [1964]; xxxv, 474 pp.), 378-422. Frontis., pls.
Pacific material comprises excerpts from Bullen and Haley, and narratives about attacks by whales on whaleships, including those of Owen Chase and John Deblois of the *Ann Alexander*.

494   SPEARS, John R. (ed.), "The log of the bark *Emily* as kept by L.R. Hale, Third Mate - 1857-60", *Harper's Monthly Magazine*, 107: 638 (July 1903), 242-51.
The *Emily*, Captain P.N. Luce, sailed from New Bedford 17 October 1857, and called at Chatham Island, in the Galápagos group, probably about mid-1859. The excerpts from Hale's log do not contain much about *Emily*'s Pacific cruising, but rather concentrate on general whaling details.

495   STACKPOLE, Edouard A., "Historic 'Essex' manuscript returns, after absence of 98 years", *Historic Nantucket*, 28:3 (1981), 6-9.
Account of the loss of the *Essex* by the last survivor of open-boat voyage, Thomas Nickerson (see above), presented to Nantucket Historical Association after discovery in a Connecticut attic.

496   THOMSON, J. Inches, "Whale fishing", chap. 10 of his *Voyages and wanderings in far-off seas and lands* (London, Headley Brothers, n.d. [1913?]; 191 pp.), 65-73.
Describes author's whaling experiences on the *Splendid* of New Bedford, on which "Frank Bullen gained much of his experience as narrated in his book 'The Cruise of the *Cachalot*' ", in whaling grounds off "the Solanders, Vau Vau, South Pacific and Australian Gulf".

497   [THRUM, Thomas G.], "Captain Thomas Spencer", *Hawaiian Almanac and Annual for 1923*, (Dec. 1922), 108-12.
Details of the capture of whaleship *Triton* of New Bedford, Thomas Spencer, master, at Sydenham's Island in 1848, from *Polynesian* of 25 March 1848, based on Spencer's private journal. See also no. 90.

498   TRIPP, William Henry, "Bill Fuller goes a-whaling", chap. 3, and "Loss of ship Holder Borden" in "Whalemen's adventures", chap. 11 of his *There goes flukes". The story of New Bedford's last whaler being the narrative of the voyage of schooner JOHN R. MANTA on Hatteras Grounds 1925, and whalemen's true yarns in old deep-sea whaling days* (New Bedford, Mass., Reynolds Printing, 1938; [xiv], 262 pp.), 15-29, partic. 23-6, 142-51. Illus. (photos) by author.

"Bill Fuller . . ." has some information on Galápagos whaling, taken from the reminiscences of Fuller, who sailed on *Osceola* of New Bedford on 1862-65 voyage to Atlantic, Pacific and Arctic Oceans. "Loss of ship Holder Borden" contains account by Captain Pell of wreck of his ship on "Pell's Island", northwest of Hawaii in 1844, and of his later visit to site of wreck in 1845, taken from *The Friend* (Honolulu) and published in the *Whalemen's Shipping List* of 25 March and 15 July 1845. Details given of position of "Pell's Island" (26° 2'N., 174° 51'W. - probably Lisianski Island, discovered by Captain Lisianski in the *Neva* in 1805). Two other items taken from *Whalemen's Shipping List* of 19 Jan. and 13 Apr. 1847 also refer to this island, "not on any chart". See also under Ralph P. Dupont, no. 460 above.

499   [VERMILYEA, Lucius H.], contrib. by Joseph B. Howerton, "A whaler's letter", *American Neptune*, 18:4 (1958), 320-3.

Letter to Lieutenant M.F. Maury, U.S.N., 31 Jan. 1859, about whaling experiences. Pacific refs. included.

500   WADDELL, James I., 1824-1886, Chaps. 8 and 9 of his *C.S.S. Shenandoah: the memoirs of Lieutenant Commanding James I. Waddell*, ed. by James D. Horan (New York, Crown Publishers Inc., 1960; 200 pp.), 139-61. Illus.

Covers sinking of four American whalers at "Punipet or Ascension, east of the Caroline Group"; includes description of meeting with "King of the Lea Harbor tribe", the landing of prisoners from the whaleships at Lea Harbor, and sinking of other whaleships in North Pacific.

501   WALKER, Eliza (dictated by, to S.K. Johnstone), "Old Sydney in the 'forties. Recollections of Lower George Street and 'The Rocks' ", *Journal and Proceedings of the Royal Australian Historical Society*, 16:4 (1930), 292-320.

See partic. pp. 309-10 for notes on whalers in the port of Sydney during the 1840s.

502   WHIDDEN, John D., Captain, b. 1832, "1846-1847: Rio de Janeiro.-Cape Horn.-Otaheite", "1847: Society Islands.-Honolulu.-California . . .", and "1847-1849: Whaling in '48.-Again Tahiti.-Escape to the hills . . .", chaps. 6-8 of his *Ocean life in the old sailing ship days: from forecastle to quarterdeck* (Boston, Little, Brown and Co., 1908, 1910; xvi, 314 pp. Reprinted with title, *Old sailing ship days. From forecastle to quarterdeck*, with intro. by Ralph D. Paine. Boston, Charles E. Lauriat Co.; London, Martin Hop-

kinson & Co. Ltd, 1925; xxiv, 314 pp.), 52-78. Frontis. port., pls. Map in
2nd ed.

Whidden shipped on the *Tsar* in Boston in 1846, and joined the whaler *Samuel
Robertson*, Captain J.K. Turner, of Fairhaven, Mass., in Hawaii (*Samuel Robertson*
left her home port on 20 June 1846), which then sailed on an unfruitful whaling
cruise. In 1848 *Samuel Robertson* put in to Papeete for repairs; Whidden deserted
ship there and joined the whaler *George*, Captain George Taber, of Stonington,
Conn., which returned to port in June 1849, via Cape Horn. (Mitchell Library; PMB
327, 775: *Samuel Robertson*)

503   WILKES, Charles, Lieutenant, U.S.N., 1798-1877, Chap. 12 of vol.
5 of his *Narrative of the United States Exploring Expedition. During the
years 1838, 1839, 1840, 1841, 1842* (5 vols.), (Philadelphia, Printed by
C. Sherman, 1844; xv, 591 pp.), 515 ff. Illus., appendices, gen. index. See
also unofficial ed., Philadelphia, Lea & Blanchard, 1845-46.

Much on American whalers and whaling in the Pacific Ocean.

504   WILLIAMS, Harold (ed.), "Whaling wife: being Eliza Williams' own
journal of her thirty-eight-month voyage with her husband, master of the
ship *Florida*, from New Bedford to Japan and the Sea of Okhotsk in pursuit
of the great whales", *American Heritage*, 15:4 (1964), 64-79.

See also no. 104, Harold Williams, *One whaling family*.

505   [WRIGHT, Elihu], 1801-1840, "The letters of a young whaleman -
1822-1824 during a voyage to the Pacific Ocean", *Historic Nantucket*, 29: 3
and 4 (1982), 21-8, 24-8.

Elihu Wright of Saybrook, Conn., birthplace of William Lay (q.v. no. 63) shipped
on board the *Enterprise* of Nantucket, Captain Reuben Weeks, for a Pacific whaling
cruise, 3 Sept. 1822-27 Jan. 1826 (introductory note gives 23 Sept. as sailing date).
Letters include one from South Pacific, 10 Feb. 1823, 1° 40' S., 120° W., one from
Oahu, 11 Apr. 1823, one from North Pacific, 33° N., 160° W., May (i.e. begun in)
1823. In this letter Wright refers to the *Globe*, spoken 31 Aug. [1823]: ". . . all
well 450 bbls. Jno. received a letter by William Lay who I was much disappointed
not to see". Another letter is apparently from Sandwich Islands, and is undated [ca.
Dec. 1823]. In it Wright mentions the arrival of the *Globe* on "7th" [Dec.?].

(C) General studies.

506   ABBOT, Willis J., "The whaling industry . . .", chap. 4 of his *Amer
ican merchant ships and sailors*, illus. by Ray Brown (New York, Dodd, Mead
& Co., 1902; x, 372 pp.), 121-51. Frontis., pls., illus.

507   "ABOARD A SPERM-WHALER," *Chamber's Journal*, 1, ns 21 (1854),
52-5.

Sperm whaling in the Pacific.

508 "ACCOUNT OF THE WHALE-FISHERY," in *The mariner's library, or voyager's companion: containing narratives of the most popular voyages from the time of Columbus to the present day: with accounts of remarkable shipwrecks, naval adventures, the whale-fishery, & c. . . . , illustrated by fine engravings* (Boston, Lilly, Wait, Colman & Holden, 1833; C. Gaylord, 1834; 1840; xiv, 492 pp.), 331-46. Frontis., illus., pls.

509 ALBION, Robert G., "*Acushnet*" and "*Charles W. Morgan*" in his *Five centuries of famous ships from the Santa Maria to the Glomar Explorer,* with foreword by Benjamin Labaree (New York, St Louis etc. McGraw-Hill Book Co., [1978]; viii, 435 pp.), 174-9. Illus., index.

510 ————, William A. BAKER and Benjamin W. LABAREE, "Distant seas and whaling" in chap. 3, "The golden age, 1815-1865" of their *New England and the sea,* American Maritime Library, vol. 5 (Middletown, Conn., Wesleyan. University Press for the Marine Historical Association Inc., Mystic Seaport, 1972; xiv, 299 pp.), 105-18. Endp., map, frontis., illus., index.

511 "THE AMERICAN WHALE FISHERY," review (art. VIII) of *Discovery and adventure in Polar seas and regions, with an account of the whale fishery* (New York, Harper, 1833) and *Scientific tracts, nos. 1824: whale fishery* (Boston, 1833), *Monthly Review,* ns, ser. 4, 1:3 (March 1834), 347-53.
Includes statistics for the American whale fishery, and ref. to mutiny on the *Globe.* Also contains excerpt from Owen Chase's account of the attack on the *Essex* by a sperm whale (Chase is spelt "Clave" in text).

512 ANTHONY, Irvin, "Thar she blows!", chap. 10 of his *Down to the sea in ships* (Philadelphia, The Penn Publishing Co., 1924; 358 pp.), 163-83. Frontis., illus.

513 ————, "The *Globe* goes whaling", chap. 11 of his *Revolt at sea: a narration of many mutinies* (New York, G.P. Putnam's Sons, "A Minton Balch Book", [1937]; London, Putnam, [1938]; xi, 296 pp.), 117-30. Frontis., pls., map, bibliog.

514 ————, "The Sharon", chap. 17 of his *Revolt at sea . . .,* q.v. above, 188-96.
Note: Anthony places *Sharon* (of Fairhaven, Mass.) mutiny in Atlantic Ocean. Philip Purrington in "Anatomy of a mutiny", q.v. below, gives evidence for correct location in Pacific.

515 "THE ART OF WHALING, *The Boston Pearl and Literary Gazette,* 4: 45-46 (18, 25 July 1835), 359, 369-70.

Description of the spermaceti whale and the technique of whaling, cutting in and trying out; see also no. 377, "Whaling in the Pacific", for which this article serves as an introduction.

516   "ASSOCIATIONS FOR WHALING IN THE SOUTH SEAS: THE BRITISH WHALE AND SEAL FISHERY COMPANY", *New Zealand Journal*, 6:180 (1846), 278-80.

517   "AUSTRALIAN SPERM WHALE FISHERY", *Australian Quarterly Journal of Theology, Literature & Science*, ed. by Rev. Charles P.N. Wilton, 1 (1828), 86-94. (National Library of Australia - Ferguson 1171)

518   ARGYLE, E.W., "The Enderbys of London", *Sea Breezes* (Liverpool), 10? (Jan. 1956), 56-9.
The Enderbys and British whaling in the South Pacific.

519   BACH, John, "Internal shipping 1788-1850", chap. 4 of his *A maritime history of Australia* ([West Melb., Vic.], Nelson, 1976; xvi, 481 pp.), 70-92, partic. 74-7. Illus., maps, notes, bibliog., indexes. Reprinted Sydney and London, Pan Books, [1982].

520   BAKER, Benjamin, "History of the bark Lagoda of New Bedford, Mass., one of New Bedford's most successful whaling vessels", *Old Dartmouth Historical Sketches*, 45 (Nov. 1916), 33-47.
Lists *Lagoda*'s whaling cruises between 1841-1886, many which were to the Pacific Ocean.

521   BAKER, Veronica F. and Ian A.D. BOUCHIER, "The polymath practitioners: Thomas Beale, M.D. (1807-1849) and Frederick Debell Bennett, M.D. (1806-1859), *Practitioner*, 217: 1299 (1976), 428-34.
Sheds light on the careers of the authors of *The natural history of the sperm whale . . .* and *Narrative of a whaling voyage . . . ,* q.v. nos. 4, 5 and 7.

522   BECK, Horace, The *Essex* story in "Legends and tales", chap. 13 of his *Folklore and the sea*, American Maritime Library, vol. 6 (Middletown, Conn., Wesleyan University Press for the Marine Historical Association Inc., Mystic Seaport, [1973]; xvii, 463 pp.), 378-9. Port., pls., notes, bibliog., index.

523   BECKE, Louis, "Leviathan" in his *Wild life in southern seas* (London, T. Fisher Unwin, 1897; 369 pp.), 222-47.
Whaling in the Southern Ocean from 1791.

524   BIRGE, William S., "The whale and the whaleman", *New England Magazine*, 34:3 (1906), 265-72.
General survey of New England participation in whaling.

525 BLAINEY, Geoffrey, "Technology in Australian history", *Business Archives and History*, 4:2 (1964), 117-37, partic. 120-2.

526 ———, "Whalemen", chap. 5 of his *The tyranny of distance: how distance shaped Australia's history* (Melbourne, Sun Books, 1966; x, 365 [+7] pp.), 99-117. Pls., maps, notes, index. First hard cover ed., Melbourne, Macmillan Co. of Australia, 1968. Reprinted 1977.

527 BLOND, Georges, "The era of the cachalot", chap. 3 of his *The great story of whales*, trans. by James Cleugh of *La grande aventure des baleines* (Paris, Fayard, 1953; 244 pp.), (New York, Hanover House [Doubleday and Co., Inc.], 1955; 251 pp.), 85-173. Illus. Also pub. London, Weidenfeld and Nicolson, 1954; 213 pp., with title *The great whale game*.
Partic. ref. to Nelson C. Haley and the *Charles W. Morgan*, q.v. no. 51.

528 BOGGS, S. Whittemore, "American contributions to geographical knowledge of the Central Pacific", *Geographical Review*, 28: 2 (1938), 177-92.
See partic. "American whaling", pp. 184-8, which suggests that claims for American whalers' discoveries of some 200 small islands in the Central Pacific are exaggerated.

529 BONHAM, Julia C., "Feminist and Victorian: the paradox of the American seafaring woman of the nineteenth century", *American Neptune*, 37: 3 (1977), 203-18.
Includes discussion of whaling wives.

530 BONNER, W. Nigel, "The right whale fishery: the beginnings of commercial whaling" and "The yankee whalers: the sperm whale fishery", chaps. 10 and 11 of his *Whales* (Poole, Dorset, Blandford Press, [1980]; x, 278 pp.), 212-25, partic. 216-18, 222-4. Pls., illus., bibliog., index.

531 BOSSIÈRE, René E., "Les navires baleiniers 1830-1930", *Bulletin Officiel du Yacht Club de France*, 132 (1930), 503-10 + 6 (illus.).
General historical survey, but with special emphasis on French whaling (pp. 503-6).

532 BRADDLEY, Harold W[hitman], "Thomas ap Catesby Jones and the Hawaiian Islands, 1826-1827", *Thirty-Ninth Annual Report of the Hawaiian Historical Society for the Year 1930*, (1931), 10-26.
Jones was sent to Hawaii in response to an appeal to the U.S. Govt. by "numerous groups of Nantucket seamen interested in whaling" to protect American citizens, vessels and commerce against lawless deserters, mainly from whalers.

533 ———, "The commercial frontier", chap. 5 of his *The American frontier in Hawaii: the pioneers 1789-1843* (California, Stanford University

Press; London, Humphrey Milford, Oxford University Press, [1942] and new ed. [1944]; xii, 488 pp.), partic. 214-28, and refs. 79-82. Endp., map, bibliog. footnotes, index.

534   BRIERLY, O[swald] W[alter], 1817-1894, "Whales and whaling" (correspondence), *Athenaeum*, 1762 and 1767 (3 Aug. and 7 Sept. 1861), 160, 320-21.
Refs. to whales Brierly observed off east coast of Australia and in Pacific Ocean, and to whaling in these regions.

535   BRIGHAM, William T., "Whales and the whaling industry" in his *An index to the islands of the Pacific Ocean: a handbook to the chart on the walls of the Bernice Pauahi Bishop Museum of Polynesian Ethnology and Natural History*, Memoirs, B.P. Bishop Museum, vol. 1, no. 2 (Honolulu, Bishop Museum Press, 1900; iv, 172 pp.), 105-6. Frontis., maps.

536   BROEZE, F.J.A., "Whaling in the southern oceans: the Dutch quest for southern whaling in the nineteenth century", *Economisch- en Sociaal-Historisch Jaarboek*, 40 (1977), 66-112.

537   BROOKES, Jean Ingram, "Trader, whaleman and missionary, 1800-1820" and ". . . 1820-1840", chaps. 2 and 3 of her *International rivalry in the Pacific Islands 1800-1875* (Berkeley, University of California Press, 1941; x, 454 pp.), 10-42. Appendices, bibliog., index.
See also whaling refs. in "The island world, 1840-1850", p. 169 ff and Appendix 2 (an attack on a whaler), p. 421.

538   BROWN, Alexander Crosby, "Attacks on vessels by enraged whales", *American Neptune*, 1: 4 (1941), 293-4.
Includes refs. to *Essex* and *Ann Alexander*.

539   BROWN, James Templeman, 1842-1886, "The whalemen, vessels and boats, apparatus, and methods of the whale fishery", 2nd sect. of pt. 15, "The whale-fishery" of George Brown Goode et al., *The fisheries and fishery industries of the United States*, sect. 5, vol. 2 (Washington, Government Printing Office, 1887; xx, 881 pp.), 218-93.
See also his *The whale fishery and its appliances* (Washington, Government Printing Office, 1883), 116 pp., pub. for the Great International Fisheries Exhibition, London, 1883.

540   BROWNING, Mary A., "The blue & gray in Ponape", *Glimpses of Guam*, 16:1 (1976), 24-31, 66.
Confederate raider *Shenandoah* and the sinking of four whaleships at Ponape in 1865 (*Pearl* of New London, *Harvest* of Honolulu, *Hector* of New Bedford and *Edward Carey* of San Francisco).

541   CALLAHAN, James Morton, "Early relations of whalers and traders with the natives", chap. 4 of his *American relations in the Pacific and the Far East 1784-1900*, Johns Hopkins University Studies in Historical and Political Science, series 19, nos. 1-3 (Baltimore, Johns Hopkins Press, 1901; 177 [+10] pp.), 37-48. Footnotes, appendices, index.

See also other whaling refs. interspersed in text.

542   CARANO, Paul and Pedro C. SANCHEZ, "Whalers visit Guam" in chap. 5, "Final century of Spanish rule" of their *A complete history of Guam* (Rutland, Vt. and Tokyo, Charles E. Tuttle Co., [1964]; xvii, 452 pp.), 145-7. Illus., frontis., map, bibliog., index.

543   CÉCILLE, J.B.T., "Extrait du rapport adressé à M. le Ministre de la Marine par M. Cécille, capitaine de vaisseau, commandant la corvette l'*Héroïne* envoyée dans l'hémisphère austral à la protection de la pêche de la baleine pendant les années 1837, 1838 et 1839. Partie nautique et pêche", *Annales Maritimes et Coloniales*, 72:2, vol. 1 (1840), 180-260.

544   CHURCHWARD, L.G., "Notes on American whaling activities in Australian waters 1800-1850", *Historical Studies*, 4:13 (1949), 59-63.

545   ――――, "Whaling and trading", chap. 2 of his *Australia & America 1788-1972: an alternative history* (Sydney, Alternative Publishing Cooperative Limited, 1979; xxix, 261 pp.), 20-40. Notes, bibliog., index.

546   CLARK, A[lonzo] Howard, 1850-1918, "History and present condition of the fishery", 1st sect. of pt. 15, "The whale-fishery" of George Brown Goode et al., *The fisheries and fishery industries of the United States*, sect. 5, vol. 2 (Washington, Government Printing Office, 1887; xx, 881 pp.), 3-218.

See partic. "Development of the sperm-whale fishery", pp. 63-73, "List of whaling voyages from American ports, 1870 to 1880", pp. 174-92 and sections on French and Australian fisheries, pp. 207-13.

547   CLEMENT, Ernest W., "Mito samurai and British sailors in 1824", *Transactions of the Asiatic Society of Japan*, 33:1 (1905), 86-131.

Japanese accounts of landings on the coast of Japan in Hitachi region, of sailors from British vessels, appparently whalers, amongst them a Captain Gibson. Appendix contains list of shipping, mainly whalers out of London, at Bonin Islands, 1833-35.

548   COLWELL, Max, "To seek it at a distance", chap. 9 of his *Whaling around Australia* (Adelaide, Rigby Ltd., [1969]; [viii], 168 [+10] pp.), 90-105. Illus., pls., bibliog., index. Reprinted as a Rigby "Seal Book", 1977.

549 _____, "Whaling" in his *Ships and seafarers in Australian waters* ([Melbourne], Lansdowne Press, [1973]; 127 pp.), 40-55. Illus., "further reading" list.

Some material, including illustrations, on pelagic whaling from Australia.

550 "COMMERCIAL PROSPECTS OF NEW ZEALAND. NO. V. THE FISH-ERIES", *New Zealand Journal*, 1:12 (1840), 152-3.

551 CONGDEN, J. B., "New Bedford, Massachusetts", *National Magazine and Industrial Record*, 1: 4 (Sept. 1845), 328-43.

See partic. pp. 337-40 for refs. to whaling activities of New Bedford.

552 CREIGHTON, Margaret S., "The captains' children: life in the adult world of whaling, 1852-1907", *American Neptune*, 38:3 (1978), 203-16.

Footnotes contain useful refs. to unpublished material.

553 CRISP, Frank, "The sperm whale hunters", chap. 8 of his *The adventure of whaling*, illus. by Winston Megoran (London, Macmillan & Co.; New York, St. Martin's Press, 1954; 143 pp.), 69-98. Illus.

554 CROWTHER, W. Lodewyk, 1887-1981, "Notes on Tasmanian whaling", *Papers and Proceedings, Royal Society of Tasmania*, (1919), 130-51.

Material on sperm whaling in the South Pacific Ocean as well as Tasmanian bay whaling.

555 DAKIN, W.J., "Whaling - and Australia", *Walkabout*, 12:11 (1946), 4-12.

See partic. pp. 4-7 for 19th century refs.

556 _____, "Australia and the golden age of Pacific whaling", chap. 4 of Charles Barrett (ed.), *The Pacific: ocean of islands* (Melbourne, N.H. Seward Pty. Ltd., [1950]; [viii], 176 pp.), 41-54. Frontis., pls., illus.

557 DALLAS, K.M., "The whaling industry 1770-1800" and "The prosperity of whaling", chaps. 5 and 6 of his *Trading posts or penal colonies: the commercial significance of Cook's New Holland route to the Pacific* (Hobart, Fullers Bookshop, [1969]; 132 pp.), 57-90. Illus., footnote refs., appendix, index.

Chaps. cited deal particularly with the significance of whaling to early Australian settlement.

558 DAMON, Ethel M., "The Seamen's Bethel at Honolulu", *The Friend*, 103 (June 1933), 124-31.

559   DAWS, Gavan, "Honolulu in the 19th century: notes on the emergence of urban society in Hawaii", *Journal of Pacific History*, 2 (1967), 77-96.

Refs. to effects on Honolulu of Pacific whaling industry.

560   ———, "Whales" in "A new society, a new economy 1855-1876", chap. 5 of his *Shoal of time: a history of the Hawaiian Islands* (New York, Macmillan Co., [1968]; xv, 494 pp.), 169-72; see also 166-7, 173. Endp., maps, pls., bibliog., notes, indexes. Reprinted paperback ed., Honolulu, University Press of Hawaii, [1974].

561   DE JONG, C[ornelis], "Walvisvaart in de Zuidzee", pt. (B) of chap. 25 in his *Geschiedenis van de oude Nederlandse walvisvaart*, vol. 2: *Bloei en achteruitgang 1642-1872* (Johannesburg, [C. de Jong], 1978; xii, 536 pp.), 463-9. For notes, tables, bibliography and summary in English, see vol. 3: *Noten bij deel twee, tabellen, grafieken, bijlagen*, "A short history of old Dutch whaling" . . . (Johannesburg, [C. de Jong], 1979; x, 409 pp.), partic. 132-4, 310, 321-3.

562   DEMOLIÈRE, P., "La pêche à la baleine", *Mémoires de la Société Dunkerquoise pour l'Encouragement des Sciences, des Lettres et des Arts*, 50 (1909), 115-48 (+ annexes).

History and description of Dunkirk whale fishery, with partic. ref. to the influence of Nantucket whalemen on the industry after 1788.

563   DESTRUCTION OF THE *ESSEX* in "An account of the whale-fishery; with anecdotes of the dangers, & c. attending it", in *Ocean scenes, or, The perils and beauties of the deep; being interesting, instructive, and graphic accounts of the most popular voyages on record, remarkable shipwrecks, hair-breadth escapes, naval adventures, the whale fishery, etc., etc.* (Dublin, James M'Glashan, 1849; 326 [+ 2] pp.), 318-9. Illus. 1st pub. New York, Leavitt Allen, [1847]. 490 pp. Repub. New York, 1855.

Very brief ref., in section (pp. 302-20) dealing generally with northern fishery, to wreck of the *Essex* and its aftermath.

564   "DESTRUCTION OF THE ESSEX BY A WHALE. As related by her commander, Captain George Pollard" in *The mariner's chronicle: containing narratives of the most remarkable disasters at sea, such as shipwrecks, storms, fires, and famines: also, naval engagements, piratical adventures, incidents of discovery, and other extraordinary and interesting occurrences* (New-Haven, Durrie and Peck, 1834; xii, 504 pp.), 398-402. Illus. Other eds. of this work pub. in New Haven, 1834, by George W. Gorton, R.M. Treadway and A.B. Wilcox, and in Philadelphia by G.N. Loomis.

See also no. 644 below under "Loss of the whale ship Essex".

565   DODGE, Ernest S., "Early American contacts in Polynesia and Fiji", *Proceedings of the American Philosophical Society*, 107:2 (1963), 102-6. See partic. "Whaling", pp. 105-6.

566   ———, "Whalers ashore", chap. 5 of his *Islands and empires: western impact on the Pacific and East Asia*, vol. 7 of Boyd C. Shafer (ed.), *Europe and the world in the age of expansion* ([Minneapolis], University of Minnesota Press; [London], Oxford University Press, 1976; xvi, 363 pp.), 69-84. Pls., refs., bibliog., index.

567   DORSETT, Edward Lee, "Hawaiian whaling days", *American Neptune*, 14:1 (1954), 42-6.

568   DOTY, Richard G., "Guam's role in the whaling industry", *Guam Recorder*, ns 2:4 (1972), 20-7.

569   DULLES, Foster Rhea, "Early contacts with Hawaii", chap. 9 of his *America in the Pacific: a century of expansion* (Boston and New York, Houghton Mifflin Co., 1932; xiii, 299 pp.; 2nd ed. 1938), partic. 141-54. Bibliog. notes, index.

570   DUMONT D'URVILLE, J[ules] S[ébastian] C[ésar], 1790-1842, "Pêche de baleines", in chap. 56, vol. 2 of his *Voyage pittoresque autour du monde: résumé général des voyages de découvertes . . .* (2 vols.), (Paris, L. Tenre, 1835; 584 pp.), 535-7.

571   DUNBABIN, Thomas, "Whalers, sealers, and buccaneers", *Journal and Proceedings of the Royal Australian Historical Society*, 11:1 (1925), 1-32.

572   ———, "Spiking the guns at Nukahiva", chap. 7 of his *Sailing the world's edge: sea stories from old Sydney* (London, Newnes, [1931]; 283 pp.), 78-88.
Refs. to Eber Bunker's whaling enterprises.

573   ———, "New light on the earliest American voyages to Australia", *American Neptune*, 10: 1 (1950), 52-64.
Covers period up to 1812. Of some whaling interest.

574   ("T D "), "Whaling industry", in vol. 9 of *The Australian Encyclopaedia* (Sydney, Grolier Society of Australia, [1965]; 547 pp.), 273-6.

575   DUPETIT-THOUARS, A[bel] A[ubert], 1793-1864, "Rapport à M. le Ministre de la Marine sur la pêche de la baleine dans l'Océan Pacifique", in vol. 3 of his *Voyage autour du monde sur la frégate la* Vénus *pendant les* *années 1836-1839* . . . *Relation* (4 vols.), (Paris, Gide, 1841; 490 pp. + 6 tables), 345-96. Dated 24 June 1839. 5 tables attached.

576   EAGLESTON, John H., ["Long voyages of the whalers"], in George Granville Putnam, *Salem vessels and their voyages: a history of the European, African, Australian and South Pacific Islands trade as carried out by Salem merchants, particularly the firm of N.C. Rogers & Brothers*, series 4 (Salem, Essex Institute, 1930; 8, 175 pp.), 137-42. Frontis., pls., ports.
Eagleston lists whalers seen at Papeete in 1837 while visiting there in command of brig *Mermaid* of Salem.

577   ENDERBY, Charles, 1798?-1876, "British southern whale fisheries" [Oct. 1848], *New Zealand Journal*, 8:232 (1848), 246-7.

578   ENGLE, Eloise and Arnold S. LOTT, "Whaling", in chap. 7, "All ships - all seas" of their *America's maritime heritage* (Annapolis, Md., Naval Institute Press, [1975]; xii, 392 pp.), 118-22, 124. Illus., bibliog., index.

579   FAIVRE, Jean-Paul, "La pêche baleinière" in his *L'expansion française dans le Pacifique de 1800 à 1842* (Paris, Nouvelles Éditions Latines, [1953]; 550 pp.), 404-7, 409-10. Maps, bibliog., index.
See also other entries listed in index under "Baleiniers, Baleine (pêche à la)".

580   FINNIS, Harold J., "Whaling" in his *Captain John Finnis 1802-1872: a brief biographical sketch*, Pioneers' Association of South Australia Publication no. 32 (Adelaide, The Association, 1958; 19 pp.), 4.
Finnis was joint owner, with J. Montefiore, of the Sydney whaling barque *Elizabeth*, in which he went whaling to the Southern fishery in the 1830s. He was also master of the *William Wallace*, whaling in 1836. Hezel, *Foreign ships in Micronesia*, q.v. no. 120, p. 117, refers to incident involving *Elizabeth*, Capt. Finnis, at Ebon, Marshall Islands, 16 Oct. 1833, reported in *Sydney Herald*, 2 Dec. 1833.

581   FLOWER, William, 1831-1899, "Whales, and British and colonial whale fisheries", *Proceedings of the Royal Colonial Institute*, 26 (1894-95), 80-100, partic. 96 ff.

582   FREYCINET, L[ouis-Claude de Saulces] de, 1779-1842, "Pêche de la baleine" (with partic. ref. to whaling from Sydney), in vol. 2, pt. 3 of his *Voyage autour du monde, entrepris par ordre du Roi* . . . *exécuté sur les corvettes de S.M. l'*Uranie *et la* Physicienne, *pendant les années 1817, 1818, 1819 et 1820* . . . *Historique* . . . (2 vols. in 4), (Paris, Pillet Aîné, 1839; pp. 917-1470), 964-6.
See also "Détails sur la pêche de la baleine" in the above, vol. 1, pt. 2 (Paris, 1828; pp. 543-734), 501-7, for information on sperm whaling techniques etc. with partic. ref. to area near Timor.

583 GALLAGHER, Robert S., "Castaways on forbidden shores", *American Heritage*, 19:4 (1968), 34-7.
Wreck of whaleship *Lawrence* on Etorofu, Kuriles, 1846.

584 GILL, J.C.H., "Genesis of the Australian whaling industry: its development up to 1850", *Royal Historical Society of Queensland, Year Book of Proceedings*, 8:1 (1965-66), 111-36.

585 GOODRICH, Frank B[oot], 1826-1894, Pacific whaling refs. in chap. 49 of his *Man upon the sea: or, A history of maritime adventure, exploration, and discovery, from the earliest ages to the present time* (Philadelphia, J.B. Lippincott & Co., 1858; 544 pp.), 495-507, partic. 504 ff. Another ed. with title *Remarkable voyages: or, Man upon the sea* . . . , 1873; 560 pp. (same pagination for chap. 49).
Discusses the appearance of revenge-seeking whales in the 1820s, "Mocha Dick", and the sinking of the *Essex* and *Ann Alexander*.

586 GRATTAN, C. Hartley, "Sealing . . . whaling . . . guano . . . gold . . . trade . . .", chap. 9 of his *The United States and the Southwest Pacific*, American Foreign Policy Library (Cambridge, Mass., Harvard University Press, 1961; xii, 273 pp.), 83-103. Endp. map, bibliog., notes, index.

587 ———, References to whaling in "The islands as No Man's Lands" and "The islands enter world politics", chaps. 11 and 12 in his *The Southwest Pacific to 1900: a modern history*, University of Michigan "History of the Modern World" series (Ann Arbor, University of Michigan Press, [1963]; xiv, 558 + xvii), 179-220. Maps, "suggested readings", index.

588 GREENWOOD, Gordon, "The contact of American whalers, sealers and adventurers with the New South Wales settlement", *Journal and Proceedings of the Royal Australian Historical Society*, 29:3 (1943), 133-56.
Also printed as chap. 3 of his *Early American-Australian relations from the arrival of the Spaniards in America to the close of 1830* ([Carlton, Vic.], Melbourne University Press in assoc. with Oxford University Press, 1944; x, 184 pp.), 63-96. Pls., bibliog., index.

589 GUÉRIN, Fernand, "Robert Surcouf, armateur à la pêche à la baleine", *Courrier Maritime de France*, 40: 7 (1 Feb. 1936), 3-4.
Although not related directly to whaling in the Pacific, this article contains important documentary material on the equipping and crew of the *Victor* and the *Africain* of Saint-Malo, owned by Robert Surcouf, in period 1819-22.

590 GUNSON, W.N., "Europeans in the Pacific Islands: beachcombers, whalers and traders", series no. 821 in *World conference on records: preserving our heritage August 12-15, 1980*, vol. 10, Australasian and Polynesian family and local history (Salt Lake City, Utah, Corporation of the President of the Church of Jesus Christ of Latter-day Saints, 1980; various pagings), 1-14.

591   HACKLER, Rhoda E.A., "The voice of commerce", *Hawaiian Journal of History*, 3 (1969), 42-9.
Discusses career of John Coffin Jones, U.S. agent for commerce and seamen, Hawaii, 1820-39.

592   HADFIELD, Robert L., "The hero of the 'Sharon' ", chap. 8 of his *Mutiny at sea* (London, Geoffrey Bles, 1937; New York, E.P. Dutton & Co., 1938; vii, 246 pp.), 134-56. Frontis., pls. Reprinted Stanfordville, N.Y., Earl M. Coleman Enterprises, 1979.
Hadfield places *Sharon* mutiny in the Atlantic. Philip F. Purrington, in his "Anatomy of a mutiny", q.v. below, no. 693 gives evidence for its location in the Pacific. See also Irvin Anthony, "The Sharon", no. 514 above.

593   [HAMILTON, Robert, M.D.], "Third genus - cachalot: the spermaceti whale", "South Sea fishery", in his *The natural history of the ordinary cetacea*, vol. 6 of *Mammalia* in *The naturalist's library*, conducted by Sir William Jardine (Edinburgh and London, W.H. Lizars; Dublin, W. Curry, Jun. and Co., 1837; xv [xii], 17-264 [+ 24, 12] pp.), 154-80, partic. 169 ff. Illus. (col. engravings). Reprinted 1840, 1846?, 1852, 1861.
Much information from Beale's whaling voyage on British, American and N.S.W. whaling.

594   HARMER, Sidney F., 1862-1950, "History of whaling", *Proceedings, Linnean Society of London*, 140 (1927-28), 51-95, partic. 62-6. Appendix, bibliog.
Presidential address.

595   HARRIS, Sheldon H., "Mutiny on *Junior*", *American Neptune*, 21:2 (1961), 110-29. Reprinted in Ernest Dodge (ed.), *Thirty years of The American Neptune*. (Cambridge, Mass., Harvard University Press, 1972; xiii, 300 pp.), 163-82.
Mutiny culminating off southeast coast of Australia late in 1857 on *Junior* of New Bedford. See also no. 85.

596   HARROP, A.J., "France and New Zealand", chap. 5 of his *England and New Zealand: from Tasman to the Taranaki War* (London, Methuen & Co. Ltd, [1920]; xxiv, 326 pp.), partic. 107-14. Bibliog., index.
French colonisation ambitions and the desire to protect whaling interests in New Zealand waters discussed.

597 HART, Francis R[ussell], "The New England whale-fisheries", *Publications of the Colonial Society of Massachusetts*, 26 (1924), 65-79. Pls., facsims.
Read at meeting of the Society, 24 April 1924. See partic. p. 74 ff. for Pacific whaling refs.

598 HARTWELL, R.M., "Whaling and sealing", chap. 7 of his *The economic development of Van Diemen's Land 1820-1850* ([Carlton, Vic.], Melbourne University Press, [1954]; xii, 273 pp.), 139-43, partic. 142-3. Maps, tables (see partic. Table 19, p. 40), bibliog., index.

599 HARTWIG, Georg, "Der Pottfischfang im grossen Ocean", chap. 2 of his *Die Inseln des grossen Oceans im Natur- und Volkerleben* (Wiesbaden, C.W. Kreidel, 1861; xvi, 544 pp.), 15-17. Maps. See also Swedish ed. of the above, *Söderhafvets öar framställda i natur- och folklif* (Stockholm, Tryckt Hos P.G. Berg, 1862; xvi, 512 pp.), 14-25. Frontis., maps.

600 HAWES, Charles Boardman, "The story of the ship Globe of Nantucket", *Atlantic Monthly*, 132:6 (1923), 769-79.

601 HEAD, Timothy E. and Gavan DAWS, "The Bonins—isles of contention", *American Heritage*, 19:2 (1968), 58-64, 69-74.
See partic. pp. 58-64 for whaling refs.

602 HEGEMANN, Fr[iedrich], Captain, "Der Walfang im Stillen Ozean und nördlich der Berings-Strasse während der sechziger Jahre dieses Jahrhunderts', *Annalen der Hydrographie und Maritimen Meteorologie*, 21 (1893), 65-7.

603 HEINE, William C., "*Charles W. Morgan*: United States", in his *Historic ships of the world* (Adelaide, Rigby; New York, G.P. Putnam's Sons, 1977; 156 pp.), 31-7. Illus., bibliog., index.

604 HEIZER, Robert F. (ed.), "Techniques and implements of the American whale fishery: from a early Japanese account", *California Historical Society Quarterly*, 32:3 (1953), 225-9 + 4 pls.
Based on account in vol. 3 of *Bandan* - observations made by Jirokichi, the only literate member of a group of 13 fishermen from Toyama, whose ship became derelict between Hakodate (Hokkaido) and Edo (Tokyo) in 1838, and who were rescued by an American whaler in April 1839.

605 HERMAN, Louis M., "Humpback whales in Hawaiian waters: a study in historical ecology", *Pacific Science*, 33:1 (1979), 1-15. Bibliog.

606 HEZEL, Francis X. and M.L. BERG (eds.), "Wood, water and women: whaling days at Ponape and Kosrae 1840-1860", [chap. 8] of their [*Micro-

nesia: winds of change.] *A Book of readings on Micronesian history*, ESEA title IV-B (Saipan, Omnibus Program for Social Studies Cultural Heritage, Trust Territory of the Pacific Islands, 1979; iii, 538 pp.), 172-99. Illus., maps, appendices, source refs.

607   [HODGKINSON, Richard], "Eber Bunker - whale ship captain of Parramatta", *Newsletter, Royal Australian Historical Society*, 158 (1976), 4-5.

608   HOEHLING, A.A., "The *Essex*", chap. 2 of his *Great ship disasters*, 1st ed. (New York, Cowles Book Co., Inc., [1971]; vi, 250 pp.), 19-26. Bibliog. refs.

609   HÖVER, Otto, "Walfang", "Weltreise der 'Virginia' ", "Südseewalfang" and "Südseeverein" in his *Von der Galiot zum Fünfmaster: unsere Segelschiffe in der Weltschiffahrt 1780-1930* (Bremen, Angelsachsen-Verlag, [1934]. Reprinted Norderstedt, Chronik-der-Seefahrt-Verlag Heinemann, 1975; 518 pp.), 194-200. Illus., map.
Discusses role of Bremen whalers in South Sea whaling, 1830s-1850s.

610   HOHMAN, Elmo P., "Wages, risk, and profits in the whaling industry", *Quarterly Journal of Economics*, 40 (1926), 644-71.

611   JANSSEN, Albrecht, "Südseefischerei" in his *Tausend Jahre deutscher Walfang* (Leipzig, F.A. Brockhaus, 1937; 260 pp.), 176-84. Illus., pls., maps, bibliog., glossary.

612   JEFFERY, Walter, 1861-1922, "The Americans in the South Seas" in Louis Becke and Walter Jeffery, *The tapu of Banderah* (London, C. Arthur Pearson; Philadelphia, Lippincott, 1901; vi, 315 pp.), 245-57.
Importance of American whaling and sealing enterprise in the Pacific from the time of the first settlement in New South Wales. Note: Jeffery's authorship of this sketch is confirmed in A. Grove Day, *Louis Becke* (Melbourne, 1967), p. 156, n. 15.

613   JENKINS, James Travis, "The American sperm whale fishery", in chap. 4 of his *Whales and modern whaling* (London, A.F. & G. Witherby, [1932]; 233 pp.), 99-112. Frontis., pls., bibliog.

614   JOHNSTON, George H., "The colonial whalers", *Blue Peter: the Magazine of Sea Travel*, 13:133 (1933), 162-6.
Partic. ref. to Tasmanian whalers, but includes deep sea whaling.

615   JONES, A.G.E., "Captain Peter Kemp and Kemp Land", *Mariner's Mirror*, 54:3 (1968), 233-43.
Includes some information on British South Seas whaling activities.

616 ———, "The British southern whale and seal fisheries", Pts. 1 and 2 (Pt. 2 subtitled: "The principal operators"), *Great Circle*, 3:1 and 2 (1981), 20-9, 90-102. Notes on sources.

617 ———, "The South Seas whaling voyage of the 'Comet', 1812-1815", *Great Circle*, 5: 2 (1983), 98-104 (includes 2 appendices. App. 2 lists ships spoken by *Comet* during cruise).
The *Comet* of Hull, Captain Scurr, sailed to South Seas 5 Sept. 1812 and arrived home 9 December 1815. Reached Pacific Ocean via Cape Horn early 1813 and cruised on Galápagos grounds, returning to England via Cape Horn. Captain Scurr died at Talcahuano on 17 June 1815.

618 JONES, Maude, "Whaling in Hawaiian waters", *Paradise of the Pacific*, 50 (Apr. 1938), 20.
Brief outline of whale fishery grants in Hawaiian waters 1847-58.

619 JÜRGENS, Hans Peter, "Der Walfang in der Südsee", in his *Abenteuer Walfang: Wale, Männer und das Meer* (Herford, Koehlers Verlagsgesellschaft MBH, [1977]; 136 pp.), 105-13. Pls., illus., bibliog., index.

620 KENDALL, Henry, 1839-1882, "Sperm whaling", *Australian Journal* (Melbourne), 5:54 (Nov. 1869), 150-1.

621 KENNY, Robert W., "Yankee whalers at the Bay of Islands", *American Neptune*, 12:1 (1952), 22-44.
Refs. to the career of James Reddy Clendon, a British subject, who received a "recess appointment" as American Consul at Bay of Islands in Oct. 1838, and who served there from 27 May 1839 to 31 Dec. 1842.

622 KING, William H.D., "Arctic whaling fleet disaster", *Sixty-Third Annual Report of the Hawaiian Historical Society for the Year 1954*, (1955), 19-28.
Only one out of the seven Hawaiian whalers registered under the Hawaiian flag with the fleet escaped from ice (1871).

623 KOSTER, John, "The whales' best friend: Confederate captain who would not surrender", *Oceans*, 12:3 (1979), 3-7.
Captain Waddell of the Confederate raider *Shenandoah*, and his attacks on the New England whaling fleet, as well as the sinking of four whaleships at Ponape in 1865. See also Mary A. Browning, no. 540 "The blue & gray in Ponape", above.

624 KUGLER, Richard C., "The penetration of the Pacific by American whalemen in the 19th century", in *The opening of the Pacific: image and reality*, Maritime Monographs and Reports, 2 (London, National Maritime Museum, 1971; 27 pp.), 20-7.

625   KUYKENDALL, Ralph S. (with intro. chaps by Herbert E. Gregory), "The whaling era", chap. 17 of their *A history of Hawaii* (New York, Macmillan Co., 1926; x, 375 pp.), 189-97. Frontis., illus., maps, appendix, index, "further reading" for each chap. Later eds. 1927, 1928, 1938, 1940.

See index for other whaling refs. Note: This work prepared under direction of Historical Commission of the Territory of Hawaii.

626   _____, "The whaling industry", in chap. 16, "Commercial and agricultural progress" of his *The Hawaiian kingdom 1778-1854: foundation and transformation* (Honolulu, University of Hawaii Press, 1938; vii, 453 pp.), 305-14. Frontis., illus., endp., maps, footnotes, appendices, index. Later eds. 1947, 1957, 1968, 1978 (University Press of Hawaii, with preface by Gavan Daws).

See index for other whaling refs.

627   _____, "Decline of the whaling industry" in chap. 5, "From whales to sugar" of his *The Hawaiian kingdom 1854-1874: twenty critical years* (Honolulu, University of Hawaii Press, 1953; x, 310 pp.), 135-40. Illus., refs, endp. maps, index.

See index for other whaling refs.

628   LACOUTURE, J.E., Captain, U.S.N. (Retd.), "Lahaina - the whaling capital of the Pacific" *Historic Nantucket*, 29: 4 (1982), 16-22 (incl. note on author).

Survey of Lahaina's whaling history, with concluding section on work of Lahaina Restoration Foundation.

629   LAJONKAIRE, Paul de, "Des primes à la pêche", *Journal des Économistes*, 2 (1852), 80-5.

See partic. p. 82 ff for refs to whaling and need to encourage French whaling.

630   LANDAUER, Lyndall B., "Charles M. Scammon: from seaman to civilized whaler to naturalist", *California History*, 61: 1 (1982), 46-57.

Scammon became a whaler of necessity from about 1853-63, and was engaged in whaling on Pacific coast of U.S., Bering Sea and all areas of Pacific Ocean. See no. 713 below under Charles M[elville] Scammon, "The American whale-fishery".

631   LANG, John Dunmore, 1799-1878, Accounts of the sperm and black-whale fishery of New South Wales in chap. 8, "View of the present state of the colony under Major-General Bourke" in vol. 1 of his *An historical and statistical account of New South Wales, both as a penal settlement and as a British colony* (2 vols.), (London, Cochrane and M'Crone, 1834; xiv, 401 pp.), 299-308. Fold. map. See also chap. 9, "View of the amount and distribution of the colonial population, of the produce and trade, and of the revenue and expenditure of New South Wales" in vol. 1 of 2nd ed. (London, A.J. Valpy; Edinburgh, Bell and Bradfute, 1837; xii, 466 [+1] pp.), 375-83 and Appendices 14 and 15, 458-60. Fold. map. (Ferguson 1806 and 2289)

632   LANMAN, James R., "The American whale fishery", *Merchants' Magazine and Commercial Review*, 3:5 (Nov. 1840), 361-94, partic. 370 ff.

633   LAWSON, Will, "Whalers, ancient and modern", *Australian National Review*, 5:25 (1939), 55-60.

634   _____, and The Ship Lovers' Society of Tasmania, "Whale ships and whaling", chap. 4 of their *Blue gum clippers and whale ships of Tasmania*, Australiana Society Pub. (Melbourne, Georgian House, [1947]; 261 pp.), 43-80. Frontis., pls., ports., appendix, index.

635   LECUCQ, L[ouis], 1822-1855, "Pêche à la baleine", in his *Question de Tahiti* (Paris, Librairie Militaire de Blot, 1849; 126 pp.), 31-5. (Mitchell Library)

636   LEVER, R.J.A.W., "Whales and whaling in the western Pacific", *South Pacific Bulletin*, 14:2 (1964), 33-6.

637   LEVI, Werner, "Whaling and sealing", chap. 3 of his *American-Australian relations* (Minneapolis, Minn., University of Minnesota Press; London, Geoffrey Cumberlege, Oxford University Press, [1947]; [iii], 184 pp.), 25-36. Map, bibliog., index.

638   LITTEN [SILVERMAN], Jane, "Whaler versus missionary at Lahaina", *Hawaii Historical Review*, 1:4 (1963), 68-74. Bibliog. note.
Riots by whalemen at Lahaina in 1825 and 1827.

639   _____, "Lahaina anchorage", *Historic Nantucket*, 8:3 (Jan. 1961), 12-24.
Significance of Lahaina anchorage to American shipping, particularly whalers, in first half of 19th century.

640   LITTLE, Barbara, "The sealing and whaling industry in Australia before 1850", *Australian Economic History Review*, 9:2 (1969), 109-27.

641   LITTLEFIELD, L.A., "Fitting out a whaler", *Old Dartmouth Historical Sketches*, 14 (June 1906), 4-13.

642   LOCKLEY, Ronald M., "The whale hunters", [chap. 6] of his *Whales, dolphins and porpoises*, illus. by Elizabeth Sutton (Newton Abbot and London, David & Charles, [1979]; [Sydney], Methuen of Australia, 1979; 200 pp.), 107-21, partic. 116 ff. Pls., illus., refs., index.

643   "Loss of the Essex and other vessels by attacks of whales", chap. 11 of *Voyage and venture: or, The pleasures and perils of a sailor's life* (Philadelphia, H.C. Peck and T. Bliss, 1854 and 1857; viii, 300 pp.), 157-60. Frontis., illus.

This book should not be confused with *Voyage and venture: or, Perils by sea and land*, q.v. no. 764 below under "The whale fishery and its hazards". (Huntress, *Checklist*, 404c)

644   "Loss of the whale ship Essex", in *The mariner's chronicle, of shipwrecks, fires, famines, and other disasters at sea; containing narratives of the most noted calamities and providential deliverances which have resulted from maritime enterprise, both in Europe and America; together with an account of the whale fishery, sketches of nautical life, steam boat disasters, &c. . . .* , 2 vols. (Boston, Charles Gaylord, 1834; viii, 335; vi, 336 pp.), I, 34-6. Illus., pl.

This is a much briefer account than that published in the one vol. edition of *The mariner's chronicle*, q.v. above under "Destruction of the *Essex* . . .", which was based on Captain Pollard's narrative. It is in the third person, omits any mention of cannibalism, and has less detail about the survivors. For further information about the publishing history of the American editions of *The mariner's chronicle* see R.J. Silveira de Braganza, *The Hill Collection*, 2, 486-7. For details of Alexander Duncan's *The mariner's chronicle . . .* (6 vols., London, [1808?]), on which the American eds. were based, see Ferguson, *Bibliography of Australia*, 1, 462.

645   Lydgate, J.M., "Hilo fifty years ago", *Hawaiian Almanac and Annual for 1923* (Dec. 1922), partic. 101-2, 106.

Refs. to Thomas Spencer, a well-known Hawaiian whaling figure in the 1850s. See also under Thomas G. Thrum, "Thomas Spencer . . .", no. 747 below.

646   Macdonald, Barrie, "Early contacts and the beginnings of trade", chap. 2 of his *Cinderellas of the Empire: towards a history of Kiribati and Tuvalu* (Canberra, London and Miami, Australian National University Press, 1982; xx, 335 pp.), 14-30, partic. 16-26. Map, notes, bibliog., index.

Discusses importance of whalers in early trading contacts, particularly with southern Kiribati and Ocean Island.

647   McKee, Linda, " 'Mad Jack' and the missionaries", *American Heritage*, 22:3 (1971), 30-7, 85-7.

Lieutenant Jack Percival of the *Dolphin*, who was sent in pursuit of the *Globe* mutineers. See partic. pp. 30-5 for whaling refs. Article concentrates mainly on events on Oahu after *Dolphin*'s arrival there in 1826.

648   McKibben, Frank P., "The whaling disaster of 1871", *New England Magazine*, 18:4 (June 1898), 490-5.

Loss of 34 whaleships from San Francisco, Honolulu and New England near Bering Strait. Over 1,200 survivors landed on Hawaiian shores in October 1871.

649 McNab, Robert, "First whaling trade, 1801 to 1806", chap. 8 of his *From Tasman to Marsden: a history of northern New Zealand from 1642 to 1818* (Dunedin, J. Wilkie & Co., Ltd., 1914; xiv + i, 236 pp.), 95-108.

650 Marshall, Mac and Leslie B., "Holy and unholy spirits: the effects of missionization on alcohol use in eastern Micronesia", *Journal of Pacific History*, 11: 3-4 (1976), 135-66.
Includes discussion of the part played by whalers in the introduction of alcohol in eastern Micronesia.

651 Martin, Kenneth R., "The successful whaling voyage of the *Lucy Ann*, of Wilmington, 1837-1839", *Delaware History*, 15:2 (1972), 85-103.

652 _____, "Yankee whalemen and the enigma of the avenging whale", *Mankind* (Los Angeles), 3:11 (1973), 54-61.

653 _____, "Wilmington's first whaling voyage, 1834-1837", *Delaware History*, 16:2 (1974), 152-70.
Voyage of the *Ceres* to the Pacific Ocean.

654 _____, "A whale attack on the whale ship *Joseph Maxwell*, 1845", *Melville Society Extracts*, 27 (Sept. 1976), 1-4.
Joseph Maxwell, Captain William H. Perry, of Fairhaven on whaling voyage 13 Dec. 1843 to 27 Nov. 1847. During cruise in Pacific in 1845, somewhere on Off-shore grounds east of Nukuhiva, encountered rogue whale. Incident described in logbook of first mate, W.M. Christ. Author also discusses generally incidence of whale attacks on ships.

655 _____, "Let the natives come aboard; whalemen and islanders in Micronesia", *Glimpses of Micronesia and the Western Pacific*, 18:3 (1978), 38-44.

656 _____, "Information wanted: respecting Micronesia's beachcombers", *Glimpses of Micronesia and the Western Pacific*, 19:4 (1979), 79-83.
The whalemen - beachcombers of Micronesia.

657 _____, "American whaleships in the Mariana Islands", *Guam Recorder*, 9 (1979), 3-9.

658 _____, "Maui during the whaling boom: the travels of Captain Gilbert Pendleton, Jr.", *Hawaiian Journal of History*, 13 (1979), 59-66.

659 Marvin, Winthrop L., "The Yankee whalemen", chap. 8 of his *The American merchant marine: its history and romance from 1620 to 1902*

(London, Sampson Low, Marston & Co. Ltd.; New York, Charles Scribner's Sons, 1902; xvi, [ii], 444 pp.), 132-72. Index. Reprinted New York, Charles Scribner's Sons, 1919, with bibliog. refs.

660   MASON, John Thomson, "Formerly midshipman of the 'Shenandoah' ", "The last of the Confederate cruisers," sect. 4 of "Confederate commerce-destroyers", *Century Illustrated Monthly Magazine*, 56, ns 34 (Aug. 1898), 600-10, partic. 608.
Contains ref. to the destruction of four whaleships at Ponape in 1865.

661   MAUDE, H. E., "Whaling discoveries", in chap. 3 "Post-Spanish discoveries in the Central Pacific" of his *Of islands and men: studies in Pacific history* (Melbourne, Oxford University Press, 1968; xxii, 397 pp.), 121-32. Pls., endp., maps, bibliog.
Other whaling refs. interspersed in text.

662   MAURY, M[atthew] F[ontaine], Lieutenant, U.S. Navy, 1806-1873, "Letters from whalemen" in his *Explanations and sailing directions to accompany the wind and current charts . . .* , 7th ed., enlarged and improved (Philadelphia, E.C. and J. Biddle, 1855; xxxvi, 869, 34 pp.), 257-87. See also earlier and later eds.
These are general accounts of whales and whaling, not referring to the Pacific area exclusively.

663   MICHENER, James A. and A. Grove DAY, "Rascals in paradise: the *Globe* mutineers", chap. 1 of their *Rascals in paradise* (London, Secker & Warburg, 1957; 384 pp.; New York, Random House, Inc., [1957]; 374 pp.), 13-50 (Lond. ed.). Endp., map, bibliog. Other eds., New York, Bantam Books, 1958; 325 pp.: London, Transworld Publishers, [1960]; 443 pp.

664   MILLAR, David P., "Whalers, flax traders and Maoris of the Cook Strait area: an historical study in cultural confrontation", *Dominion Museum Records in Ethnology* (Wellington), 2:6 (1971), 57-64, partic. 57-60.

665   MOMENT, David, "The business of whaling in America in the 1850s", *Business History Review*, 31:3 (1957), 261-91.

666   MOOREHEAD, Alan, "The bloodstained ice", chap. 2, pt. 3 of his *The fatal impact: an account of the invasion of the South Pacific 1767-1840* (London, Hamish Hamilton, [1966]; xiv, 230 pp.), 191-204. Pls., maps, appendix, bibliog., index.
See partic. pp. 197-204 for refs. to pelagic whaling in the South Pacific.

667   MORGAN, Theodore, "Whaling" and "The peak of the whaling trade, and collapse", chaps. 5 and 9 of his *Hawaii: a century of economic change*

1778-1876 (Cambridge, Mass., Harvard University Press, 1948; xi, 260 pp.), 74-85, 140-53. Appendices, bibliog., index.

668   MORISON, Samuel Eliot, "The whalers, 1815-1860", chap. 20 of his *The maritime history of Massachusetts 1783-1860* (Boston and New York, Houghton Mifflin Co., 1921; xiv, 401 pp. Boston, Houghton Mifflin - Cambridge, Riverside Press, 1941; xii, 2, 421 pp.), 314-26 (1941 ed.). Frontis., pls., illus., appendices, bibliog. 1921 ed. reprinted 1922, 1924, 1925, and pub. London, Heinemann, 1923. 1941 ed. reprinted 1961 Boston, Houghton Mifflin etc. and Toronto, Thomas Allen as "Sentry" ed.; 1979, Boston, Northeastern University Press in Northeastern Classics ser.

669   MORSE, Abner, Reverend, "New missionary field among seamen", extract of a letter from Rev. A. Morse of Nantucket, dated 20 Oct. 1821, taken from the *Religious Intelligencer, Christian Spectator* (New Haven), 4:1 (1822), 46-7.
Discusses formation of Bible and Tract Society to supply whale ships with such material, and the influence of whalemen on pagan natives of the Pacific and elsewhere.

670   MORTON, Harry A., "Whaling", chap. 10 of his *The wind commands: sailors and sailing ships in the Pacific*, with drawings by Don Hermansen and Paul Dwillies from orig. drawings and research by Peggy Morton (Middletown, Conn., Wesleyan University Press and Vancouver, The University Press of British Columbia, [1975]; St. Lucia, Qld., University of Queensland Press, 1980; xxvii, 498 pp.), 136-47 and notes 413-5. Pls., illus., figs., endp. map, bibliog., index.

671   "NARRATIVE OF ACCIDENT AND DISASTER" - "Destruction of a large whale ship", *Household Narrative of Current Events*, (28 Sept. - 28 Oct. 1851), 251-2.
Report of *Ann Alexander*'s sinking by sperm whale.

672   NEWMAN, C.E.T., "Taking over", chap. 15 in sect. E, "The stewardship of Charles Hook" of his *The spirit of Wharf House: Campbell enterprise from Calcutta to Canberra 1788-1930* ([Sydney], Angus & Robertson Ltd, 1961; xvi, 260 pp.), 94-101. Frontis., port., illus., pls., refs., index.
See partic. pp. 98-101 for activities of the whaler *Spring Grove* in 1810.

673   NEWTON, A.P., "Forgotten deeds of the Empire: whalers of the South Pacific", *Saturday Review*, 160 (28 Sept. 1935), 253.

674   NICHOLAS, William H., "American pathfinders in the Pacific", *National Geographic Magazine*, 89:5 (1946), 617-40.
Impact of whalers on Pacific discovery and exploration discussed *inter alia*.

675   NORMAN, L[eslie], "Colourful days", chap. 2 of his *Pioneer shipping in Tasmania: whaling, sealing, piracy, shipwrecks, etc. in early Tasmania* (Hobart, J. Walch & Sons, [1938]; reprinted Hobart, Drinkwater Publishing Co., 1979; 220 pp.), 22-35, partic. 27-30. Pls., illus., charts.

Includes some material on sperm whaling.

676   ———, "Whaling from earliest times", chap. 11 in pt. 2 of his *Sea wolves and bandits: sealing, whaling, smuggling and piracy, wild men of Van Diemen's Land, bushrangers and wreckers* (Hobart, J. Walch & Sons, 1946 [i.e. 1947]; reprinted Hobart, Drinkwater Publishing Co., 1979; 208 pp.), partic. 196-200.

677   ———, "The zenith of Tasmanian whaling" and following sections in chap. 3, "Trypots" of his *Haunts of the blue whale* (Hobart, O.B.M. Publishing, 1978; xv, 156 pp.), 31-50.

Contains account of the voyage of the Hobart whaling brig *Grecian*, 1861-64, and its part in the removal of Tongans to work in Fiji.

678   NORTHEY, Richard P., "A brief account of the whaling industry in Salem, 1820-1860, with some excerpts from the logs of Salem whalers", *Collections, Essex Institute*, 75 (July 1939), 234-48.

679   NOUGARET, Jules, "La pêche de la baleine", *Revue des Deux Mondes*, 39: 83 (1869), 707-29.

Mainly concerned with rise and decline of French whaling, with description of whaling operations. See p. 717 for Pacific refs.

680   OLIVER, Douglas L., "Whalers, traders, and missionaries: 1780-1850", chap. 8 of his *The Pacific Islands* (Cambridge, Mass., Harvard University Press, 1951; [xi], 313 pp.), 73-86. Rev. ed., Garden City, N.Y., Anchor Books, Natural History Library, Doubleday & Co. Inc. in cooperation with American Museum of Natural History, 1961; (xxiii, 456 pp.), 97-116. Illus., "principal sources and additional reading", index.

Note: Rev. ed.. also pub. Cambridge, Mass., Harvard University Press, 1962; Honolulu, University Press of Hawaii, 1975, 1977.

681   O'MAY, Harry (comp.), "Offshore whaling" in his *Wooden hookers of Hobart Town* (Tasmania [sic], L.G. Shea, Government Printer, n.d.; reprinted Hobart, T.J. Hughes, Government Printer, 1978; 137 + vi pp.), 29-31. Pls.

682   OMMANNEY, F.D., "Yankee sperm whaling", "Yankee whaling ships", "The kill" and "The decline of Yankee whaling" in chap. 4, "History of whaling" of his *Lost leviathan* (London, Hutchinson, [1971]; 280 pp.), 84-92. Illus., pls., appendix, list of refs., index.

See also refs. to sperm whales, bay whaling, in index.

683   OWEN, Russell, "American claims in the Pacific: discoveries of early American whalers cited in island dispute with Britain", *Far Eastern Review*, 34:5 (1938), 173.

684   PALAU COMMUNITY ACTION AGENCY, "Traders and whalers", chap. 4 of its *A history of Palau*, vol. 2, *Traders and whalers. Spanish administration. German administration* ([Koror, Palau], Palau Community Action Agency, [1977]; x, 133-271), 133-79. Illus., notes, bibliog.

685   PEARSON, Michael, "The technology of whaling in Australian waters in the 19th century", *Australian Journal of Historical Archaeology*, 1 (1983), 40-54.

Examines whaling techniques and artifacts used in shore-based and ship-based whaling in Australia in 19th century.

686   PEASE, Z[ephaniah] W., "The history of the building of the Bourne Whaling Museum. With reminiscences of old counting rooms", *Old Dartmouth Historical Sketches*, 44 (Apr. 1916), 13-21.

Includes information about Jonathan Bourne, whaling merchant and ship-owner, and his ships, partic. the *Lagoda*, many of which went whaling in the Pacific.

687   "PÊCHE FRANÇAISE DE LA BALEINE DANS LES MERS DU SUD EN 1829", *Le Navigateur: Journal des Naufrages et des Autres Événements Nautiques*, 1:6 (Sept. 1829), 293-335.

No specific Pacific refs., but general survey of French whaling - history, methods, armaments, whaleboats; types of whales and places of resort; comparison between French and American usages; plea for greater French enterprise. (Library, University of California, Berkeley)

688   PERRY, John W., "The gallant huntress: the whaleship *Charles W. Morgan* in Micronesia, 1852", *Micronesian Reporter*, 23:4 (1975), 35-7.

689   ———, "Conflicts of interest: four case studies of clashes between whalers and Micronesians", *Glimpses of Micronesia and the Western Pacific*, 18:3 (1978), 20-4.

690   PHILP, J.E., "Whaling days of the past", *Bookshelf Miscellany* (Hobart), (1933-34), 49-53.

691   PINSEL, Marc I., "The wind and current chart series produced by Matthew Fontaine Maury", *Navigation: Journal of the Institute of Navigation*, 28:2 (1981), 123-37.

See partic. pp. 130, 133-4 for refs. to Maury's whale charts (q.v. under M.F. Maury, above).

692   PURCELL, H.G., "Hawaii and the whaling fleet", *Nautical Research Journal*, 7:1-2 (1955), 2-6.

Includes material on Hawaiian whalers lost in Bering Strait in 1871.

693   PURRINGTON, Philip F., "Anatomy of a mutiny", *American Neptune*, 27:2 (1967), 98-110.

Account of mutiny on board the *Sharon* on a whaling voyage in the Pacific, 1841-4.

694   RABLING, Harold, "The great age of whaling", chap. 7 of his *The story of the Pacific: explorers of the earth's mightiest ocean* (New York, W.W. Norton & Co. Inc., 1965; 191 [+1] pp.), 121-44. Illus., notes.

695   "THE RESOLUTE WHALE", *Chambers's Pocket Miscellany*, 2 (1852), 167-71.

Describes the sinking of the *Ann Alexander* by a whale in the Pacific Ocean. Quoted in full in Janez Stanonik, *Moby-Dick: the myth and the symbol* . . . , Appendix 2, 199-202 (see no. 305).

696   REYNOLDS, J[eremiah] N., 1799-1858, "Report on islands discovered by whalers in the Pacific", House Executive Documents, 23rd Congress, 2nd Session, vol. III, Doc. no. 105. (1835), 1-28.

Report of investigation completed by 1828, drawn up from conversations with whaling captains. See also Reynolds's *Address on the subject of a surveying and exploring expedition* . . . , no. 233.

697   RICHARDS, Rhys, "American whaling on the Chatham grounds", pts. 1 and 2, *Historic Nantucket*, 18:2 (1970), 26-35; 18:3 (1971), 29-40.

See also nos. 234 & 235.

698   RIENZI, G[régoire] L[ouis] Domeny de, 1789-1843, "Pêche du cachalot . . .", sect. 107 of "Malaisie" in vol. 1 of his *Océanie ou cinquième partie du monde: revue géographique et ethnographique de la Malaisie, de la Micronésie, de la Polynésie et de la Mélanésie* . . . (3 vols.), in "L'univers. Histoire et description de tous les peuples" series (Paris, Firmin Didot Frères, 1836; 399 [+2] pp.), 214-220. Fold. maps, illus., gen. index (vol. 3).

Whaling and the whale fishery in the South Seas generally as well as in the Molucca Sea discussed. (Australian National University Library - Rare Book Collection)

699   RIESENBERG, Felix, "Sealers and whalers", [chap. 13] of his *Pacific Ocean* (New York, London, Whittlesey House, McGraw-Hill Book Co., Inc.,

[1940]; 322 pp.), 226-45. Another ed. London, Museum Press, [1947]; 284 pp., 200-16. Illus., maps (by Stephen J. Voorhies), index.

700   "RISE AND PROGRESS OF SPERM WHALE FISHERY" (from Beale's *Natural History of the sperm whale*), *New Zealand Journal*, 2:30 (1841), 69-71.

701   ROBOTTI, Frances Diane, "Whalers as explorers and discoverers of the Pacific", *Nautical Research Journal*, 7:1-2 (1955), 23-5.

702   RONCK, Ronn, "Thaaar she blooooows! A chronicle of whaling in Micronesia", *Glimpses of Micronesia and the Western Pacific*, 18:3 (1978), 20-4.

703   ROE, Michael, "Australia's place in the 'Swing to the East', 1788-1810", *Historical Studies*, 8:30 (1958), 202-13.
Includes discussion of British whaling background in settlement of Australia.

704   ROSENHOUSE, Leo, "Whaling: from New Bedford to Sausalito", *Compass* (Mobil Oil Corp.), 44:3 (1974), 29-33.
Explains departure of many New Bedford whalemen to Californian coast to escape taxation and other disadvantages in late 18th and early 19th centuries.

705   ROSS, Irwin, "The strangest mutiny", *Compass*, 44:4 (1974), 26-30.
Mutiny on board New Bedford whaler *Junior* in 1857 and events thereafter, with conclusion of affair off Cape Howe, S.E. Australia. See no. 82.

706   RUSSELL, M[ichael], Right Reverend, LL.D., D.C.L., 1781-1848, South Sea whale fishery in chap. 11, "General remarks on the past and present condition of Polynesia" of his *Polynesia: or An historical account of the principal islands in the South Sea, including New Zealand; the introduction of Christianity; and the actual condition of the inhabitants in regard to civilization, commerce, and the arts of social life* (Edinburgh, Oliver & Boyd; London, Simpkin, Marshall & Co., 1842, 1843, 1845, 1847?, 1849, 1850; 440 pp.), 420-5. Fold. map, index. Am. eds, New York, Harper & Row, 1842?, 1843, 1845, 1848; xv, 17-362 pp. Note: rev.ed., London and Edinburgh, Nelson and Sons, 1852; 486 pp., has no significant whaling refs.

707   RYDELL, Raymond A., "The whaling industry", chap. 4 of his *Cape Horn to the Pacific: the rise and decline of an ocean highway* (Berkeley and Los Angeles, University of California Press, 1952; xii, 213 pp.), 58-75. Maps, chap. notes, bibliog., index.

708   ST. CLAIR, Henry [comp.], "Mutiny on board the ship Globe", in his *The criminal calendar; or, An awful warning to the youth of America;*

being an account of the most notorious pirates, highwaymen and other male-
factors who have figured in this hemisphere. Compiled from the best au-
thorities (Boston, Frederic S. Hill, 1831; 356 pp.), 233-43. Pls. Later eds.
have title *The United States criminal calendar . . .; being an account of the*
most horrid murders, piracies, highway robberies, &c. &c. . . . (Boston,
Charles Gaylord, 1832, 1833, 1834 1835; Boston and New York, 1840).
(American Imprints 9077; Sabin 75023)

709   SAKAMAKI, Shunzo, "Japan and the United States, 1790-1853: a study
of Japanese contacts with and conceptions of the United States and its people prior to the American expedition of 1853-4", *Transactions of the Asiatic*
Society of Japan, 2nd series, 18 (1939), 1-204.
See partic. pp. 11-86 for refs. to American whaleships in contact with Japan or with
shipwrecked Japanese seamen.

710   SANDERSON, Ivan T., "A-h-h, blo-o-o-w-s!", *American Heritage*, 12:1
(1960), 48-54, 63-4.
Note: Between pp. 54-63 is portfolio of scenes from "The panorama of a whaling
voyage round the world", painted by Benjamin Russell in collaboration with Caleb
Purrington, first exhibited in Dec. 1848. Canvas is 102 in. high and 1275 ft. long.

711   SANFORD, F.C., "Notes upon the history of the American whale
fishery", *Report of the Commissioner of Fish and Fisheries for 1882* (Washington, 1884), 205-20.

712   SAY, Horace, "Des primes d'encouragement pour les grandes pêches
de la morue, de la baleine et du cachalot", *Journal des Économistes*, 10: 1
(Jan. - May 1851), 87-93, partic. 92-3.

713   SCAMMON, Charles M[elville], Captain, U.S. Revenue Marine, 1825-
1911, "The American whale-fishery", pt. 3 of his *The marine mammals of*
the north-western coast of North America, described and illustrated. To-
gether with an account of the American whale-fishery (San Francisco, John
H. Carmany and Co.; New York, G.B. Putnam's Sons, 1874; 319, v pp.),
185-276, partic. 209 ff. Illus., appendix (of 4 pts.), index. Reprinted with
new intro. by Victor B. Scheffer and portrait of Scammon, New York, Dover
Publications, Inc.; Toronto, General Publishing Co. Ltd; London, Constable and Co., Ltd, [1968]. X, 319, v pp. Also Riverside, Calif., Manessier
Publishing Co., 1969; xlvi, 319, v pp., with new intro.
Appendix includes "Glossary of words and phrases used by whalemen" and "List of
stores and outfits for a first-class whale-ship, for a Cape Horn voyage . . . .". Note:
"The sperm whale", chap. 8 of this work has refs. to sinking of *Essex* and *Ann Alex-*
ander, pp. 78-9.

714   SCHMITT, Frederick P., "Oh, what a wild one he must have been!", *Yankee*, 36:6 (1972), 102-7.

"From the inception of whaling as an industry, it had been the custom to stamp a ship's name into every harpoon. As a result, many 'rogue' whales carried a record of their violent history in their flanks . . ." - from introduction to article.

715   [SEWARD, William H., 1801-1872], The whale fishery in the Pacific Ocean, in "Survey of the whaling grounds and routes of commerce on the Pacific Ocean", *Congressional Globe*, 32nd Congress, 1st session, vol. 24, pt. 3 (1852), 1074-5.

Seward's speech of 29 July 1852 to U.S. Senate. See also no. 246.

716   SHAFTER, Richard A., "Last of the spouters", *Trident*, 4: 39 (1942), 736-7.

Brief history of the *Charles W. Morgan*.

717   SHAW, Dale, "The savage sea", *True: The Man's Magazine*, (Oct. 1958), 31-33, 88-92, 94, 96-7. Illus., map.

Detailed narrative of the *Essex* story.

718   SHERMAN, Stuart C., "Preface to the third issue" in vol. 1 of Alexander Starbuck, *History of the American whale fishery from its earliest inception to the year 1876*, 2 vols. (New York, Argosy-Antiquarian Ltd, 1964; vii (+iii), 407 pp.), i-vii.

See also no. 149, under Alexander Starbuck.

719   SHERRIN, R.A.A., 1832-1893, "Whaling" and "Whaling in New Zealand", chaps. 9 and 19 in Thomson W. Leys (ed.), *Early history of New Zealand. [Pt. 1], From earliest times to 1840*, Brett's Historical series (Auckland, New Zealand, H. Brett, 1890; 728, xliii, [1] pp.), 99-102, 155-76. Illus., appendices, index.

Chap. 9 refers to first whalers in Australian waters; chap. 19 includes refs. to whaleships and whaling in New Zealand waters as well as to shore-based whaling.

720   "A SHIP SUNK BY A WHALE" (from the *Panama Herald*), *Littell's Living Age*, 31:393 (29 Nov. 1851), 415-6.

Destruction of *Ann Alexander* of New Bedford, Captain John S. Deblois, in 1850. This report was also published in the *Daily Evening Traveller* (Boston), 3 Nov. 1851, under heading, "Thrilling account of the destruction of a whale ship by a sperm whale".

721   "SHIPWRECKS AND DISASTERS" (loss of the ship *Essex*), in *Stories about the whale; with an account of the whale fishery, and of the perils attending its prosecution* (Concord, N.H., Merriam & Merrill, 1854; 24 pp.), 16-19. Illus. Earlier ed., Concord, Rufus Merrill, 1850, with "Museum of

Natural History" on cover title. 1854 ed. has cover title, "Merrill's toys: stories about whales", with "Concord, N.H., Rufus Merrill, 1853" beneath. Sabin records an earlier ed. with title *Stories about whales*, Concord, R. Merrill, [1842?]. (Sabin 92207, 92208)

722   SLIJPER, E.J., "Historical introduction", in his *Whales*, trans. by A.J. Pomerans from orig. Dutch ed., *Walvisson*, pub. Amsterdam, 1958 (London, Hutchinson; New York, Basic Books, 1962; 475 pp. 2nd ed. with new foreword, concluding chap. and bibliog. by Richard J. Harrison, London, Hutchinson; Ithaca, N.Y., Cornell University Press, 1979; 511 pp.), 11-57. Illus., bibliog., index.

723   SMITH, J[erome] V[an] C[rowninshield] (ed.), 1800-79, "Whale fishery", *Scientific Tracts, Designed for Instruction and Entertainment, and Adapted to Lyceums and Families*, 1:18 (1833), 425-47. Three vols. in this series pub. between 1831-33, with 24 nos. a year. 1832-33 vols. have imprint: Boston, Allen and Ticknor. 1831-32 vols. ed. by Josiah Holbrook and others. This article reviewed in *Monthly Review*, 1:3, ns 4 (1834), 347-53. (Earl Gregg Swem Library, College of William & Mary).

724   SNOW, E.R., "Tragedy out of New Bedford", in his *New England sea tragedies* (New York, Dodd, Mead, ; 310 pp.), 108-33.
Mutiny on the *Junior* in 1857. See no. 82.

725   SNOW, Philip and Stefanie WAINE, "Traders and whalers", chap. 7 of their *The people from the horizon: an illustrated history of the Europeans among the South Sea Islanders* (Oxford, Phaidon Press; New York, E.P. Dutton Co., Inc., 1979; 296 pp.), 110-22. Illus., bibliog., index. "List of illustrations and their sources" also included.

726   A SON OF THE OCEAN, "An account of the whale fishery; with anecdotes of the dangers &c. attending it", in his *A home on the deep; or the mariner's trials on the deep blue sea* (Boston, Bradley, Dayton & Co., 1859; xii, 483 pp.), 331-46. Frontis., illus.
Essex story, pp. 344-5.

727   "A SPERM-WHALER", *National Magazine: Devoted to Literature, Art, and Religion*, 4 (May 1854), 414-8.
Deals particularly with South Sea whalers, "smart, well-formed, thoroughly rigged ships and barques", the crews of which "are remarkably shrewd, intelligent men".

728   "SPERM WHALING", *South - Asian Register*, 2 (Jan. 1828), 119-23.
"We shall here attempt a short sketch of the history, and circumstances, of South Sea Whaling." (National Library of Australia - Ferguson 1143).

729   STACKPOLE, Edouard A., "The whalemen of Nantucket and their South Sea Island discoveries", *Proceedings, Nantucket Historical Association*, (1944-45), 48-55.

730   [_____] ("E.A.S."), "George A. Grant - whaleman: first curator of the Whaling Museum", *Historic Nantucket*, 28:1 (1980), 16-21.
George Grant was born at Upolu, Samoa, and was later whaler in the Pacific. Son of Captain Charles Grant, whose 3 children all born on his Pacific whaling voyages.

731   STACKPOLE, Renny A., "The Whaling Museum", *Historic Nantucket*, 28:1 (1980), 6-9.

732   STEIN, Douglas, "Paths through the sea: Matthew Fontaine Maury and his wind and current charts", *Log of Mystic Seaport*, 32:3 (1980), 99-107.
Maury obtained considerable amount of his data on winds and currents in the Pacific Ocean from masters of whaleships.

733   STEVEN, M.J.E., "Exports other than wool", chap. 15 in G.J. Abbott and N.B. Nairn (eds.), *Economic growth of Australia 1788-1821* (Carlton, Vic., Melbourne University Press, 1969; x, 361 pp.), 285-307, partic. 298 ff.
Refs. to early Australian whaling industry.

734   STEWART, J.J., " 'Thar' she blows.' Australian whaling in the last century", *Walkabout*, 6:4 (1940), 36-40.

735   STOKESBURY, James L., "Saga of the Yankee whalers", *American History Illustrated*, 9:7 (1974), 6-11, 43-50.

736   STONE, Thomas, "Whalers and missionaries at Herschel Island", *Ethnohistory*, 28: 2 (1981), 101-24.
Impact of the liquor trade on relations between missionaries and whalers in the 19th century Arctic whaling post of Herschel Island is contrasted with the case of the beach communities and whalers in eastern Micronesia.

737   STONES, William, "At sea - the captain's story - whaling", chap. 3 of his *My first voyage. A book for youth*; later eds. titled *What I learned at sea: or, My first voyage. A book for youth* (London, Simpkin, Marshal & Co., 1854; London, Ward, Lock & Tyler, n.d. [1870?]; iv, 239 pp.), 16-25. Illus.
Written for young sea travellers. Contains instructive material on sperm and black whales and on whaling activities, with ref. to visit to island in Torres Strait in whaleship, where narrator was attacked by natives and "left for dead". (Ferguson 16291, 16293; Australian National University Library - Mortlake Collection, 2nd ed.).

738   "THE STORY OF THE WHALE", *Harper's New Monthly Magazine*, 12: 70 (March 1856), 466-82.

General survey of whales and whaling, but with references in concluding section to cruising "under 'the line' ", Mocha Dick, the loss of the *Essex* and *Ann Alexander*.

739   STRAUSS, W. Patrick, "The heyday of the whaler, 1835-1862", chap. 3 of his *Americans in Polynesia 1783-1842* (East Lansing, Michigan State University Press, 1963; [v], 187 pp.), 34-42. Frontis., map, chap. notes, appendix, index.

See also other refs. to whalers and whaling in the index.

740   STUER, Amy P. L., "Whalers", in her *The French in Australia*, Immigration Monograph series 2 (Canberra, Australian National University, Institute of Advanced Studies, Department of Demography, 1982; xv, 249 pp.), 59-61. Maps, illus., tables, appendices, bibliog.

741   "TEMPERANCE", review of *Fifth Annual Report of the New York State Society for the Protection of Temperance, presented by the Executive Committee, Feb. 25, 1834, North American Review*, 39 (Oct. 1834), 494-510.

Temperance on American ships discussed - whaleships included. Out of 186 whalers from New Bedford, 168 were reported to be Temperance ships.

742   THOMAS, R., A.M., "Loss of the whale ship Essex" in his *Interesting and authentic narratives of the most remarkable shipwrecks, fires, famines, calamities, providential deliverances, and lamentable disasters on the seas, in many parts of the world* (Hartford, Conn., Ezra Strong, 1836; [2], 359 + 1 (index) pp.), 323-5. Pls. Orig. pub. as part 2 of *An authentic account of the most remarkable events, containing the lives of the most noted pirates and piracies*, 2 vols. in 1, New York, Ezra Strong, 1836. Other eds. of the Hartford one vol. ed. include Columbus, J. & H. Miller, [183 ?]; [Boston ?, E. Strong, 1836 ?]; New York, E. Strong, 1837; Hartford, E. Strong, 1839; Hartford, S. Andrus & Son, 1847, 1848, 1850, 1852. (See also Sabin, 95441, 95444)

743   THOMPSON, Lindsay G., "The whale fishery", chap. 7 of his *History of the fisheries of New South Wales; with a sketch of the laws by which they have been regulated . . . Compiled from official and other authentic sources* (Sydney, Charles Potter, Government Printer, 1893; 128 pp.), 76-88. Fold. maps at end.

"Published by authority of the New South Wales Commissioners for the World's Columbian Exposition, Chicago, 1893. Maps include "Map shewing whaling grounds in portion of the Southern Hemisphere. By Captain J.B. Carpenter". Note: This work was printed also in *Pamphlets issued by the New South Wales Commissioners for the World's Columbian Exposition, Chicago, 1893 for the information of visitors to that exhibition . . . .*, vol. 1 (Sydney, Charles Potter, Government Printer, 1893).

744   THOMSON, Basil, 1861-1939, "In the old whaling days", [chap. 11] of his *South Sea yarns* (Edinburgh and London, William Blackwood and Sons, 1894; xv, 326 [+2] pp.), 173-94. Frontis., pls.
Whaling ships in Fijian waters.

745   THRUM, Thos.[Thomas] G., "Honolulu's share in the Pacific whaling industry of by-gone days", *Hawaiian Almanac and Annual for 1913*, (Dec. 1912), 47-68.
General survey, with list of Honolulu whalers with annual catches since 1832.

746   ———, "When sailors ruled the town", *Hawaiian Almanac and Annual for 1921*, (Dec. 1920), 62-8.
Sailors' riot in 1852 in Honolulu - many from whaleships.

747   ———, "Thomas Spencer; master mariner - merchant - sugar planter", *Hawaiian Almanac and Annual for 1924*, (Dec. 1923), 117-25.
Continuation of author's article "Captain Thomas Spencer", q.v. no. 90, above. Describes Spencer's career in Hawaii where he was an important figure in whaling circles in the 1850s and later.

748   TOMPKINS, E. Berkeley, "Black Ahab: William T. Shorey, whaling master", *California Historical Quarterly*, 51:1 (1972), 75-84.
Shorey, born Barbados 1859, shipped on first whaling voyage in 1876 from Provincetown, Mass. Third mate on *Emma F. Herriman* of Boston on 1880 voyage, which included a Pacific cruise, and on her later voyages from San Francisco, finally as master in 1886. Later master of other vessels whaling in North Pacific.

749   TRIPP, George H., b. 1853, "Whaling ventures and adventures", *One Hundred and Eighth Anniversary Celebration of the New England Society in the City of New York*, (1913), 22-41.

750   TRUBY, J. David, "The turbulent wars that whales have fought against man", *Smithsonian*, 3:2 (1972), 58-65.
Refs. to whaling and whaleships, partic. the *Essex*.

751   TWAIN, Mark (pseud. of Samuel L. Clemens), 1835-1910, "Mrs. Jollopson's 'gam' " (letter dated April 1866 and reprinted from the *Sacramento Weekly Union*, 26 May, 1866) in *Letters from the Sandwich Islands written for the Sacramento Union by Mark Twain*, with intro. and conclusion by G. Ezra Dane and illus. by Dorothy Grover (San Francisco, Grabhorn Press (lim. ed.), 1937; Stanford, Cal., Stanford University Press; London, Humphrey Milford, Oxford University Press, [1938]; xii, 224 pp.), 62-71. Reprinted New York, Haskell House Publishers, 1972. Illus.

A description of some of the whaling vocabulary widely used in Honolulu. Printed as Letter 9 "Sad accident", no. 753 below, *Mark Twain's letters from Hawaii*, ed. by A. Grove Day.

752   ———, "The whaling trade" [Letter 10, April 1866] in *Letters from Honolulu, written for the Sacramento Union by Mark Twain*, intro. by John W. Vandercock; limited ed. of 1000 copies (Honolulu, Thomas Nickerson, 1939; xvi, 101 pp.), pp. n.a.
Four letters only printed; others deal with sugar industry, *Hornet* disaster and importance of Hawaiian trade.

753   ———, "Sad accident" and "The whaling trade", Letters 9 and 10 dated Honolulu, April 1866, in A. Grove Day (ed. with intro. by), *Mark Twain's letters from Hawaii* (New York, Appleton-Century, [1966]; xix, 298 pp.), 77-95.
See "A note on this edition of the Letters", pp. xix, for publication details of Twain's whaling letters.

754   VAUCAIRE, Michel, "Les Mers du Sud", chap. 7 of his *Histoire de la pêche à la baleine*, Bibliothèque Géographique series (Paris, Payot, 1941; 262 pp.), 140-92. Illus., pls., diagrs., bibliog.
Chap. includes sections on "Les Américains", "La pêche du cachalot et les Anglais," "La pêche du cachalot et les Français".

755   VILLIERS, Alan, "The whalers", book 3 of his *Vanished fleets* (London, Geoffrey Bles, [1931]; xi, 269 pp.), 113-99. Frontis., pls., appendices. Also pub. with subtitle *Ships and men of old Van Diemen's Land* (Garden City, N.Y., Garden City Pub. Co., Inc. [1931]; viii [+iii], 297 pp.), 153-237. Endp. map, pls., appendices. Rev. ed., Cambridge and London, Patrick Stevens Ltd; Hobart, Cat & Fiddle Press, 1974, with title *Vanished fleets: sea stories from old Van Diemen's Land*. [13], 297 pp.
Includes "From Captain Tregurtha's log", chaps. 13-14, q.v. no. 97, and "The adventure of the 'Essex' ", chap. 15, which gives details of the role of Captain Raine and the *Surry* in the *Essex* story. Second appendix consists of "Copy of whaling agreement", Hobart Town, 1855.

756   ———, "Whales and whaling", chap. 14 of his *Oceans of the world: man's conquest of the sea*. (London, Museum Press, [1963]; 159 pp.), partic. 135-8. Frontis., pls., maps, bibliog., index.

757   WÄTJEN, Hermann, "Zur Geschichte der bremischen Südseefischerei im 19. Jahrhundert", *Bremisches Jahrbuch*, 25 (1914), 138-66.

758   WALLACE, Frederick William, "In the wake of the wind-ships", pt. 1 of his *In the wake of the wind-ships; notes, records and biographies per-*

taining to the square-rigged merchant marine of British North America
(London, Hodder and Stoughton Ltd.; New York, George Sully & Co., [1927];
xii, 282 pp.), 1-26.

Deals with the whale-fishery of British North America, which included voyages to
the Pacific. Partic. ref. to the adventures of the St. John whaler *James Stewart*,
Captain Kenny, in the Gilbert Islands, 1846.

759   WARDEN, _____, "Îles nouvellement découvertes, sur la côte du
Japon", *Bulletin de la Société de Géographie*. (Paris), 1st. ser., 9:60-61 (1828),
208-9.

Note on the discovery of six islands in the Bonin group by "le Capitaine Coffin, de
Nantucket" (James Coffin, in the British whaler *Transit*), in September, 1824.

760   WATSON, Arthur C., "The paths of the whalemen", *Yachting*, 45:5
(1927), 53-6, 88.

Partic. ref. to whalers in the Pacific and their contribution to the work of the hy-
drographer Matthew F. Maury.

761   "THE WHALE AND WHALE FISHERIES", in vol. 1 (?) of William and
Robert Chambers (eds.), *Chambers's Information for the People*, new and
improved ed., 2 vols. (Edinburgh, William and Robert Chambers, 1842; viii,
800 pp.), 417-32.

Uses Beale as a source of information on sperm whale fishery. (Mitchell Library has
extract only, with *Chambers's Information for the People*, issue no. 27 ns [1842?]
cited; see also Ferguson 3575)

762   "THE WHALE FISHERIES", in Art. IV: "New Zealand", *Quarterly
Review*, 68 (1841), 142-4.

General survey of the state of the South Seas fishery in a review of several books
on the Australian colonies and New Zealand, with partic. ref. to evidence given by
Charles Enderby to committee of House of Commons on subject.

763   "THE WHALE FISHERY", *Merchants' Magazine and Commercial Review*, 2:4 (Apr. 1840), 338.

Report of Dupetit-Thouars and D'Urville on the French whale fishery in the South
Seas to the Minister of the Marine.

764   "THE WHALE FISHERY AND ITS HAZARDS", in *Voyage and venture;
or, Perils by sea and land*, illus. by William Harvey (London, [New York?],
George Routledge and Co., 1853; new ed. 1858; 380 pp.), 95-113.

Includes material on the wreck of the *Essex* as well as "A whalers' inn at New Bedford", which is taken from chaps. 2 and 3 of *Moby Dick* (unacknowledged). (Huntress, *Checklist*, 383c; Mitchell Library)

765   WHIPPLE, A.B.C., "Three-month ordeal in open boats: sinking of the "Essex" became climax of "Moby Dick"; here is tragic aftermath novel left out", *Life*, 33:19 (10 Nov. 1952), 144-6, 149-50, 152, 154, 156. Illus., map.

766   _____, "The golden age", chap. 7 of his *Vintage Nantucket* (New York, Dodd, Mead & Company, [1978]; xi, 260 pp.), 126-52. Illus., index.
Chap. 8, "The matriarchy", pp. 152-69, part of which refers to whaling wives, is also of interest.

767   WILLIAMS, C.A., "Early whaling industry of New London", *Records and Papers of the New London County Historical Society*, 2:1 (1895), 3-22.

768   WILLIAMS, Harold, "Yankee whaling fleets raided by Confederate cruisers: the story of the bark *Jireh Swift*, Captain Thomas W. Williams", *American Neptune*, 27:4 (1967), 263-78.
See partic. pp. 268-70 for *Jireh Swift's* whaling voyage in the Pacific.

769   [WILLIAMS, J.R.], "The whale fishery", *North American Review*, 38 (Jan. 1834), 84-115.
Although mainly reviewing works on Arctic whaling by William Scoresby and others, article includes many refs. to Pacific whale fishery. Quoted in Olmsted, *Incidents of a whaling voyage . . .* (see no. 76, 123-9).

770   _____, "New Bedford, Massachusetts", *Fisher's National Magazine and Industrial Record*, (Sept. 1845), 329-43.
Includes review of New Bedford whaling, and data on whale fishery products in 1844.

771   "WONDERFUL EXPLOIT OF BENJAMIN CLOUGH", *Littell's Living Age*, 4: 45 (22 Mar. 1845), 710-12.
Mutiny on *Sharon* of Fairhaven in Pacific Ocean, west of Gilbert Islands, in 1842, and the actions of Clough, third mate, resulting in saving of ship, crew and cargo. Note: This account also published in *Hunt's Merchants' Magazine*, 26: 3 (March 1852), 334-7, under title, "Fearless feat of an American whaleman".

772   WORTH, Henry B., "Voyages of ship 'Bartholomew Gosnold' ", *Old Dartmouth Historical Sketches*, 44 (Apr. 1916), 11-12.
Bartholomew Gosnold made 10 out of total of 13 whaling voyages to the Pacific.

773   WRIGHT, Harrison M., "Traders and whalers", chap. 2 of his *New Zealand, 1769-1860: early years of western contact* (Cambridge, Mass., Harvard University Press, 1959; xi, 225 [+3] pp.), 19-39. Map, bibliog. essay, index.
Partic. ref. to whalers at Bay of Islands and Kororareka.

774 WYLLIE, Robert Crichton, 1798-1865, "Notes on the Sandwich, or Hawaiian Islands", *Simmond's Colonial Magazine*, 5:19 (July 1845), 253-68. Includes information and statistics on the whale fishery. Dated Honolulu 10 Jan. 1845.

(D) Scrimshaw and marine art.

775 "ACQUISITION" [of piece of scrimshaw depicting Newport whaleship *John Coggeshall* in the Pacific Ocean, north of New Zealand, by Mystic Seaport Museum], *Log of Mystic Seaport*, 33:3 (1981), 106-7.

776 "THE ASSOCIATION ACQUIRES THE PORTRAIT OF A WHALING MASTER'S WIFE", *Historic Nantucket*, 29: 3 (1982), 6-9. Portrait of Mary Coffin Nichols of Nantucket, whose husband, Capt. James Nichols, was master of the *Neptune* of Sag Harbor and the *Lion* of Providence, R.I., which was whaling in the Pacific Ocean 1850-53 (sailed 15 Sept. 1849, returned 23 Oct. 1853). Mrs. Nichols accompanied him on this voyage. In 1878 Capt. Nichols and his brother Capt. Charles Nichols put on display their collection of South Sea artifacts and shells acquired during their voyages.

777 BANKS, Steven, "Bone, ivory, horn and shells", chap. 5 of his *The handicrafts of the sailor* (Newton Abbot, London, David & Charles, [1974]; 96 pp.), 69-81. Illus., bibliog., index.

778 BARBEAU, Marius, " 'All hands aboard scrimshawing' ", *American Neptune*, 12:2 (1952), 99-122. Separately published in 1973. See no. 275.

779 _____, "Seafaring folk art", *Antiques*, 66:1 (1954), 47-9. Art of scrimshaw, practiced by seamen and also by Pacific Islanders, Eskimos and Indians of the Pacific Northwest.

780 BECK, Horace, Scrimshaw discussed in "Art", chap. 7 of his *Folklore and the sea*, American Maritime Library vol. 6 (Middletown, Conn., Wesleyan University Press for the Marine Historical Association Inc., Mystic Seaport, [1973]; xvii, 463 pp.), 187-92. Port., pls., notes, bibliog., index.

781 BIGELOW, Ethel, "Scrimshaw work of the early days", *House Beautiful*, (Aug. 1920), 95, 130. Partic. ref. to scrimshaw pie-wheels made by whalemen.

782 BRANNING, Timothy, "Ivory artistry of the Yankee whaler", *National Wildlife*, 19:2 (1981), 12-14, 17.

783 BURROWS, Fredrika A., " 'Susan's' teeth", *Antiques Journal*, 35 (May 1980), 20-2, 48.

Partic. ref. to the scrimshaw work of Frederick Myrick on the *Susan* of Nantucket, Captain F. Swain, voyaging to the Pacific 1826-29.

784   CHAPLIN, Richard, "The De Blois collection of scrimshaw", *Newport History*, 44:3 (1971), 69-76.
A scrimshaw collection which originated during the Pacific voyage of the New Bedford whaler *Merlin*, Captain John Scott De Blois, 1856-59; the captain was accompanied by his wife Henrietta Tew De Blois, who kept a journal during the voyage and described the scrimshaw collected.

785   CHILDS, Charles D., " 'Thar she blows'. Some notes on American whaling pictures", *Antiques*, 40 (July 1941), 20-3.
No specific Pacific refs., but useful outline of work of prominent whaling artists of the 19th century.

786   COMSTOCK, Helen, "Scrimshaw: an art now lost", *Connoisseur*, 96 (Aug. 1935), 97-8.

787   CROSBY, Everett U., "Ship Spermo of Nantucket: an unusual early American primitive", *Historic Nantucket*, 4: 3 (Jan. 1957), 25 + illus.
Ref. to painting "Ship Spermo of Nantucket in a heavy thunder squall on the coast of California - 1822" (during Pacific Ocean whaling cruise 27 Aug. 1820-24 Mar. 1823 under command of Captain James Bunker).

788   DALAND, Edward L. (pseud. of Edward Baland Lovejoy), "Engraved types of scrimshaw", *Antiques*, (Oct. 1935), 153-55.

789   DILLARD, William T., "The history of scrimshaw", *Creative Crafts*, 8 (June 1982), 57.

790   EVANS, Vaughan, "Scrimshaw: the art of the whaleman", *Australasian Antique Collector*, 20 (1980), 53-8.

791   FRAUDREAU, Martin and Philip JODIDIO, "Nantucket et l'art du scrimshaw", *Connaissance des Arts*, 307 (Sept. 1977), 82-7.

792   HALEY, Paul C., "Scrimshaw and the Yankee whaler", *Sea Frontiers*, 22:3 (1976), 150-3.

793   HANSEN, Hans Jurgen (ed.), "Seamen's crafts: scrimshaw, wood, paper and rope work, ships in bottles, panoramic models" in *Art and the seafarer: a historical survey of the arts and crafts of sailors and shipwrights*, trans. of *Kunstgeschichte der Seefahrt: Kunst und Kunsthandwerk der Seeleute und Schiffbauer* (Oldenbourg & Hamburg, Gerhard Stalling Verlag, 1966) by James and Inge Moore (London, Faber and Faber, [1968]; 296 pp.), 251-2, 261-4, 269-70. Pls. (273, 276-7, 280), bibliog., index. See also "Ship portraiture", p. 201, for refs. to paintings of American whaleships, and pls. and illus., pp. 204, 227-8, 231.

794   HAZE, Wellington, "Jagging wheels", *Antiques*, 2 (June 1922), 260-2.
Scrimshaw jagging or pie wheels made by American whalemen.

795   HOWARD, Margaret Ann, "Scrimshaw", *Lapidary Journal*, 33 (May 1979), 550-4.
A general survey of development of scrimshaw, and types of articles made.

796   HUSTER, H. Harrison, "Scrimshaw: one part whalebone, two parts nostalgia", *Antiques*, 80:2 (1961), 122-5.

797   JOHNSON, Barbara, "The Barbara Johnson whaling collection: 're-spect for the man, respect for the whale' ", *Sea History*, 29 (1983), 32.
Note on the development of the author's collection, with partic. ref. to scrimshaw pieces.

798   LIPTON, B., "Whaling days in New Jersey", *Newark Museum Quarterly*, 26:2-3 (1975), 1-73.
Article gives background for Newark Museum's first bicentennial exhibition, which presented New Jersey's whaling industry over 200 years. Items on show included prints, paintings and scrimshaw.

799   MALLEY, Richard C., "False teeth: new problems with plastic scrimshaw", *Log of Mystic Seaport*, 32:3 (1980), 83-9.

800   MARTIN, Kenneth R., "Whalemen's views of Lahaina", *Lahaina Jottings*, (Apr. 1974), 2 pp.

800a   _____, "Glimpses of the old South Seas: whalers depict their landfalls", *Oceans*, 13:6 (1980), 7-13.

801   MEYER, Charles R., "Whaling and the art of scrimshaw", *Conservationist*, 31:3 (1976), 29-32.

802   PEASE, Z[ephaniah] W., ["Scrimshaw"], editorial in *New Bedford Mercury*, 2 Dec. 1920, reprinted in *Old Dartmouth Historical Sketches*, 50 [Dec. 1920?], 4-5.

803   PRINCE, Daniel, "Scrimshaw: art of the Yankee whaler", *Art and Antiques*, 4:3 (1981), 108-13.

804   PURRINGTON, Philip F., "Around the world in eighty rods: New Bedford's whaling panorama", *Antiques*, 80:2 (1961), 142-5.

[RUSSELL, Benjamin], See under Ivan T. Sanderson, no. 710, above.

805   SHEPPARD, T., "Whaling relics", *Mariner's Mirror*, 6:5 (1920), 142-9. Illus.
Engraved whales' teeth and whalebone objects acquired by Hull Museum described. No specific Pacific refs.

806   SPENCE, W.D., "Scratched on whalebone: the art of scrimshaw", *Country Life*, 155:4014 (1974), 1473-4.

807   STACKPOLE, Edouard A., "The 'Ann Alexander's' scrimshaw set tells the story of a ship sunk by a whale", *Historic Nantucket*, 27:3 (1980), 6-12.

808   TORDOFF, Ruth E., "Scrimshaw: Alaskan or whaler art?", *Alaska Journal*, 2:3 (1972), 54-6.

809   WATSON, Arthur C., "Scrimshaw - the perfect hobby: whalemen found it a triumphant answer to an acute problem", *Technology Review*, (March 1938), 221-24, 245-6.
History of the development of scrimshaw. Possibility of Pacific Island influence discussed.

810   WEST, Janet, "Scrimshaw: recent forgeries in plastic", *Mariner's Mirror*, 66:4 (1980), 328-30.
See author's bibliography for other refs. on this topic.

811   _____, "Scrimshaw: facts and forgeries", *Antique Collecting*, 16:10 (1982), 17-21.

812   _____, "Scrimshaw: old, new or plastic?", *Australasian Antique Collector*, 27 (1984), 48-51.

813   "WHALING PAINTINGS" (from Kendall Whaling Museum, Sharon, Mass.), *American Neptune*, 22:1-4 (1962), 16-17, 108-9, 200-1, 292-3.
63 paintings and prints reproduced—some of Pacific interest.

814   WILSON, Claggett, "Scrimshaw, the whaleman's art", *Antiques*, 46 (Nov. 1944), 278-81.

815   WINN, Thea, "Scrimshaw, the whalers' art", *Relics: A Link to Our Pioneer Heritage*, 2:4 (1969), 8-9, 26, 30.
History and technique of scrimshaw.

(E) Literary material: Melville, *Moby-Dick*, reviews of works on whaling. See also WORKS OF FICTION, sect. A.

816   ARVIN, Newton, "The whale", [chap. 5] of his *Herman Melville*, "American Men of Letters" series ([New York], William Sloane Associates, [1950]; xiii, 312 pp.), 143-93. Bibliog. notes, index.

817   BABCOCK, C. Merton, "Herman Melville's whaling vocabulary", *American Speech*, 2:3 (1954), 161-74.

818   BIRSS, John Howard, " 'Moby-Dick' under another name", *Notes and Queries*, 164 (25 Mar. 1933), 206.
Refs. to *Péhe Nù-e, the tiger whale of the Pacific* by "Captain Barnacle" and the influence of Melville's *Moby-Dick* on it: see no. 324.

819   [BRODERIP, W.J.], " 'The natural history of the sperm whale &c. &c. . . .' by Thomas Beale", *Quarterly Review*, 63 (March 1839), 318-41.

820   CHASE, Richard, "Light in the morning", chap. 11 of his *Herman Melville: a critical study* (New York, Macmillan Co., 1949; xiii [+ ii], 305 pp.), 43-102. Index.
Partic. emphasis on Melville's use of folklore in creating *Moby-Dick*.

821   "THE CRUISE OF THE 'CACHALOT' ROUND THE WORLD AFTER SPERM WHALES. By Frank T. Bullen, first mate", *Athenaeum*, 3718 (28 June 1899), 107.
For other reviews of this work in English journals, see *Academy*, 57 (9 Dec. 1899), 690-1; *Critic*, 34 (April 1899), 353; and *Outlook*, 61 (4 March 1899), 563.

822   DAHL, Curtis, "*Moby Dick* and reviews of *The cruise of the Cachalot*", *Modern Language Notes*, 67:7 (1952), 471-2.

823   DAWS, Gavan, "Herman Melville" in his *A dream of islands: voyages of self-discovery in the South Seas* (Milton, Qld., Jacaranda Press; New York, W.W. Norton, 1980; xviii, 289 pp.), partic. 74-9. Endp. maps, ports., illus., "note on sources", index.

824   FRÉDÉRIX, Pierre, "L'aventurier des îles" [Herman Melville], *La Revue. Littérature, Histoire, Arts et Sciences des Deux Mondes*, 21-3 (1 and 15 Nov., 1 Dec. 1949), 39-55, 236-59, 446-68.
Refs. to Melville's whaling experiences partic. in Pts. 1 and 2.

825   GARNETT, R.S., "Mocha Dick, or the white whale of the Pacific" (letter), *Times Literary Supplement*, 1228 (30 July 1925), 509.

826   ———, "Moby-Dick and Mocha-Dick. A literary find", *Black-wood's Magazine*, 226:1370 (1929), 841-58.

Includes sections of J.N. Reynolds's "Mocha-Dick . . .': see no. 371-4.

827   GROBMAN, Neil R., "The tall tale telling events in Melville's *Moby-Dick*", *Journal of the Folklore Institute*, 12:1 (1975), 19-27.

828   HAYFORD, Harrison, "Hawthorne, Melville, and the sea", *New England Quarterly*, 19:4 (1946), 435-52.

Possible influence of Jeremiah Reynolds on Melville and Hawthorne discussed *inter alia*.

829   HEFLIN, Wilson L., "Melville's third whaler", *Modern Language Notes*, 64:4 (1949), 241-45.

830   ———, "Melville and Nantucket", [chap. 9] in Tyrus Hillway and Luther S. Mansfield (eds., with intro. by), *Moby-Dick: centennial essays*, ed. for the Melville Society (Dallas, Southern Methodist University Press, [1953]; xiv, 182 pp.), 165-79. "Third printing, 1965".

Originally appeared in *Proceedings of the Nantucket Historical Association* (1951), 22-30.

831   ———, "New light on Herman Melville's cruise on the *Charles and Henry*", *Historic Nantucket*, 22: 2 (1974), 6-27.

The *Charles and Henry*, of Nantucket, Captain John B. Coleman, sailed for the Pacific in December 1840, returning 8 March 1845. Article includes list of original ship's company, books in ship's library, provisions taken aboard.

832   ———, "Researching in New Bedford, circa 1947", *Melville Society Extracts*, 42 (May 1980), 1-4.

833   ———, "More researching in New Bedford", *Melville Society Extracts*, 43 (Sept. 1980), 11-14.

834   HOWARD, Leon, "A predecessor of Moby-Dick", *Modern Language Notes*, 49:5 (1934), 310-11.

Influence of sections of *Miriam Coffin: or, The whale-fishermen* by Joseph C. Hart on Melville's work: see no. 360.

835   ———, "The Pacific: outward bound" and sect. 1 of "The Pacific: recoil", chaps. 3 and 4 of his *Herman Melville: a biography* (Berkeley and Los Angeles, University of California Press, [1951]; new ed. 1981; xi, 354 pp.), 40-71.

836   Hoyt, Helen P., "Captain Robert Barnacle (pseud. of Charles Martin Newell): whaleman, author, doctor of medicine", *Fifty-Ninth Annual Report of the Hawaiian Historical Society for the Year 1950*, (1951), 12-18.

Newell wrote novels about Hawaii as well as whaling stories. He served on whalers from the age of 15, and became master of several whalers which visited the Pacific, such as the *Copia* of New Bedford. See also nos. 324, 368-9.

837   "Huntsmen of the sea", *Harper's New Monthly Magazine*, 49: 293 (Oct. 1874), 650-61.

Commentary on W.M. Davis, *Nimrod of the sea; or, The American whaleman* (New York, 1873), q.v. no. 36.

838   Jaffé, David, "The captain who sat for the portrait of Ahab", *Boston University Studies in English*, 4 (1960), 1-22.

Influence of Wilkes's *Narrative of the U.S. Exploring Expedition . . .* on *Moby-Dick*. See also no. 300, David Jaffé, *The stormy petrel and the whale*.

839   Lane, Lauriat, Jr., "Melville's second whaler", *Melville Society Extracts*, 43 (Sept. 1980), 14-15.

Discussion of the possible origin of the *Lucy Ann*.

840   Lecomte, Jules, "Études maritimes, de quelques animaux apocryphes et fabuleux de la mer: le cachalot blanc", *Musée des Familles*, 4 (Jan. 1837), 97-104.

Quoted in full in Janez Stanonik, *Moby-Dick: the myth and the symbol . . .* (q.v. no. 305), 32-8 and Appendix 1, 189-95 (in original French).

841   Leeson, Ida, "The mutiny on the *Lucy Ann*", *Philological Quarterly*, 19:4 (1940), 370-79.

Melville joined the Sydney whaler *Lucy Ann* at the Marquesas in August 1842. Less than two months later, at Tahiti, a number of seamen, including Melville, were put ashore, charged with mutiny.

842   Leimberg, Inge, "*Moby Dick*. Der weisse Wal historisch betrachtet", *Literatur in Wissenschaft und Unterricht*, 5:1 (1972), 7-21.

843   Loving, Jerome M., "Melville's pardonable sin", *New England Quarterly*, 47:2 (1974), 262-78.

The development of *Moby-Dick* from whaling yarn to allegory.

844   McCormick, Edgar L., "Melville's third captain", *Historic Nantucket*, 9:4 (1962), 61-5.

Captain John B. Coleman, of the *Charles and Henry*, who also made five earlier whaling voyages into the Pacific.

845   MacMechan, Archibald, " 'The best sea story ever written' ", *Queen's Quarterly*, 7:2 (1899), 120-30. Also printed in the author's *The Life of a little college, and other papers* (Boston, Houghton Mifflin Company, 1914; 308 pp.), 179-98.
On *Moby-Dick*.

846   [Melville, Herman], Review of "*Etchings of a whaling cruise, with notes of a sojourn on the island of Zanzibar. To which is appended, a brief history of the whale fishery; its past and present condition. By J. Ross Browne . . .* Harper & Brothers: 1846", *Literary World*, 6 (6 Mar. 1847), 105-6.

847   Monteiro, George, "On the author of the 'greatest sea-book known': commentary on Herman Melville at the turn of the century", *Papers of the Bibliographical Society of America*, 73 (1979), 115-20.
Partic. ref. to critical notices of Frank T. Bullen's *Cruise of the "Cachalot"* (q.v.) and comparison with Melville.

848   Montillier, Pierre, "Le séjour d'Herman Melville à Tahiti en 1842", *Journal de la Société des Océanistes*, 15:15 (1959), 365-71.

849   "A narrative of the shipwreck, captivity, and sufferings of Horace Holden and Benjamin H. Nute . . .", *North American Review*, 43 (July 1836), 206-26.
A detailed notice of the above work.

850   Pitt, A. Stuart, " 'A semi-romance of the sea': *Miriam Coffin* as precursor of *Moby-Dick*", *Historic Nantucket*, 19:4 (1972), 15-30.
Discussion of Joseph Hart's *Miriam Coffin*, no. 360, and the parallels in it to *Moby-Dick*.

851   Pommer, Henry F., "Herman Melville and the wake of the *Essex*", *American Literature*, 20:3 (1968), 290-304.
Study of Melville's use of the *Essex* story; ref. to Melville's meeting with Captain Pollard, probably in July 1852.

852   Stewart, George R., "The two *Moby-Dicks*", *American Literature*, 25 (Jan. 1954), 417-48.
Discussion of the hypothesis that Melville conceived *Moby-Dick* originally as a simple whaling story (as suggested in chaps. 1-15), before reconceiving it in its final published form.

853   Weaver, Raymond M., "Blubber and mysticism" and "Leviathan", chaps. 7 and 8 of his *Herman Melville: mariner and mystic* [with intro. by Mark Van Doren, 1961 ed.], (London, Humphrey Milford, Oxford University Press; New York, George H. Doran Co., [1921]; 399 pp.), 128-69.

Frontis., port., pls., illus., bibliog., index. Reprinted New York, Pageant Books Inc., [1961].

854   "WHALING VOYAGE, &C.", review (Art. XII) of *Narrative of a whaling voyage round the globe from the year 1833 to 1836* by F.D. Bennett, *Monthly Review*, ns 4, 2:2 (June 1840), 272-9.

VI.

Newspapers and periodicals.

This list is not a comprehensive one. It includes 19th century journals and newspapers which published, in many cases on a regular basis, shipping information, reports, news items and comments relating to various aspects of whaling in the Pacific Ocean. Those marked with an asterisk are the most important sources of whaling news and of data on whaleships.

855   ATLAS. *Sydney Weekly Journal of Politics, Commerce, and Literature.* 30 Nov. 1844 - 30 Dec. 1848. Weekly. (Ferguson 3775)

856   *AUSTRALIAN* (Sydney). 14 Oct. 1824 - 28 Sept. 1848. Weekly, semi-weekly, 3 weekly. (Ferguson 931)

857   *AUSTRALIAN ALMANACK AND GENERAL DIRECTORY* (Sydney). Various versions of title. Before 1822 *NEW SOUTH WALES POCKET ALMANACK.* 1806 - 1835. No issue 1807. Annual.
Includes shipping arrivals and departures for each year from Sydney. (See Ferguson, vol. 1, Index, under "Almanacs".)

858   *BRITANNIA AND TRADES' ADVOCATE* (Hobart). 1 Jan. 1846 - 3 July 1851. Weekly, semi-weekly (from 24 Aug. 1846). Incorporated in *TASMANIAN COLONIST*, q.v. no. 891 below. (Ferguson 4242)

859   *COLONIAL ADVOCATE, AND TASMANIAN MONTHLY REVIEW AND REGISTER. Devoted to News, Politics, Agriculture, and Commerce* (Hobart). 1 March - 1 October 1828. Monthly. (Ferguson 1181)

860   *COLONIAL MAGAZINE AND COMMERCIAL-MARITIME JOURNAL* (London). Jan. 1840 - June 1842 (8 vols.). Becomes *FISHER'S COLONIAL MAGAZINE AND COMMERCIAL MARITIME JOURNAL*, Aug. 1842 - Dec. 1843 (4 vols.), then *FISHER'S COLONIAL MAGAZINE AND*

JOURNAL OF TRADE, COMMERCE AND BANKING, 1844-45 (2 vols.). (Ferguson 2957)

Refs. to Pacific whaling, American whale fishery etc. Continued as *SIMMONDS' COLONIAL MAGAZINE . . .* , q.v. no. 866 below.

861   *COLONIAL TIMES, AND TASMANIAN ADVERTISER* (Hobart). See also under *HOBART TOWN GAZETTE.* 19 Aug. 1825 - 22 Aug. 1857. Weekly, semi-weekly, 4 weekly, 3 weekly, 5 weekly, daily, 3 weekly. (Ferguson 1004a)

"Sydney extracts" contain shipping / whaling information.

862   *COLONIST AND VAN DIEMEN'S LAND COMMERCIAL AND AGRICULTURAL ADVERTISER* (Hobart). 6 July - 16 Nov. 1832; 23 Nov. 1832 - 7 July 1834. Weekly. Thereafter becomes *TRUE COLONIST . . .* , q.v. no. 892 below. (Ferguson 1524a)

863   **THE FRIEND: a Journal Devoted to Temperance, Seamen, Marine and General Intelligence* (Honolulu). Also has titles *TEMPERANCE ADVOCATE* (Jan. 1843) and *TEMPERANCE ADVOCATE AND SEAMEN'S FRIEND* (Mar. - Dec. 1843). Jan. 1843 - May/ June 1854. Frequency varies.

Major source of whaling information for the Pacific generally.

864   *HOBART TOWN COURIER.* Various versions of title. 20 Oct. 1827-31 May 1859. Weekly, semi-weekly, 3 weekly, daily. (Ferguson 1126a)

"Trade and shipping" section.

865   *HOBART TOWN GAZETTE, AND SOUTHERN REPORTER* (Hobart). Also with titles *COLONIAL TIMES* (20 Aug. - 31 Dec. 1825) and *HOBART TOWN GAZETTE AND VAN DIEMEN'S LAND ADVERTISER* (20 Jan. 1821 - 24 June 1825). 1 June 1816 - 20 Oct. 1827. Thereafter official gazette of Tasmanian Govt. to 31 Dec. 1889. (Ferguson 649)

866   *HOWE'S WEEKLY COMMERCIAL EXPRESS [AND MISCELLANEOUS INTELLIGENCER]* (Sydney). No. 1-22, 2 May - 26 Sept. 1825. Weekly. (Ferguson 1026)

867   **HUNT'S MERCHANTS' MAGAZINE* (New York). Also has title *MERCHANTS' MAGAZINE AND COMMERCIAL REVIEW.* July 1839 - Dec. 1870. Monthly.

Issues in the 1840s in partic. have regular items and statistics on whaling, particularly American.

868   **JOURNAL DU HAVRE Commercial, Maritime et Littéraire, Annonces Légales et Avis Divers* (Le Havre). Also has title *JOURNAL DU HAVRE, Commercial et Politique* (from 1838). 1826-1858. Daily.

869   *LAUNCESTON ADVERTISER*. 9 Feb. 1829 - Jan. 1847. Weekly, semi-weekly - frequency varies. Also published with weekly supplement: "Launceston Prices Current and Shipping List". (Ferguson 1278)

870   *[LLOYD'S] REGISTER OF SHIPPING* (London). Instituted 1760. Annual. 1800 - 1833 (Underwriters / Shipowners). Becomes *LLOYD'S REGISTER OF BRITISH AND FOREIGN SHIPPING*, 1834 + . Reprinted London, Gregg Press, n.d., [196-?]
Important source of information about British whaleships.

871   *MAGASIN PITTORESQUE* (Paris). 1833 - 1923. Annual.
Vols. 1, 2, 4, 6, 19, 28 and 43 in partic. have items of whaling interest.

872   *NANTUCKET INQUIRER*. Also has title *INQUIRER AND MIRROR* (after 1865). 23 June 1821 +. Weekly. Semi-weekly 1833 - 41, Oct. 1860; 3 weekly 1852.
Major source of information on whaleships and whaling.

873   *NAUTICAL MAGAZINE* (London). March 1832 + . Monthly.
Numerous refs. to whaleships and whaling. An "Index to the Nautical Magazine" based on holdings in the Sydney Public Library which lists references of Australasian and South Seas interest in the *Nautical Magazine* for the period 1832 - 94 is available on microfilm in the Department of Pacific & Southeast Asian History, Research School of Pacific Studies, Australian National University. (Typescript, 393 pp. "Whaling", pp. 378-9.)

874   *NEW-BEDFORD DIRECTORY* (New Bedford, to 1867; thereafter Boston). Various versions of title. 1836 + . Irregular annual. (Sabin 52492)
Issues for 1836, 1838, 1839 and 1841 (all comp. by Henry H. Crapo) contain "List of whale ships, belonging to the United States".

875   *NEW-BEDFORD MERCURY*. 7 Aug. 1807 - 1895. Weekly; daily after 28 Feb. 1831.
Numerous whaling references.

876   *NEW-BEDFORD REPORTER AND SEAMAN'S WEEKLY VISITOR*. Also has titles *NEW BEDFORD REPORTER AND FAMILY WEEKLY VISITOR* and *NEW BEDFORD REPORTER AND WHALEMAN'S WEEKLY VISITOR*. 30 July? 1846- ?. Weekly.

877   *NEW-ENGLAND ALMANACK, AND FARMER'S FRIEND* (New London). Published with this title 1823-89. Annual. Previously *NEW-ENGLAND ALMANACK*.
Lists whaleships belonging to New London, Stonington, Mystic and Sag Harbor.

878   *NEW ZEALAND JOURNAL* (London). 8 Feb. 1840 - 6 Nov. 1852. Fortnightly.

Written in interests of the New Zealand Company until July 1850. Regular whaling news. (Hocken, *Bibliography of . . . New Zealand*, pp. 84-5.)

879   *NORTH AMERICAN REVIEW* (Boston/New York). Also has title *NORTH-AMERICAN REVIEW AND MISCELLANEOUS JOURNAL* (May 1815 - Apr. 1821). May 1815 - Winter 1939/40. Monthly.

Issues in 1830s and 1840s in partic. have material on whaling.

880   *PACIFIC COMMERCIAL ADVERTISER* (Honolulu). 2 July 1856 - 21 May 1888. Weekly.

881   *POLYNESIAN* (Honolulu). 6 June 1840 - 11 Dec. 1841; 18 May 1844 - 23 Apr. 1863. Weekly.

Official journal of the Hawaiian Govt.

882   *SAILORS' MAGAZINE AND NAVAL JOURNAL* (New York: American Seamen's Friend Society). Also has titles *SAILORS' MAGAZINE* (Sept. 1857 - Aug. 1864) and *SAILORS' MAGAZINE AND SEAMEN'S FRIEND* (Sept. 1864 +). Sept. 1828 +. Monthly.

883   *SAILOR'S MAGAZINE AND NAVAL MISCELLANY* (London: British and Foreign Seamen's Friend Society and Bethel Union). Also has title *SAILOR'S MAGAZINE, AND NAUTICAL INTELLIGENCER*. 1820-1853? Monthly.

Regular whaling refs. - see index to each volume.

884   *SANDWICH ISLAND GAZETTE, & JOURNAL OF COMMERCE* (Honolulu). 30 July 1836 - 27 July 1839. Weekly. Becomes *SANDWICH IS-LAND MIRROR AND COMMERCIAL GAZETTE*, 15 Aug. 1839 - 15 July 1840. Monthly.

"Marine Intelligence" column for Port of Honolulu contains much whaling information, especially in "Memoranda" section.

885   *SANDWICH ISLAND NEWS* (Honolulu). 2 Sept. 1846 - 24 Aug. 1847; 5 Nov. 1847 - 14 Apr. 1849. Weekly.

886   *SIMMOND'S COLONIAL MAGAZINE AND FOREIGN MISCEL-LANY* (London). 1844 - 48 (15 vols.). Continued as *COLONIAL MAGA-ZINE AND EAST INDIA REVIEW*, 1849 - 51 (8 vols.) and combined with *ASIATIC JOURNAL* to form *COLONIAL AND ASIATIC REVIEW*, 1852 - 53 (2 vols.). (Ferguson 3903).

887 *SYDNEY GAZETTE AND NEW SOUTH WALES ADVERTISER.* 5 Mar. 1803 - 20 Oct. 1842. Weekly, semi-weekly, 3 weekly, daily. Suspended 30 Aug. 1807 - 15 May 1808. (Ferguson 383)
Major source of whaling information, shipping reports in and out of Sydney and in the Pacific area.

888 *SYDNEY GENERAL TRADE LIST.* Also with titles *SYDNEY GENERAL TRADE LIST, MERCANTILE CHRONICLE AND ADVERTISER* and *SYDNEY GENERAL TRADE LIST AND MERCANTILE ADVERTISER.* No. 1-6, 17 May - 20 Dec. 1828; no. 1-31, 16 July 1829 - 1 Feb. 1830; ns no. 1-3, 29 Apr. - 14 May 1830; vol. 2-9, 3 Jan. 1835 - 31 Dec. 1842. First 6 nos. irregular, then weekly. Incorporated into *SHIPPING GAZETTE AND SYDNEY GENERAL TRADE LIST*, vol. 1-17, Mar. 1840 - 1860. Weekly. (Ferguson 1216)
Detailed information on prices, shipping, exports, imports, etc.

889 *SYDNEY HERALD.* From 2 Aug. 1842 *SYDNEY MORNING HERALD.* 18 Apr. 1831 +. Weekly, semi-weekly, 3 weekly, daily. (Ferguson 1480)
Shipping lists and regular reports of Pacific whaling interest.

890 *SYDNEY MONITOR.* Also has title *MONITOR* (To 9 Aug. 1828) and *SYDNEY MONITOR AND COMMERCIAL ADVERTISER* (1834-41). 19 May 1826 - 29 Dec. 1841. Weekly and semi-weekly. (Ferguson 1087)

891 *TASMANIAN COLONIST* (Hobart). 1 Jan. 1846 - 30 July 1855. Twice weekly. 3 July 1851 incorporates *BRITANNIA AND TRADES' ADVOCATE*, q.v. no. 858 above.

892 *TRUE COLONIST AND VAN DIEMEN'S LAND POLITICAL DESPATCH AND AGRICULTURAL AND COMMERCIAL ADVERTISER* (Hobart). 5 Aug. 1834 - Dec. 1844. Weekly, daily (2 Jan. - 20 Mar. 1835), weekly. (Ferguson 1858a)

893 *WHALEMEN'S SHIPPING LIST* (New Bedford). Also has title *WHALEMEN'S SHIPPING LIST AND MERCHANTS' TRANSCRIPT* (1843-1883). 17 Mar. 1834 - 29 Dec. 1914. Weekly.

Appendixes

Appendix 1
Pacific Island names used in the nineteenth century and mentioned in the bibliography, and their modern equivalents

Amargura	Fonualei, Tonga
Ascension Island	Ponape, Caroline Islands
Byron's Island	Nikunau, Kiribati
Charles Island	Floreana, Galápagos Islands
"Cohannah" Island	Unidentified, possibly Guam, Marshall Islands
De Peyster ("Duprester's") Island	Nukufetau, Tuvalu
Duke of York's Island	Moorea, Society Islands
Dundas Island	Abemama, Kiribati
Eimeo	Moorea, Society Islands
Ellice Islands	Tuvalu
Farewell Island	Cikobia, Fiji
Friendly Islands	Tonga Islands
Georgian Islands	Society Islands (Windward Group)
Gilbert Islands	Kiribati
Gilbert's Island	Islet in the north Tarawa Atoll, Kiribati
Hervey's Island(s)	Manuae, Cook Islands
Hope Island	Arorae, Kiribati
James Island	San Salvador, Galápagos Islands
Keppell's Island	Tafahi, Tonga
Kingsmill Islands	Southern group of Kiribati
Ladrones Islands	Marianas Islands
Lord Chatham's Island	Chatham Island
MacAskill's Island	Pingelap, Caroline Islands
Mangea	Mangaia, Cook Islands
Marshall's Island	Islet in the north of Tarawa Atoll, Kiribati
Matthew's Island	Abaiang or Marakei, Kiribati
Morgan Island	Unidentified, probably Little Makin, Kiribati

Mulgrave or Mulgrave's Islands	Mili, Marshall Islands
Navigators' Islands	Samoa Islands
New Hebrides	Vanuatu
"Orrori" Island	Arorae, Kiribati
Otaheite	Tahiti
Owhyhee	Hawaii
Pearl Islands	Tuamotu Archipelago
Pell's Island	Probably Lisianski Island, Hawaii
Pleasant Island	Nauru
Pylstaart's Island	Ata, Tonga
Ralick Islands	Ralik Chain, Marshall Islands
Raven's Island	Ngatik, Caroline Islands
Rematura Island	Rimatara, Tubuai (or Austral) Islands
"Reupore" Islands	Probably Reitoru, Tuamotu Archipelago
St. Augustine Island or San Augustin	Nanumea, Tuvalu
Sandwich Islands	Hawaiian Islands
Simpson's (or Roger Simpson) Island	Abemama, Kiribati
Strong's Island	Kusaie, Caroline Islands
Sydenham's (or Sydenham Teast's) Island	Nonouti, Kiribati
Terrapin Island	Unidentified, possibly in Galápagos Islands
Turtle Island	Vatoa, Fiji
Wahoo	Oahu, Hawaii
Wallis Island	Uvea, Wallis and Futuna Islands
Wellington Island	Mokil, Caroline Islands
Whytotacke	Aitutake, Cook Islands
Woodle's Island	Kuria, Kiribati

Sources:

Forster, H., Discoveries in the Pacific after 1779 (unpublished MS., Department of Pacific and SE Asian History, Australian National University).

Hezel, F.J., *Foreign ships in Micronesia* (Saipan 1979).

Langdon, R. (ed.), *American whalers and traders in the Pacific* . . . (Canberra 1978), Part VI: "A gazetteer of obsolete/alternative names of the Pacific Islands with their current equivalents".

Maude, H.E., *Of islands and men* . . . (Melbourne 1968), Chap. 3: "Post-Spanish discoveries in the Central Pacific", pp. 84–133.

Nicholson, I.H., *Gazetteer of Sydney shipping 1788–1840* . . . (Canberra 1981).

Appendix 2
The major whaling grounds of the Pacific Ocean, and the whales hunted in them in the nineteenth century

On-Shore	Situated between the southern boundary of Chile and the northern limits of Peru, extending to the coasts of the southern part of modern Ecuador, west to the Juan Fernández and Galápagos Islands. (Sperm and right)
Off-Shore	Between latitude 5° to 10° south, and longitude 90° to 120° west. (Sperm)
On-the-Line	These grounds followed the Equator from the coast of South America approximately to the waters around the islands of southern Kiribati (Kingsmill Islands). (Sperm)
Middle	Situated between northern New Zealand and the east coast of Australia, particularly between about 29° to 35° south and 159° to 172° east. (Sperm and right)
Japan and Coast of Japan	The east coast of Japan, extending south to the Bonin Islands, between latitude 28° - 40° north and eastwards to approximately 170° (east). (Sperm)
Vasquez	The area north of New Zealand, including the seas around Fiji and Tonga. (Sperm, right and humpback)

Other important areas

South Pacific	Between parallels 21° - 27° south. (Sperm)
North Pacific	Between parallels 27° - 35° north. (Sperm and right)
Northern Tuvalu	(Sperm)
Samoa Islands	(Sperm)
Tuamotu Archipelago	(Sperm)
Southern Kiribati	(Sperm)
Off east and south coasts of New Zealand, to Chatham Islands and Auckland Islands	(Sperm and right)
North coast of New Guinea from 140°-146° 146° east	(Sperm)
Bismarck Archipelago, Bougainville and Solomon Islands, south to Chesterfield Islands	(Sperm and humpback)

Northern Vanuatu	(Sperm)
Solander ground, south of South Island, N.Z., and west of Stewart Island	(Sperm)

Note also:

Hawaiian Islands	(Humpback - shore stations)
California ground	(Gray)

Sources:

Beale, T., *The natural history of the sperm whale* . . . (London 1839), chap. XV, "Of the favourite places of resort of the sperm whale", pp. 188–91.

Carpenter, J, "Map shewing whaling grounds in portion of the Southern Hemisphere" in L.G. Thompson, *History of the fisheries of New South Wales* (Sydney 1893).

Hohman, E.P., *The American whaleman* . . . (New York 1928), pp. 148–52.

Maury, M.F., *Whale chart* . . . (Washington 1851). Note: This chart is reproduced in colour in A. B. C. Whipple and Editors of Time-Life Books, *The whalers* (Amsterdam 1979), pp. 70–1.

Morton, H., *The whale's wake* (Dunedin 1982), front endpaper map, showing main whaling grounds in the southwest Pacific area.

Sanderson, I.T., *Follow the whale* (London 1956), partic. "The world, showing the true oceans with the major sperming grounds", pp. xxvi-ii and "The South Pacific, as seen by Samuel Enderby", pp. 233–4.

Scammon, C.M., *The marine mammals of the north-western coast of North America* . . . (New York 1968), p. 214.

Appendix 3
A list of general reference books and articles used in the compilation of the bibliography

N.B.: Bibliographic references under author's name only, as given in Section I, are cited in full below.

Albion, Robert Greenhalgh, "Writings on maritime history", *American Neptune*, 10 (1950), 12–18 (1952–8). Note: 17 (1957) prepared by L. Shields.
Annual bibliographic listing of writings on all aspects of maritime history.

Andrews, Barry G. and William H. Wilde, *Australian literature to 1900: a guide to information sources*, American Literature, English Literature, and World Literatures in English Information Guide series vol. 22. Book Tower, Detroit, Mich., Gale Research Co., 1980. xxii, 472 pp.

Ash, Lee (comp.), *Subject collections: a guide to special book collections and subject emphases as reported by university, college, public, and special libraries and museums in the United States and Canada.* New York and London, R.R. Bowker Co., 1978. 1184 pp.

See section on "Whales and whaling".

Book Review Digest. Vol. 1, 1906 +. Minneapolis (1906–12), New York (1913 +), H.W. Wilson Co.

British Museum, *General catalogue of printed books.* Photolithographic edition to 1955, 263 vols. London, The Trustees of the British Museum, 1965–66.

Day, A. Grove, *Pacific Islands literature: one hundred basic books.* Honolulu, University Press of Hawaii, 1971. xxii [+ii], 176 pp. Appendix, index.

Ferguson, John Alexander, *Bibliography of Australia, 1784–1900,* 7 vols. Sydney, London, Angus & Robertson Ltd, 1941–69. Illus., indexes. Reprinted Canberra, National Library of Australia, 1975–77.

Fonda, Douglass C., Jr., *Catalogue . . . : a selection of books and manuscripts relating to ships and the sea, and voyages to distant lands . . .* (title varies). Mountshannon, Co. Clare, Ireland, Douglass C. Fonda, [197–]- 1982. Various pagings. See also *Supplement number one,* [1982]

Numerous whaling items, listed under "Whales and whaling", "the whale fishery", etc., with annotations.

France - Ministère de l'Instruction et des Beaux-Arts, *Catalogue général des livres imprimés de la Bibliothèque Nationale.* Auteurs, 230 vols. Paris, Imprimerie Nationale/Paul Catin, 1897–1980.

Hocken, T[homas] M[orland], *A bibliography of the literature relating to New Zealand.* Wellington, John Mackay, Government Printer, 1909. xii, 619 pp. Index.

Kaplan, Louis, et al. (comps.), *A bibliography of American autobiographies.* Madison, University of Wisconsin Press, 1961. xii, 372 pp.

Lefkowicz, Edward J., *Catalogue . . .* and *Bulletin . . .:* "Rare books and manuscripts relating to the sea and its islands and to nautical science". Fairhaven, Mass., Edward J. Lefkowicz Inc., [198–] +. Various pagings.

Many whaling items listed, with annotations.

Library of Congress, *The National Union Catalog: pre-1956 imprints. A cumulative author list . . . ,* 685 vols. [London and Chicago], Mansell [Information/Publishing Ltd], 1968–80.

Library of Congress, Catalog Publication Division, Processing Dept., *Newspapers in microform. United States 1948–1972*. Washington, Library of Congress, 1973. xxiii [+ ii], 1056 pp. Index.

Lorenz, Otto, et al. (eds.), *Catalogue général de la Librairie française, 1840–1925*, 34 vols. Paris, O. Lorenz/D. Jordell/E. Champion/Hachette, 1867–1945.

Miller, E. Morris, *Australian literature from its beginnings to 1935: a descriptive and bibliographical survey of books by Australian authors in poetry, drama, fiction, criticism and anthology with subsidiary entries to 1938*, 2 vols. Melbourne, Melbourne University Press in association with Oxford University Press, 1940. xi, 484; , 485–1074 pp. Reprinted Sydney, Sydney University Press, 1973.

Muir, Marcie, *A bibliography of Australian children's books*, "A Grafton Book"; 2 vols. Vol. 1, London, Andre Deutsch, [1970]. 1038 pp. Vol. 2, Ultimo, N.S.W. and London, Andre Deutsch, 1976. 554 pp. Pls., illus., index (vol. 2).

See partic. Vol. 1, "A select bibliography of the South West Pacific area", and Vol. 2, "Supplementary bibliography of the South West Pacific area".

National Library of Australia, *Newspapers in Australian libraries. A union list. Part 2. Australian newspapers*, 3rd ed. Canberra, National Library of Australia, 1975. xxii, [190] pp.

O'Reilly, Patrick and Édouard Reitman, *Bibliographie de Tahiti et de la Polynésie française*, Publications de la Société des Océanistes, no. 13. Paris, Musée de l'Homme, 1967. xvi, 1046 pp.

Philbrick, Thomas, *James Fenimore Cooper and the development of American sea fiction*. Cambridge, Mass., Harvard University Press, 1961. xviii, 329 pp. "Works cited", notes, index.

Polak, Jean, *Bibliographie maritime français depuis les temps les plus reculés jusqu'à 1914*. Grenoble, Éditions des 4 Seigneurs, 1976. 367 [+ 3] pp. Bibliog., pls., indexes.

———, and Michèle Polak, *Supplément*. Grenoble, 1983. 110 [4] pp.

Over 1400 additions and corrections to original work.

Poole, William Frederick and William I. Fletcher, et al., *Poole's index to periodical literature, 1802–1906*, 6 vols. in 7. Boston, J.R. Osgood Co./Houghton Mifflin Co., 1882–1908. Reprinted 1938, 1958.

Quérard, Joseph Marie, et al., *La littérature française contemporaine. XIXe siècle. Le tout accompagné de notes biographiques et littéraires*, 6 vols. Paris, Daguin Frères/Delaroque Aîne, 1842–57.

Reitman, Édouard, Patrick O'Reilly, and Renée Heyum, "Bibliographie de l'Océanie", 1939–44 - 1971, *Journal de la Société des Océanistes*, 1:1 (1945) - 30: 43–44 (1974).

First bibliography covers period 1939–44, then annual listing.

Sabin, Joseph, [et al.], *Bibliotheca Americana: a dictionary of books relating to America, from its discovery to the present time*. Begun by Joseph Sabin, continued by Wilberforce Eames and completed by R. W. G. Vail for the Bibliographic Society of America, 29 vols. New York, Sabin and Bibliographic Society of America, 1868–1936. Reprinted Amsterdam, N. Israel, 1961–2.

St. John, Judith, *The Osborne collection of early children's books: a catalogue*, 2 vols. Vol. 1, 1566–1910, with intro. by Edgar Osborne. Vol. 2, 1476–1910, with assistance of Dana Tenny and Hazel I. MacTaggart. Toronto, Toronto Public Library, 1975 (vol. 1 lst pub. 1958 and reprinted with corrections, 1966).

Sealts, Merton M., Jr., *Melville's reading: a check-list of books owned and borrowed*. Madison, Milwaukee and London, University of Wisconsin Press, 1966. x, 134 pp. Illus., notes.

Shaw, Ralph Robert and Richard H. Shoemaker, *American bibliography: a preliminary checklist, 1801–19*, items 1– 50192, 22 vols. New York, Scarecrow Press, Inc., 1958–66.

Shoemaker, Richard H., et al. (comps.), *A checklist of American imprints, 1820–33*, items 1–22795, 16 vols. New York and London/Metuchen, N.J. and London, Scarecrow Press, Inc., 1964–79. (Note: continuing series.)

Silveira de Braganza, Ronald Louis and Charlotte Oakes (eds.), *The Hill Collection of Pacific voyages*, [vol. 1], with annotations by Jonathan A. Hill; limited ed. of 1000 copies. San Diego, Calif., University of California, University Library, 1974. xv, 333 pp. Pls., facsims., illus. endp. maps.

Silveira de Braganza, Ronald Louis (ed., annot. and comp.), *The Hill Collection . . .* , vol. 2, and Indexes vol.; limited eds. of 800 and 950 copies. San Diego, Calif., University of California, University Library, 1982, 1983. xviii, 337–627; x, 629–766 pp. Pls. (vol. 2), illus., endp. maps.

Spence, Sydney A., *A bibliography of selected early books and pamphlets relating to Australia 1610–1880*. London, The Compiler [Sydney A. Spence], 1952. 88 pp. *(Supplement) to 1610–1880 (and extension from):- 1881–1900* [of the above]. London, The Compiler, 1955. 100 pp.

Tanselle, G. Thomas, *A checklist of editions of Moby-Dick 1851–1976. Issued on the occasion of an exhibition at the Newberry Library commemorating the 125th anniversary of its original publication*. Evanston and Chicago, Northwestern University Press and the Newberry Library, 1976. vii, 50 pp.

Titus, Edna Brown (ed.), *Union list of serials in libraries of the United States and Canada*, 3rd ed.; 5 vols. New York, H.W. Wilson Co., 1965.

Wright, Lyle H., *American fiction, 1774–1850: a contribution toward a bibliography*, Huntington Library Publications; 2nd rev. ed. San Marino, Calif., The Huntington Library, 1969 (lst pub. 1948). xviii, 411 pp. Indexes.

Appendix 4
The Pacific Manuscripts Bureau and the New England Microfilming Project

In 1970 and 1976, the Pacific Manuscripts Bureau, Research School of Pacific Studies, Australian National University, Canberra, organised two projects under the general title of the New England Microfilming Project. Each was under the direction of Dr. John S. Cumpston, a specialist in early Australian maritime history, and resulted in the acquisition of 420 reels of microfilm logbooks, account books, correspondence, charts, newspaper clippings, shipping records, and other information. Whaling logbooks, mainly dating from the second and third quarters of the nineteenth century, made up the greater part of the records, all of which were selected for their bearing on the history of Australia, New Zealand, the Pacific Islands and the Pacific basin generally.

More than 40 libraries, museums and private individuals in New England made their records available to Dr. Cumpston for microfilming or provided him with copies of the material on film where microfilming projects had already been carried out. Their names and addresses are listed in the introduction to *American whalers and traders in the Pacific: a guide to records on microfilm*, edited by the Executive Officer of the Pacific Manuscripts Bureau, Mr. Robert Langdon (see Section II-A). The first New England Microfilming Project, which is a non-profit enterprise, was sponsored by 12 libraries in Australia, New Zealand and Hawaii; and the second by ten. Copies of the films obtained are deposited in each of these libraries, as appropriate. The ten libraries which sponsored both projects are: The National Library of Australia, Canberra; the Library, Australian National University, Canberra; the Mitchell Library, Sydney; the Library, University of Sydney; the State Library of South Australia, Adelaide (in association with the libraries of the University of Adelaide and the Flinders University of South Australia); the State Library of Tasmania, Hobart; the State Library of Victoria, Melbourne; the Library Board of Western Australia, Perth; the National Library of New Zealand, Wellington; and the Library, University of Hawaii, Honolulu. The two libraries which sponsored the first project only are: the Library, University of Newcastle, New South Wales, and the State Library of Queensland, Brisbane.

Two hundred fourteen reels of microfilm numbered PMB 200 to 412 were obtained under the first New England Project. 206 reels, numbered PMB 540–45, 571–80, 671–99 and 720–900 were obtained under the second. *American whalers and traders in the Pacific* contains indexes to the logbooks copied on the 420 microfilms, according to ships, with dates of voyages, captains and/or logkeepers, with names of ships and dates of voyages, and places visited by the ships, in Australia, New Zealand the Pacific Islands.

Indexes to "Personal Accounts" (Sections I and V-B)

N.B.: All references are to entry numbers, and not to page numbers.

Index to Islands, other place names
(See Appendix I for modern equivalents of island names cited)

Index to Whaling Captains

Sea of
Okhotsk   Kamchatka

Bering   Bering Strait

Sea of   Sea
Japan

ALEUTIAN IS

KURILE IS

Northern   Grounds

Sea of
Japan

KOREA

JAPAN

CHINA

Coast
of Japan
Ground

Japan
Ground

Hong Kong

BONIN IS

HA

H

MARIANA IS

South

China   PHILIPPINES

Sea   Guam

CAROLINE IS

MARSHALL IS

Ponape

BORNEO

NAURU

On - the Line

KIRIBATI

PHOENIX IS

INDONESIA   NEW GUINEA   Bismarck Sea

PAPUA

NEW

Bougainville
SOLOMON   IS

TUVALU

TOKELAU IS

GUINEA

SANTA
CRUZ IS

WALLIS &
FUTUNA

SAMOA IS

JAVA

Upolu

VANUATU

FIJI

NIUE

TONGA IS

CHESTERFIELD IS

LOYALTY
IS

Tongatapu

CO

NEW
CALEDONIA

Vasquez

Ground

NORFOLK I

KERMADEC IS

AUSTRALIA

Middle Ground

Sydney

New Zealand

Ground   CHATHAM IS

NEW
ZEALAND

Tasman Sea

TASMANIA   Hobart   Solander

STEWART I

Ground

AUCKLAND IS

140°   160°   180°